D0630165

JOHN M. WATKINS
Publishers and Booksellers
21, CECIL COURT,
LONDON, W.C.2.
TEMple Bar 2182.

ESSAYS AND ADDRESSES

ON THE

PHILOSOPHY OF RELIGION

(SECOND SERIES)

ESSAYS & ADDRESSES
ON THE
PHILOSOPHY *of* RELIGION
SECOND SERIES

BY

BARON FRIEDRICH von HÜGEL
LL.D., D.D.

BL
51
.H9
2nd ser.

LONDON
J. M. DENT & SONS LIMITED
NEW YORK: E. P. DUTTON & CO. INC.

All rights reserved
Made in Great Britain
by
The Temple Press Letchworth
for
J. M. Dent & Sons Ltd.
Aldine House Bedford St. London
First published 1926
Last reprinted 1951

INDIANA-P
PURDUE
LIBRARY
JUL 1 9 1979
FORT WAYNE
WITHDRAWN

Z 57/5 III

ll 7-16

To

THE MEMBERS

OF

THE LONDON SOCIETY FOR THE

STUDY OF RELIGION

INTRODUCTORY NOTE

It will be seen that the following Essays and Addresses were composed or delivered at various dates between 1904 and 1922. The second and sixth have already been privately printed; the ninth and tenth, of a slighter character than the others, appeared in *The Student Movement* and *The Challenge* respectively. The rest, as far as I have been able to ascertain, are now published for the first time. The earliest of these, "Official Authority and Living Religion," was revised by Father George Tyrrell, and the author incorporated some of Tyrrell's suggestions into the substance of the essay. The address to which Baron von Hügel himself would probably have attached the most importance is the seventh, "Suffering and God," which was prepared for the London Society for the Study of Religion, although only certain portions of it were actually read at the meeting. I feel confident that I am interpreting the Baron's wishes in dedicating the whole volume to the members of that Society, of which he was one of the founders, to which he devoted so much loving care and thought, and which so often had the inestimable privilege of listening to his words.

The Editor.

15 *August*, 1926.

CONTENTS

I
OFFICIAL AUTHORITY AND LIVING RELIGION

I

OFFICIAL AUTHORITY AND LIVING RELIGION [1]

THE practically perennial mental and moral warfare which man wages for or against or around religion is quite evidently concentrated, for the present, and for us Western Europeans and Northern Americans, neither upon Theism (witness the deadness of Huxley and of Spencer), nor upon Catholicism (witness the intellectual emptiness of pure, militant Protestantism); but upon that very middle ground or level, hitherto common to all Historical Christians, from which they all argued back to God and on to the Church —upon what we may shortly term Christianity. And hence the very stress of the times can and does bring those together who continue to cling to Historical, Institutional, organised Christianity. But since the battle is, here and now, in great part a battle as to method—historico-critical method; or, rather, as to the right and duty of the application of this method to the historic records and phenomenal facts and products of Christianity: there is a further sifting out and regrouping of combatants; and an inevitable drawing together, among the greater body of Historical Christians, of those who, though loyal members of their respective Christian churches, hold in common a belief both in this method and in its inevitable application in the sense described.

Yet it will be well if all such Institutional Christians wake up to so keen a vision of the difficulties special to their position, as of itself already to bring, if not their partial solution, yet at least that rest and bracing of soul,

[1] Written in 1904.

3

which (to those who can bear such high air and such giddy downlooks and outlooks) ever accrues from facing, and from feeling that they are facing, things as they really are, and not as they would wish them to be. Now the point I would specially dwell on here, is not the apparently irrevocable committal of all such Churches to much that now clamours for a large discrimination and restatement (and this precisely in that middle ground and level, the whole Christological question)—a committal which may well make an explicit and definite subscription to at all detailed formularies of all such bodies appear to many difficult or impossible. Nor would I consider the further conflict, ever possible and largely actual, in all such times of transition, which is introduced into the situation by the fact that, over and above any pressure from the formularies themselves, we have a majority of officials, incapable of, or hostile to, such larger and more critical interpretations as are loyally possible, but which require, for their conception or even their toleration, men keenly awake to the mental and spiritual necessities of our times. I want to push still farther back, and study a little, not the context, the *matter* (to speak scholastically), of the difference between officialism on the one hand and the living forces of religion around us and within us on the other; but the very frame, the *form*, of this difference. And to this end I shall assume an agreement as to the *matter* of religious truth which does not, but might, obtain. I shall next try and show how the very acuteness of the conflict and pressure suggests, not only certain irrepressible rights and functions of officialism, but also certain abiding, immanental discriminations and limitations. And I shall finally try to show how these discriminations and limitations are reinforced, and rendered quite inevitable, by the clear results of historico-critical research.

I

Now to bring home vividly to our apprehension the essential and abiding divergence between the very "form" of the deepest action and experience of the mind and spirit, and the very "form" of official activity as such, let us picture to ourselves a state of things which has existed in the past, for all men of education in Western Europe; which still exists now, for many intellectually half-awake souls in the same regions; which will, thank God, certainly obtain again, for all educated men willing to believe—a state of things in which the "matter," if not of the official formularies, at least of the current official interpretation of them, harmonises with (even whilst rightly transcending) all that is recognised at the time as otherwise assured truth by the average educated man, in his average moods and moments. And I would then ask: Does this average educated man, in proportion as he truly and deeply (though, perhaps, quite partially and intermittently) lives the life of the mind and of the spirit—does he apprehend and discover, feel, think, will and act; does he suffer, love, rejoice, produce in the same manner, with the same forms and categories, as officialism seems to do and to direct him to do? The question readily answers itself: there is no kind of similarity here, between these two series of activities, in any single respect. Many as are the analogies between the spirit, life and action of a corporation, or fictitious collective personality, and those of a living indivisible person, the differences are most profound and significant. The former is necessarily mechanical and impersonal to a large extent; and the official *as such* speaks, thinks and acts, as the organ and expression of the corporate speech, thought and action. Precisely *as* official he is determined rather than self-determining; and so far non-personal. I take it, then, that seven characteristics

B

ever mark all such a man's deepest moments and efforts;
and that seven contrary peculiarities ever characterise
official acts, as such.

1. Whenever such a man most deeply, most self-
obviously thinks, wills; prays, adores; suffers, rejoices;
produces: *that* act, *that* state, *that* result, *that* very man,
are truly *new* and original. For however identical may
seem the compound of motives, apprehensions, willings,
spiritual lights and graces, moral capacities, weaknesses
and virtues, in any peasant's act of faith, of hope, of love
or trust, whether in the midst of pain, or of death, or of
spiritually creative action of any kind—however identical
this compound may seem with previous acts of that same
simple personality, and even with the similar acts of
numberless other representatives of the majority of hidden
souls that make up the Invisible Church; yet that compound, that state and act, is *new*. It is new, at least, in the
very real sense of being new for that particular soul, at
that particular point of space and time; and, as a matter
of fact, it is new and unique, in every case, in countless
other ways besides. And this newness, where at all creative
and of long fruitfulness, will ever be akin to, will in
its degree actually be, a revelation not of Time but of
Eternity. Or, at least, it will be a duration of mutually
interpenetrative experiences, rather than a clear succession
of experiences in time, where one element is made to
exclude the other. For Time is that projection into space
which our imagination has to effect, when it would help
us to give some lucid, readily transferable account of
these interior apprehensions. We resolve the compound
into its elements, which we then arrange in a linear series
in the order of their dependence.

Against the *Totum Simul* of this living quasi-timeless
Present, Authority as such will ever necessarily represent
the Previous, the What-has-already-been: a Past which,
even though it have had, in its time, the "infinite variety"
of the superbly living Cleopatra, is now being thrown,

like so much mummy-dust, into the wide-open, pleading
eyes of living, light-seeking souls.

2. Secondly: in such moments of living religious effort,
the soul will be lonely and isolated; it will be estranged not
only from the average, the majority of men, including, as a
rule, even those materially nearest to it; but it will be
estranged from its own average thoughts and moments:
in a true and necessary, though usually quite unpsycho-
physical sense, it will then be ecstatic. General Gordon
and Field-Marshal Moltke, Charles Darwin and Frederick
William Robertson, Jacob Grimm and Wilhelm von Hum-
boldt, Fichte and Hegel, Pascal and Spinoza, Augustine
and Plotinus: they all, in various degrees and forms, knew
this sense well, at their deepest and best.

Against this, Authority as such ever necessarily insists
upon the majority, the Average, both of the thoughts in
any one man, and of men amongst mankind. It cannot
help being essentially Philistine, and representing directly
that "common sense" which Schopenhauer, with such
exquisite profoundness, declares to be the deepest outrage
we can offer to Our Lord's character and spirit, if we
attribute to these latter such common sense, in an at all
primary degree or in the popular interpretation of the term.

3. Thirdly: in such moments the soul will be immensely
active, overflowingly *itself*, although the very fullness of
this action will often prevent any traces of itself from
simultaneously appearing in the Agent's consciousness:
its very sense of passivity. Its apparently simple yieldings,
sufferings, non-activity will, at bottom, be acts, acts of
its entire, central self. If pain be here, it will be the pain
of expansion and of growth, of pressing against the poor
barriers opposed to this flood-tide of self-immolating, self-
constituting life—barriers which are caused by the limits
of its essential, and still more of its actual nature, by the
predominance of evil or of slovenly habits, the effects of
past cowardice and self-seeking. And, if joy be here, it
will be because of such action against what simply exists

in me, and yet dares to claim finality or completeness. And this action will mysteriously be felt to be all the more mine, because realised at the same moment to be far more truly, to be ultimately His—His in its very possibility, occasion, actuality, truth, strength and fruitfulness.

Against this, Authority as such necessarily insists upon a true Passivity; it insists upon acting for us, and upon ourselves acting only as checks upon ourselves, so as to leave room for its action; or, at most, so as to stimulate ourselves to reproduce, as mechanically and repetitively as possible, its order or action.

4. Fourthly: in such moments as we are considering, the soul necessarily risks and dares much, and is truly conscious of such risking. As breathing, eating, walking; as hospital-nursing, fire-salvage, ambulance-work; as maternity and child-birth, all involve inevitable risks, and this in proportion to the nobility of the work attempted or achieved: so every truly noble life is noble largely through its having courageously risked all risks necessary to its own expansion, growth and fruitfulness; for these latter are the only true safety attainable by man here below.

Against such interior (or formally willed) dynamic, eventual, strengthening safety, Authority necessarily insists upon predominantly external, static, immediate, weakening safety—upon the elimination, as far as may be, of risks; and thus ever tends, of itself and by such elimination, directly to produce that terrible, not risk, but reality, of stagnation and sterility.

5. Fifthly: in such moments, the soul finds that its sheet-anchor is its interior (i.e. formally willed) truthfulness—its humble, faithful, loving seeking of material, objective truth, by an ever-growing purity of disposition and intention, and an ever-increasing attempt to become and to be all that it knows. And it would rather keep on thus, seeking truth sincerely and with self-humiliation, and thus unconsciously itself grow more like the truth which it seeks and which is already inwardly impelling

such a soul; than hold truth in such a static and self-complacent manner, as to arrest its own further approximation and apprehension of that truth.

Against this, official Authority necessarily dwells upon the end and not the means, at least not on the interior means; upon objective truth rather than subjective truthfulness; and upon truth as something static, readily transferable, identical with certain formularies—an orthodoxy, a thing.

6. Sixthly: in such moments, the soul finds Beauty, Truth, Goodness, Spirit, God, to be and to energise in and behind and through all this phenomenal world and life of ours—in various degrees and ways, anywhere and everywhere; and yet to be everywhere attainable only by the soul's concentration, prayer, suffering, and self-dedication. Certain times and places, rites and forms, will no doubt prove means and channels of special help; yet all these things will ever be to the soul mediations of graces which it may and can refuse; which it can and ought to meet and utilise.

Against this, official Authority ever tends to find Beauty, Truth and Goodness as appearing phenomenally in the phenomenal world, alongside of, and on the same phenomenal level as, ugliness, error, evil—since these latter opposites are also treated by it as though phenomenal. It tends to find all this phenomenal Beauty, Truth and Goodness in some one particular place or enclosure. You need only look with your physical eyes and your average common sense out into the world, and to institute a simply demonstrative comparison; and as land contrasts with water, or the Island of Ireland is seen distinct from Great Britain, so does the phenomenal conglomeration of Truth and Goodness, the visible City of God, stand out over against the visible City of the Devil, the phenomenal congeries of all Error and Evil. It is as though a vertical, geological conception had here been replaced by a horizontal, geographical outlook; and the consequent need of

digging down in our investigations, by a simple task of
searching for what lies on the surface of life.

7. Seventhly and finally, and as an inevitable consequence of all these characteristics, the soul will, in these
its fullest moments, necessarily experience an Optimism
in and through a Pessimism. For it will never feel its own
actual average, indeed its whole tangible achievement, so
mean, so intolerably small, stained and shabby, or the
conscious and advertised average output of its fellows
so oppressive and disgusting, as when it also most fully
realises that something of an abiding Truth and Goodness is pushing and growing, working and judging within
its own poor self; and that much more of this same self-
incarnational action of God's own Spirit is mysteriously
but mightily weaving and working in His own great wide
world without—a world, at bottom, good and very good.

Against this, official Authority is necessarily optimistic
throughout, at least as regards its own action and the
results of that action, past, present, and future. It cannot
allow the tragic note, nor that of tenderness, nor that of
humour—the very salt of the earth. The sense and expression of the pathetic contrasts and noble chiaroscuro
of our lot; the dim, deep lights of Gethsemane and Calvary falling upon the figure of the Divine Excommunicate are too much for it; and the smile of the Infant
Jesus seems somehow far too little.

In a word, the soul at its deepest is ever profoundly
original, isolated, active, daring, interior, penetrative, and
superficially pessimist; it moves through suffering on to
joy. And official Authority is, as such, ever repetitive of
something past and gone; is the voice of the average
thoughts of the many; aims at limiting the action of its
subjects to a passive reception and more or less mechanical
execution of its commands; is essentially timid; cares
necessarily more for the outward appearance and material
output, than for the interior disposition and form of the
soul's activity; maps out the very phenomenal world into

visible, mutually exclusive regions of spiritual light and
darkness; and is in so far ever unreal, as it cannot but
absolutely disallow, or must at least minimise as much
as possible, all even preliminary present sins, pains and
perplexities—at least, those of its own creation.

II

The deadlock, then, would seem to be indeed complete
—at least for such souls as, fully awake, cannot allow
mere useless ballast or clogging hindrances upon or within their spiritual lives—lives already strained and difficult
in many ways. Should we not then throw all such social,
institutional, official Authority overboard? It has often
been said in the past, and is still often said in the present,
that a grown man, at least an Anglo-Saxon or Teuton,
requires no support or check except those of his own
mind and conscience. Are not such sayings true? And
note, pray, that these objections have now gained a treble
reinforcement. For first, as historians, we now know that
the institution of the Church is far less directly and completely attributable to Our Lord than used to be believed.
Secondly, as scholars, desirous, at all legitimate cost,
of being fair and candid, we feel more and more keenly
how dangerously mischievous is any direct interference
of Officiality in these delicate matters; and how perhaps
the surest way to vitiate our very capacity to learn in these
matters, is to bring to them what we should rather fight
within ourselves—an official bias. And thirdly, as students
of human nature and of its history in such-like matters,
we may now, surely more than ever, quail before the
obvious dangers and inevitable abuses incident to the
maintenance of such a privileged class, and before the
quasi-impossibility of its ever coming to be, for our
modern conditions, more of a help than of a hindrance.

And yet: no, and again, no. Such a rejection would

be an all the more dangerous mistake, as it would readily
look, and at first feel, like an act of manly simplification
and spiritual interiorisation. For let us note how, in each
of the seven antinomies which we have dwelt on, it is
not difficult to show how, in each pair, officialism
stands for something which, if necessarily unpopular and
irritating to the strenuous soul and to all souls in their
strenuous moments, is nevertheless, in those seven respects,
an essential factor in that soul's solid growth and balance
and usefulness to others.

For, first of all, the Previous, the Past, has a right and
duty either to assert clamorously its still unexhausted
existence and action, or even, within limits, to weigh and
press upon us; and thus so to force its abiding claims, its
complements and criticisms upon our attention, as to prevent too sudden a change, a rude jerk on to another level
or way, which might upset healthy progress for the many
altogether. And this Majority, the Average, both of men
in general, and of each man's ordinary thoughts and
aspirations—they, too, have certain rights, if only as rests
and fallow-times between one period of spiritual stress
and another; and as, so to speak, neutral gaps or buffers
between the otherwise too straining and conflicting personalities of intenser pitch and those of the average pitch.
And to represent and defend these rights is to help to
prevent the minority of ideas in each man, and the minority
of men in the community, from themselves becoming a
mere trick and fashion, a puerile preciousness, an inverted,
doubly base Philistinism. And safety, even of the simply
material and easily weakening, protective kind, has a certain right and claim, as, at its best, a primary (but then
simply transitional), or as an abiding (but then ever
secondary) means of helping souls, doubtless as long as
souls shall exist on earth. For, though we are bound to
instruct and interiorly to strengthen all souls as much
as may be, some considerable weaknesses will necessarily
remain more or less amongst us all, and will demand the

partial or transitional application of such protection. And the matter of our convictions and actions, as contrasted with their form and intention, is deeply important; and, indeed, neither can exist without the other, and each will absolutely require the stimulation of other leading, equal and dependent minds. For after all, in the spiritual as in the material sphere, we have to begin by trusting, imitating, being moulded by, those who know, or who declare they do; and, again, up to the very end, the actual more or less great correspondence of our notions and strivings with objective reality and its laws, is as truly important as is our faithful striving to attain it. And even where illegitimate or excessive, an official Authority, where sincerely accepted, can and does stand forth to us as the symbol, test and partial instrument of this objective Truth and of the corresponding objective, outward-moving spirit, with its noble sense of the littleness of all excessive subjectivity. And the, as it were phenomenal, juxtaposition or contrast of Truth and Error, Goodness and Evil, they too have also in so far a claim to recognition; as, though truth and goodness, together with error and evil, are no doubt present throughout all human lives and institutions, yet they are not simply evenly distributed, either in degree or in kind, throughout or behind space or time, any more than are physical health or mental endowments. Hence it is, at bottom, as really unjust and dangerous to hold all lives, doctrines, or institutions to be equally true, helpful and holy, as to deny any and every kind or degree of truth or of goodness to any man or any institution or teaching that could ever keep alive at all. And against the former of these injustices, such, as it were phenomenalist, spirituality is a useful reminder and counter-symbol. And, finally, even an Optimism inclusive of the *status quo* has got its share of truth: for if *all* that already exists and appears, even in the actual average around us, be bad and false, then all hope of a better future is cut off; since only through a growth, liberation and concentration of the germinal, imprisoned, scattered good already at work in the present can the better of the future be achieved.

But above all, and throughout all these seven points, it is clear that Officialism, of some kind or degree, is inevitable if we would make a reasonable, continuous provision for applying the motive force and light of the leading, stimulating, renovating few to the dull, average, more or less automatic many—the few highest thoughts, volitions and experiences of any one man to the multitude of his average experiences; and the predominant dispositions and actions of the few whose religious life is almost entirely first-hand to the multitude of men whose religion is average in its attainments. And such relation is not by any means only necessary for those many thoughts and many men; it is at least as, though differently, necessary for those few who gain from such communication that uniquely noble, creaturely sense of each requiring and supplementing the other. For only then shall we avoid a gnostic, esoteric, "Palace of Art" infatuation, and the loss of that greatest glory of Christianity, the corporate spirit, the love of the universal brotherhood, the sense of the indestructible, though most easily deniable, interdependence of all times and races, gifts and activities of life, the supremacy of Love over knowledge, and of Action over speculation.

III

And History seems clearly to bear out this contention. For we there find three things.

1. We see how *practically indestructible* is, in the long run, if not this or that form of religious organisation, yet at least the presence of some such form. If the Jewish official Church could deliberately try, excommunicate and virtually itself crucify Him who was its very flower, its crown, its measure and its end; if it could, soon after, have

its one great Sanctuary levelled with the ground for ever,
and could yet continue and revive, in a very appreciable
measure, in the Rabbinical schools and the Synagogal
organisation, and last to this day: then no scandal can kill
this instinct and this need. If, at the very moment of
breaking with the old organisation, St. Paul, the most
daringly free and individual of mystical-minded souls,
became the virtual founder of the more elaborate Christian
organisation, of the Church in our stricter sense of the
word: then no overflowing fullness of interior life and personal assurance will prevent a soul, large and open enough
to hear the heart-beats of the many, from realising the
essential necessity of institutionalism for all normal religious
education and for the development of even the most interior
gifts. And if well-nigh one half, and certainly the mentally
more active part, of Western Christendom could, at the
Protestant Reformation, be carried away not only from the
specifically Roman organisation, but, just at first and in
considerable part, from all deliberate and uniform organisation whatsoever; and if, after now well-nigh four centuries,
Rome lives on still, dead or a mere Antique only to those
who do not know her; whilst the various protesting or
separate groups of persons had very soon, after many a
terrible experience, to return to some kind of deliberate
organisation: then no such experiments, tried simultaneously by different races and types of men, have any
reasonable chance of succeeding.

2. And, secondly, we see how *spiritually beneficent* is
some kind and degree of organisation and officiality, or
rather how the fuller and fullest interior life not only can
thrive in, but seems actually to require, and itself to occasion, a vigorous, definite Church organisation. Certainly
Our Lord, even though in conflict with, and the final
victim of, the abuses of the Church of His age and country,
nowhere denied or ignored its legitimate authority. Certainly St. Paul was not less, but rather more interior,
from being at the same time the great organiser of the

Christian Church. Certainly the deeply interior Clement of Alexandria and Origen grew up in, and worked with and for, a very definite organisation. Certainly the beautiful simplicity and freedom of the Poverello of Assisi and of his first heroic little band will be at once misconceived and impoverished by us, if we take them as anything but the loyal children and proudly grateful products of that very Roman Church, which they loved too much not to give their all to live down the abuses that had come to disfigure its pristine and now largely latent beauty. And certainly those great Spanish mystics, St. John of the Cross and St. Teresa, flourished in the midst of what we now, practically on all sides, recognise as an excessive politico-ecclesiastical officialism.

3. Yet there remains a third thing clearly taught by History. The frequent recurrence, and in fact the abiding-ness of attempts, on the part of truly religious men, to work and propagate or awaken religion as something purely interior, individual, subjective, as something which cannot conceive the presence or influence of a fellow-man as other than a barrier between a man and God, proclaim to all not beyond the reach of learning, that there are certain profound dangers and difficulties attendant upon all officialism; certain readily, all but inevitably, forgotten laws and limits of its efficacious exercise. I take these laws to be fundamentally two; and to be completed and reinforced by two great critico-historical conclusions.

First, then, official organisation and authority are part, a normally necessary part, of the fuller and more fruitful religious life; but they are ever only a part, and a part in what is a dynamic whole—one movement and moment in what is a life, in the deepest sense of the word. The lonely, new and daring (if but faithful, reverent and loving) outgoing of the discoverer and investigator are as truly acts of, are as necessary parts of, the Church and her life as his coming back to the Christian hive and community, which latter will then gradually test his contribution by

tentative applications to its own life, and will in part
assimilate, in part simply tolerate, in part finally reject it.
And such a lonely, venturesome outgoing appears, in all
kinds of degree and form, in every sort of life. The inven-
tive, often most daring, ever at first opposed, philanthropy
of the Saints belongs entirely to this exploratory, pioneer
class of action in the rhythmic "inspiration-expiration" life,
in the breathing of the living Church. The Church is thus,
ever and everywhere, both progressive and conservative;
both reverently free-lance and official; both as it were male
and female, creative and reproductive; both daring to the
verge of presumption, and prudent to the verge of despair.
And Church officials are no more the whole Church, or a
complete specimen of the average of the Church, than
Scotland Yard or the War Office or the House of Lords,
though admittedly necessary parts of the national life, are
the whole, or average samples, of the life and fruitfulness
of the English nation. The true cure here would then be
for officials to cultivate in themselves also the non-official,
the out-going, lonely and daring, the "expiration" movement of the complete soul and community; and for the
pioneers and investigators to keep alive in themselves the
recognition and practice of the homing, the "inspiration"
movement, the patient referring back and living with the
slow-moving, mentally ruminating, socially regulative multitude, and its and their official heads.

And, next, official organisation and Authority are ever
means, necessary means, of life; means, not ends; of life,
not of death. If all life is necessarily—in the exact measure
of its fullness, persistence and reproductive power—a
unified diversity, an organism of some kind, and there
is no temporal priority on the side either of life or of
organisation, since life and organisation grow *pari passu*:
there is nevertheless, always and everywhere, a plain
priority of logic and of worth on the side of life. We do
not live our day worthily with a view to its division into
neat sections of time, or to pleasing the police: we divide

it thus and we follow the police regulations, since, by so doing, we find that we can more fully and easily live our day in a worthy manner. And although the individual man will ever give the benefit of the doubt, where doubt exists, to the rulings of the official Authority, and will have to be interiorly pressed by increasingly grave and spontaneous promptings of conscience, in proportion as he neglects or opposes it: yet it is clear that, if the *mere* Individual, the raw human article, the spiritually untrained or unenlightened man, is, as such, ever under Authority in general, and, normally, under some particular authority conceived by himself as more or less an end: yet the Person, the spiritualised and purified man, who, as such, is part and organ and product of the Invisible Church in which God's Spirit dwells, as in His very Bride, is bound to such external authority only as to an instrument, realised by himself as such, for his own further progress, and for his social-religious union with his fellowmen. And thus some degree and kind of official Authority will be, in this double way, necessary for us all, and right up to the end of life, since we ourselves will never be quite completely "personal persons," and since, even if we could be, we shall have to live with and to love, help and be helped by, a large majority who have hardly ceased to be mere individuals. And yet one of the tests of our advance will be the degree to which, in a very full and devoted life, we shall not actually require the pressure of that official Authority, whilst nevertheless never ceasing to believe in, and on occasion practising, the necessity, for our own selves as for all men, of deferring to and executing its legitimate commands and counsels.

And, thirdly, historical criticism has ended by clearly establishing how that Church organisation and Officialism, in all but the very rudimentary, Synoptic-Gospel form of their original operation—a form so akin to the Franciscan Brotherhood during the Poverello's lifetime—is not the direct and deliberate creation of Our Blessed Lord Himself.

But for the two exceptions confirmatory of the rule,
His denunciation of the official abuses, and His modest
organisation of the little preaching and curing fraternity
of His Apostles, all competent scholars are coming to see
how entirely He kept and lived and died, as far as in Him
lay, within the pale, a member of the Jewish Church—
and this if only because, whatever be the reason, He spoke
and acted according to the current belief that this Church,
indeed all earthly arrangements, would soon end at His
Proximate Second Coming. Now this conclusion necessarily
involves the recognition that all and every officialism beyond
that humble brotherhood, so simply trained, organised
and sent out by Him, can but go back germinally and not
formally and materially to Him, somewhat as the visible
universe itself was germinally created by God in the
beginning, and not in the state or form in which we
now see it. And, since all more or less largely organised
Christian bodies go almost as far beyond that first modest
confraternity, as do our secular knowledge and our religious
problems and picturings as affected by that knowledge
go beyond the knowledge of that primitive community,
it follows that this matter is a point which concerns
all Historical Christians. And such a view will, for a
man of faith, imply his profound conviction of the
identity of the God slowly working out His purposes in
history with the God incarnate in Jesus Christ. There can
be no more "pure" Christianity, in the actual practice, or
(if he is historically unprejudiced) in the reasoned conception of the modern man now, than Christ's own
Christianity was "pure"; and this for the simple reason
that Christ, though God, is not God in the sense of leaving
God no work to do in the world. God's work, before and
during and ever since the Incarnation, has been met,
taken up, and carried higher and deeper by the Christ.
But all this cannot fail to introduce width, elasticity, and
a noble humanity into our conception of the Church.
We require the Church as much as ever, it is as venerable

and sacred as ever; but, as to the form in which we now
have it, it is mostly of divine institution in the sense in
which the family and human society are—God's work,
under the immense impulsion given to humanity by Christ
Our Lord's teachings, life, death, and glorified existence
—a work built up in and through and for the abiding
necessities, aspirations and helps of men. Thus the Church
which, in proportion to our spiritual receptiveness and
vigour, we all, as the instruments of God, have made, in
return helps to make each one of us. And thus, whilst
remaining sacred, Christian and Divine, the Church will
be conceived so warmly and humanely as to put all
haughty, oppressive, Old Testament institutionalism, all
angry, hard, cold, purely or predominantly exterior rule,
out of court and practice. And thus, from out the valuable
but much-mixed ore of our present Institutionalism, the
pure dear gold of Christ's own spirit, that has been met
and reinforced by all the goodness and greatness of a
God-moved outer world, will be smelted out and more
ready for our spiritual use.

And, lastly, this same historical criticism is demon-
strating, with apparent ruthlessness, the limited and non-
infallible character of Our Lord's recorded manifestation
of human knowledge; His adoption of all the scientific,
literary, critical assumptions, picturings and beliefs of His
own age and country—even inclusive of such an apparently
spiritual belief as that in the proximity of His Second
Coming. More and more we are being driven to the conclusion that, since the effects upon and in the Humanity,
of the Divinity of Our Lord, are necessarily matters
entirely beyond our own experience or intuition, they
cannot be determined by us, either by means of such
experience, or, *a priori*, by deductive reasoning as to the
consequences of such a union; we can but get at the
effects *a posteriori* and from history, by a quite docile
adherence to the information given us by the eye-witnesses
of that Humanity.

Now this information, taken thus, ruins the old deduc-
tions and positions, in two respects. For it turns out not
to be true that human nature, in its fullest purity and
perfection, is exempt from mental growth, struggle,
obscurity; from dim and partially mistaken gropings and
guesses. Everywhere, on the contrary, it is of the very
essence of human nature as such, and one of the central
means and pathetic forms of its very greatness and nobility,
to possess such a fringe of shadow to its light—a light
ever limited, ever pushing its way and spreading, mostly
slowly and fitfully, through the gloom. And, again, it is
not true that even that unique union with, and penetration by, the Divinity, which we Historical Christians hold
and proclaim to exist in Our Lord's Humanity, abolishes
these or any characteristics which are essential to human
nature as finite. We are evidently forced to say that God
Himself could not, even by such an unique union, abolish
these characteristics; at least, if He would have a true
Incarnation, if Our Lord was to be as truly man as He
is truly God. But note that we do not, by any such admissions, cease from holding a glorious central, spiritual and
moral inerrancy of insight and instinct in Our Blessed
Lord's teaching and life. In Him as in the Son dwelt the
plenitude of that Spirit which spake by the prophets in
sundry times and divers manners. Never more fully, never
as entirely as to-day, could we say: "Thou hast the words
of Eternal life": indeed He has.

Now, immense and deeply satisfactory conclusions
follow at once from such a recognition of Our Lord's
Humanity, for that extension of the Incarnation, the
Church, and for the official Authority within it. For
the major premiss of an implied piece of theological
reasoning does, indeed, remain as true as ever, viz. that
it is truly impossible that theologians, or indeed Church
Authority generally, should have an inerrancy higher, or
more extensive in degree or kind, than Our Lord's; or,
rather, that He should be less infallible than they. But
c

the minor premiss assumes a view of religious "truth,"
i.e. of the subject-matter of infallibility, which will want
considerable remoulding. For the intellectualist view of
religion, and of the ultimate nature and worth of man,
has prevailed to such an extent as, in good part, to obliterate
the essential characteristics of human nature, and hence of
human nature's worth, in Our Lord's life and character
themselves. And now, contrariwise, a more adequate philosophy of human nature and of its special greatness will
reinforce and apply, in their various degrees, to all human
intelligences under Christ, that which we have learnt
historico-critically about Himself, our Head and Pattern.
And hence church-officialism will necessarily become de-
intellectualised—not in the pernicious sense of discouraging
speculation and learning, or of ceasing to be awake to their
important bearing upon religion, or of neglecting to watch
for the many who do not know much of earthly knowledge, either with or against those who do: but in the
more general, all-pervasive sense, that the inerrancy of
the Church, a derivative of the fuller unfailingness of
Christ, will be taken as primarily one of spiritual instinct
and affinity for and with the religious and moral direction
given to life itself; and all this as exemplified and tested
by the deepest spiritual intuitions, experiences and actions
of the most saintly of her children across the ages, and
with a slow and halting, but, in the long run, sure growth
in adaptation to the successive requirements of all that
is good and great in God's wide world outside. The intellectual will remain a most necessary part of human life
and of the Church's interest and discipline; but it will
now appear as the more or less inadequate mental scaffolding partly shaping, partly shaped by those immanent
experiences of transcendent realities, God, our own soul,
and the community of its fellow-souls—together with the
experienced relations between those living realities: sin,
contrition; grace, pardon; strength not our own; pure
love; the action of the spiritual (if from person to person,

yet through the determinism of phenomenal science) in life in general, and (through the determinism of things and forms, the Sacraments) in religion in particular.

In a word, official Authority will thus get recognised and treated both by its bearers and its subjects as a part, a normally necessary part, but ever only a part, of the total religious life; as a means, one of the normally necessary means, but not as the end or even as one end of that life; as directly Christian and Divine, only in its germinal and most elementary features and functions; and as directly busy with bearing its share in helping on that ever-growing, ever-renewed experience and embodiment of those sacred realities from which Authority itself derives all its rights and duties, and of which it is but the consecrated, ceaseless servant.

II

THE PLACE AND FUNCTION OF THE HISTORICAL ELEMENT IN RELIGION

THE PLACE AND FUNCTION OF THE HISTORICAL ELEMENT IN RELIGION[1]

IT was in 1774 that Kant wrote to Hamann: "If a religion comes to be so placed that the critical knowledge of ancient languages—philological and antiquarian learning—constitutes the basis upon which it must remain built up, throughout all ages and all races: then the man who is most at home in Greek and Hebrew and the like will drag all the orthodox believers, in spite of all their wry faces—as though they were so many children—whithersoever he may choose. For in the matter which, according to their own admission, carries with it the probative force for the whole, these believers cannot measure themselves with that scholar." It would, then, appear to be dangerous in practice to link Religion and History very closely together.

It was in 1777 that Lessing wrote to Schumann: "Contingent truths of History can never become the proof for necessary truths of Reason." It would, then, seem to be impossible in philosophy to tie Religion to History.

And it was as lately as 1873 that Paul de Lagarde wrote: "The entire Christian Church has accepted the Jewish principle of considering as the object of religious emotion a something that has occurred once for all, instead of something which is evermore happening anew —the Past instead of the Present. . . . Yet the spirit of man, essentially eternal, cannot be satisfied with what happens just once for all. It is not religion, it is sheer sentimentality, to absorb one's self in what has come and

[1] A Paper read before the London Society for the Study of Religion on Tuesday, 2 May, 1905.

gone. We require, not the mere Past of God and of the Divine, but their very Presence, here and now." It would then appear to be contrary to the very genius of religion itself to interconnect History and Religion.

Yet, since Kant and Lessing wrote, two great developments have occurred with regard to this matter. The one has now perhaps achieved maturity; the other has, as yet, reached only certain discriminations of a still tentative but already profoundly fruitful kind. The older achievement, Critical and Historical method, has, indeed, attained and perfected a whole series of results of the most striking and far-reaching kind; and the names of the great critical workers are known to all the world. But the newer investigation—as to the nature and meaning of the historical process, the possibility and conditions of a science of History, and the place of that process and of this science in Religion and Theology respectively—this is slowly but surely progressing under our very eyes. Professor Wilhelm Windelband, of Heidelberg, and Professor Heinrich Rickert, of Freiburg, Baden, are, no doubt, the chief path-finders. Yet Professor Percy Gardner here in England has merited well, in the same direction, by his continuous, and as yet far from superfluous, insistence upon the claims and place, in life and thought, of History as a process in actual life, and as a Science within the human mind.

As concerns the supposed or real antagonism between History and Religion, Plato and Plotinus, Augustine, and the great Christian Mystics, remain, for one important side of this deep question, a treasure-house of experience, analysis and stimulation, which is even now far from being exhausted. But among recent workers, I owe most, in this matter, to Professor H. J. Holtzmann, in his book on Rothe's System, 1899; to Professor Ernst Troeltsch, in numerous articles; to M. Henri Bergson, in his *Essai*, 1898; and to the second series of Professor Josiah Royce's *The World and the Individual*, 1901.

Now I propose, in this paper, first briefly to consider the specific character of History, as process and as science, in its difference from natural happenings and natural science; next, to describe the double movement of the human mind and will from History down into Religion, and up from Religion back to History; thirdly, to explain two special points connected with the relations between such phenomenal happenings and this their doctrinal interpretation; and, lastly, to elucidate the connection between History, which apparently is ever and entirely successive, and Religion, which, in its essence, is surely suffused with some apprehension—is it not even some indirect experience?—of Simultaneity and Eternity.

HISTORICAL EVENTS AND NATURAL HAPPENINGS; THE SCIENCE OF HISTORY AND THE SCIENCE OF NATURE

Now with regard to the specific nature of History, as contrasted with what in England is still alone called "Science" — viz. the Mathematico-Physical Sciences — it will be well if we are already possessed by a sense of a certain deeply significant incommensurableness, indeed antagonism, between our actually experienced experience, and all systems of general laws and abstract concepts whatsoever. As to these latter sciences and systems, we know how the greatest possible clearness, and the greatest possible universality, have, from the first, been implied, and were soon proclaimed by man when he attempted to reflect persistently at all, to be the final tests and requirements in these subject-matters. We need but remember Parmenides, with whom the Universal alone is real; Plato, who finds true Being and true Knowledge in the Universal alone; Aristotle, who denies that there is any science of the Particular; Descartes, for whom what is quite clear to our thought is also trans-subjectively real; and Schopenhauer, who refuses the claim of History to be in any sense a true science, because it ever apprehends the Particular, and never the Universal.

1. Yet, against all this mass of authority and tradition, there is every man's continuous experience, that all our ultimate interests and standards, all our valuations of life and of men, ever and intrinsically, suppose and refer to the particular and unique. "Precisely in this uniqueness, this incomparableness of the objects," says Professor Rickert, "reside all our feelings and standards as to the ultimate worth of anything and of all things. And even

the totality of the historic process derives its worth for us from its unrepeatableness; indeed, it was this principle of Uniqueness—a unique Fall, a unique Redemption, a unique life's Trial here, and a unique Judgment hereafter—which decided the victory in favour of the Christian philosophy, in its Patristic stage and form, as against Hellenism, with its ever-increasing insistence upon the Universal and upon indefinite Repetition or, at least, repeatableness."

2. Unless, then, we would constitute such a conception of Science as to have to exclude from it facts and events in precise proportion to their final interest and worth for human beings—and, among these facts, the long vicissitudes and struggles of the Natural Sciences, the martyrdom of a Galileo, the lonely patience of a Newton, the grandly loving condescension and self-oblivion of a Darwin—we must admit, with Professor Windelband, that the "Experimental Sciences consist, in reality, of two great divisions: one kind seeks, in its apprehension of Reality, the General, in the form of Natural Law; the other seeks the Particular, as this has been determined by History. The first contemplates the ever-identical Form, the second contemplates the unique, specifically differentiated Content, of the real happenings. The former sciences are the sciences of Laws; the latter sciences are the sciences of Events. The former teach that which always is; the latter, that which occurred but once. We can call them respectively the *Nomothetic* and the *Idiographic* Sciences."

3. Now Professor Rickert has penetrated further into this all-important question, and has materially improved Professor Windelband's position, by specially insisting upon the following three points.

First, it would be false, Professor Rickert thinks, to assume that certain realities are, in all their aspects and at all their levels, the exclusive objects of the Natural Sciences; and that certain other realities are, similarly, the exclusive objects of the Historical Sciences. On the contrary, "as long as we abstract from the differing worth of things, so long has every single thing in the world its 'history' as well as its 'nature.' Each individual star-fish, indeed each single pebble or bit of chalk, possesses its particular spatial and temporal position, starting-point, succession, and end: it has, then, a 'history.' And each individual human psychical organism, each individual spirit, has its generalities, qualities, and laws common to it and to all other psychic organisms and human spirits: they have, then, a 'nature.'"

Thus "Reality becomes Nature for us, when we contemplate it with reference to the General; it becomes History, when we contemplate it with reference to the Particular. We have thus not two Realities, but only one and the same Reality seen under two different aspects," or at two different levels.

Next, Professor Rickert points out how that only in proportion as we permit ourselves to be guided by values, by our consciousness of them, do we come to attribute a History, in the strict sense of the word, to some realities and not to others. Yet, in attempting to do so, we shall find that, in a certain sense (though not in the sense of Natural Science), Aristotle's position—as to the non-existence of a Science of the Individual—remains true. For the Particular, which will now be included in (Historical) Science, will have to possess a certain general importance. It is the worth, from the point of view of human culture and civilisation, of this individual act or of this individual character, which will here be the test and measure for the incorporation of these acts or characters into (Historical) Science. The Cultural Value will thus be the general principle of these historical sciences, a value which is developed and becomes real (in fact, and in our apprehension), only in and through these unique, non-interchangeable acts and personalities.

We see from this how distinct is the general principle and measure of the Historical from that of the Natural

Sciences; and how the importance even of Psychology, which, in the sense of a science of the general psychic processes, decidedly belongs, by its logical structure, to the Natural Sciences, declines in importance in the same proportion as the cultural significance of individual personality increases. In a history of Religion, of the State, of Science, of Art, the Individual, and his unique apparition and performance in the succession of time, can never be "unessential"; indeed, "here the impulses towards the elaboration of new values almost always proceed from single personalities." Surely, only doctrinaires could wish the brilliant perversity of a Buckle back again.

And thirdly, says Professor Rickert, if we would explain and justify the application of such a selective process and its principle, "we must," evidently, "not only oppose to the Nomothetic the Idiographic method; but we must oppose to the natural-science concept of Universal Law (a law represented, in identical fashion and degree, and with automatic ease, by all the items which fall under it) the concept and conviction of Cultural Worth—a worth which is slowly and ever incompletely realised, in certain spiritual types and growths, by certain difficult, costing, never identical, never simply interchangeable, ever ethically qualified, individual acts and individual personalities." Hence, a belief in the reality and value of these Cultural Forces and Ends at work in these types is as necessary to the constitution and vitality of the Historical Sciences, as a belief in the unfailing applicability of Natural Law to all happenings at their "natural" level is essential to the constitution and vitality of the Natural Sciences. In a word, without Teleological concepts and Teleological beliefs there can be no History, in the full sense of the term, either as a Process or as a Science.

And if the Natural Sciences have got the advantage over the Historical ones, in their indefinitely greater clearness and their ready transferableness from one human brain to the other, the Historical Sciences have got the advantage over the Natural ones, in their indefinitely greater vividness, depth, and reality. In the ultimate resort, room can be found for the severest natural-science methods, and for the fullest recognition of their necessity and irreplaceable importance, in a wisely cultural conception of the world and of life; whereas room cannot be found in any purely natural-science scheme of the world and of life (if that scheme be taken, not only as final at its own depth and stage of apprehension, but as ultimate altogether) for Culture and History, as possessed of objective worth.

4. But, if all this be so, then it would be inconceivable that Religion should not possess close and insuppressible relations with History. For we have seen that History itself requires, both in those who make its events, and in those who interpret those events without violation of their very mainspring, faith of a most real kind. And we see that all characteristically human activities, presuppositions and ultimate motives and ends, belong to this Cultural, Historical domain. Hence Religion will either not be a characteristic and deep human activity at all, and will have no affinity with dispositions and acts of faith; or it will at least include the Historical, and will presumably express itself, and its expressions will have to be studied, at all events in the first instance, according to the method, categories, and ideals of History.

II

THE MIND'S MOVEMENT FROM THE APPREHENSION OF HIS-
TORICAL EVENTS AT THEIR PHENOMENAL LEVEL TO
THE CONVICTION AS TO THEIR SPIRITUAL DEPTH AND
SIGNIFICANCE; AND THE MIND'S MOVEMENT BACK
FROM THIS CONVICTION TO THAT APPREHENSION

Now, given the existence of such inalienable relations
between History and Religion, we speedily find ourselves
confronted by two closely related problems.

There is the problem of the movement of the mind,
on from the apprehension of such and such a Happening,
taken as a spiritually and ethically indifferent pheno-
menon, to the conviction of such and such a super-sensible,
spiritual and ethical Reality and meaning, taken as underlying and expressing itself in that Happening. And there
is the problem of the mind's movement, back from its
spiritual, ontological interpretation and penetration of
that Happening, to the phenomenal, natural-science level
of that occurrence.

1. Now, with regard to the movement, from the
Phenomenal and the mind's apprehension of that appearance, down to the Spiritual and the whole character's
faith in this reality, it will be well for us to take note of
how the *more* and the *other* which undoubtedly exist
in the latter act as compared with the former are to be
found more or less in every fully historical act, and in
every fully historical judgment. Thus even the most
liberal Jew's religious affirmation of Jeremiah, Akiba,
or Maimonides, as figures that concern his and our
religious life and standards, is something which, whilst
it could not exist healthily and fruitfully without a
persuasion of the actual reality of those individuals, is

profoundly more and other than the simple conviction as to that reality, apprehended, so far, only as a natural item. For this latter simple conviction is possible, indeed inevitable, for any sane man to whom would be submitted the evidence for those facts, taken as so many phenomena or natural items; whilst the former affirmation requires, to come about at all, certain ethical and religious needs, experiences and aspirations, and their awakening or deepening on occasion of the mind's contact with these phenomena. It is these dispositions and requirements which, if awakened, penetrate and interpret these phenomena, and find in them so many individual expressions and realisations, more or less complete, of a spiritual type. And this type is simultaneously felt to be of supreme value, to bear with it a right to our full assent, as a condition for our own spiritual development—a development which will but be an individual variation upon that same type. And substantially the same is no doubt true of every believing Buddhist's main affirmations concerning Gautama, of every believing Mohammedan's similar affirmations concerning Mohammed, and of every believing Christian's affirmations concerning Christ.

Indeed, every man who believes with fullness and continuity in anything at all—be it the objective worth of the moral law, or the obligation of truthfulness and accuracy of mind and speech at all costs, or the more than simply empirical worth of Natural Science, or the more than merely utilitarian importance of his country's welfare, or of his wife's or daughter's chastity—every such man does not only see, he penetrates and interprets, the merely phenomenal data, the layer of undeniability which first confronts us all in the facts and persons that surround us. And it would not be difficult to show that even the purest sceptic known to history has never yet been "pure" enough not surreptitiously to practise and to utilise, in view of his scepticism, some such spiritual experience and faith, and some such consequent inter-

pretation of the happenings around him, which, if left
uninterpreted, would, for him also, be but phenomena,
natural happenings, without a trace of ethical significance.

Nor need the, at first sight, bewildering diversity and
hopeless contradiction subsisting between all these interpretations of one and the same or of similar happenings
lead us to final scepticism as to the fruitfulness and re-
liability of this general movement of the mind, and, hence,
as to the worth, the correspondence with reality, of its
most deliberate, substantial, and central affirmations. For,
as Professor Volkelt admirably puts it: "the one ideal
necessity of thought"—and this necessity we cannot but
trust, since all attempts to dissent from it always presuppose its cogency—"spreads itself out in a multiform
fullness of relative necessities of thought, pours its riches
into them, and constitutes them members of the Kingdom
of Truth which thus grows on and on. Not one of these
relative necessities of thought—in so far as they are typical
and significant—is superfluous, but each represents a
necessary link in the growth of truth; each approximates,
from this or from that side, to the ideal necessity
of thought; each can boast of having its share in
the truth."

Indeed, as Professor Volkelt points out elsewhere, a
wide survey of all the facts of the case drives us to a further
and final conviction. "It is certain, on the one hand, that
the different movements of philosophy have been largely
determined by historical currents, and that these historical currents have taken their course according to
starting-points and directions quite other than those of
logical necessity. On the other hand, it is equally certain
that these historically determined movements and modes
of thought are, after all, in the service of logical necessity,
indeed actually embody its progressive realisation. And
these two sides of the actual situation can hardly be recon-
ciled by us otherwise than by the assumption that the
forces of history are, with their real roots and energies,

D

already planned (unbeknown to their agents) in view to agreement with the requirements and objects of Thought and of Truth. In this way, each of the different spheres of mental and spiritual life and struggle, originally destined each for the others, in reality furthers the purposes of those others, even when, in its conscious strivings, this or that sphere attends exclusively to its own particular laws and standards. For, if this original teleological inter-relation were really absent, we could not understand how the historic forces, when they come to influence and determine philosophical thinking, should, instead of contaminating it, through their introduction of religious, artistic, political, or other motives, actually occasion, as undoubtedly they do, an essential progress in that think-ing." If we but substitute Religion for Philosophy in this striking passage, we shall, I think, get a very satisfactory position with regard to the possibility and *rationale* of the movement from phenomenal happenings and their apprehension on into their inner spiritual reality and meaning.

We shall, however, have continually to bear in mind a lesson writ large over the history of religion. For here, indeed, we can and should find truth, variously ample fragments of one and the same truth, in all the larger, long-lived, and ethically and spiritually fruitful religious personalities, systems, and bodies; but we can, and should perceive that we have to do with differing depths and levels of truth, and that the advance directly demonstrable in religious history is no doubt slow, intermittent, never fully balanced or completely victorious; at its best rather spiral than straight: yet that it has been, in certain great steps, truly a progress on and into greater depths of insight, into a richer and more interpenetrative variety in unity, into larger powers of adaptation to and absorp-tion of the truths found elsewhere, and into ampler ability to interpret, satisfy and transform an ever-increas-ing number of problems, aspirations, and miseries of the spiritual and ethical nature and consciousness of man. Hence, we shall neither say that God and His truth, in any degree and form, are only here or only there, for, in various degrees and forms, they are simply everywhere; nor that they are to be found in the same form, stage, and degree everywhere, for in no two individuals, religious bodies, races, or stages of history, are they to be found either identical in their respective strength and weakness, or at the same level of development, or with the same spiritual depth and fruitfulness.

If *Panentheism*, the doctrine that God is in all things, is, here also, with regard to every wholesome element in all these religions, in the right; Pantheism, the doctrine that God is *equally* in all things, is, here also, profoundly false. Indeed, we shall find that the differences between these simultaneous or successive varieties of Types, and of the realisation of these Types, are, like unto all that directly enters into full History, differences not of quantity but of quality. Is not this the ultimate philosophy underlying the utterly unique position attributed by Athanasianism to Our Lord and His life? In so far as we are spiritual personalities at all, we all are necessarily individual and unique; He would be this in a supreme manner: His very uniqueness testifying to His belonging to that Kingdom of Spirits in which to be at all is to be, in some way, unique.

2. As to the mind's movements back, from the spiritual substance and interpretation of History, to History's phenomenal surface, I would draw special attention to what is here a continuous source of complications and dangers. The human mind is so constituted that it cannot have a profound accession of spiritual or other insight or emotion, without being impelled, in some degree or way, to picture (as it were spatially to project) this truth and conviction in some vivid, dramatic configuration. Now, in the cases under consideration, it was some direct sense-impressions, the phenomenal surface of some factual

reality, which gave occasion to, and furnished the immediate material for, all that interpretative, penetrative work.
Yet those very impressions are now found (analogously to
the case in the Natural Sciences, where the particular
phenomenal item is never accepted as sufficiently expressive of the universal law, a law which, nevertheless, that
item is held to embody quite necessarily and is known to
have stimulated the mind towards the discovery of that
law) to obscure as well as to reveal, to manifest, in but a
halting manner, that which is now held to constitute their
substratum and true function. Hence will be set going,
all but inevitably, and in most cases quite automatically,
a process of modification—of transposition, omission,
addition, enlargement, development—in those phenomenal
data, and in their first organisation.

An extreme, hence specially instructive, case of this
law, is that presented by the action of St. Francis Xavier's
devotees, who cut up the less immediately religious of
his autograph letters into little squares—with one letter
in each square—and then re-arranged these little squares
as figures of the Cross, the Anchor, a Crown, in now
direct indication of the writer's most real self-immolation,
boundless hope, and rich reward.

Now the use or mischief, and the degree in the value,
of such transformations depend entirely upon three
things: upon the ultimate worth of the spiritual reality
or type expressed by them; upon the reasonableness, for
a spiritually awakened and yet critically trained mind, of
believing in a special presence and operation of that
reality within this particular set of appearances; and upon
our being free and able, in proportion to our becoming
alive to our manifold duties in the matter, to distinguish
conscientiously between the accurate apprehension of
phenomena and the profound penetration of their spiritual
meaning.

It is clear that this third condition is being already
largely accepted and observed as regards the Old Testa-

ment. But in the New, it is, most understandably, still meeting with an opposition which not infrequently defeats its own primary object. The Fourth Gospel especially presents us with a large collection of rearrangements and expansions of the phenomenal materials which had given occasion to the faith which now returns to represent, for the later generation in whose behoof this great book was written, its own spiritual apprehension and interpretation of those phenomenal facts, by means of this its transformation of them. The Cleansing of the Temple is thus thrown back, from some few days before the death of Jesus, which took place doubtless but some eight or nine months after the opening of His public Ministry, to the opening of that Ministry; and His Ministry is now made to last three and a half years—one-half the sacred number seven. The sacrifice of the Paschal Lamb is shifted from the eve before His death, to the very time when He, its true anti-type, the "Lamb of God," was dying upon the Cross. The Eucharistic Act at the Last Supper in the upper chamber at Jerusalem, an act already sufficiently recorded by the three Synoptists, is here represented by a long doctrinal prediction of the institution and nature of that Holy Eucharist, placed two years before that last scene, and in connection with the open-air feeding of the great multitude near by to Capernaum, at the zenith of the popularity of Him Who here appears as the Bread of Life. And the emphatic insistence of the Appendix (chap. xxi. 11) upon the number 153 of the fishes, caught after the Resurrection on the Lake of Galilee, no doubt here means (as we can find from the still extant *Halieutica* of Oppianus Cilix, composed under Marcus Aurelius, where the number of all extant kinds of fishes is given at that figure) that *all kinds* of fishes were caught. The writer of that Johannine Appendix, or some previous writer copied by him, has thus added to the original factual material what looks, at first, as though but an actual, accidental number, but which is here simply a detail in the dramatic presentation of the doctrine that the Church's Apostolate extends to all kinds of human souls.

The precise difficulty occasioned for us poor moderns by all this shall be considered again in connection with the following further points.

III

TWO DIFFICULTIES CONNECTED WITH THE DISCRIMINATION
BETWEEN REALITY AT ITS PHENOMENAL LEVEL, AND
REALITY IN ITS DEPTH AND SPIRITUAL SIGNIFICANCE

I would, then, draw forcible attention to two points.

1. There is first what Wellhausen somewhere insists upon so strongly—the very slow, very late, very difficult, never simply spontaneous growth and persistence, in the human race and in any one human soul, of the sense and practice of mental accuracy, with regard to the apprehension and attestation of *factual* things and events. Indeed, even the instinct is of late growth that such accuracy is an ideal as difficult of close approach as, proportionately to our becoming aware of it, it is binding upon us all.

It is, indeed, impossible for any careful and candid student not to feel that not only our present-day answers and solutions, but our present-day questions and problems, were simply unknown to, or were considerably different for, those observers, thinkers, and recorders of antiquity (upon whom, after all, we depend for the presentation of our historical materials), in this matter of the distinction between the phenomenal surface of factual reality, and the interpretation of this reality's depths in doctrinal expansions and pictures. Let any candid reader ask himself, e.g., how far the authors of the Book of Henoch held that this or that most precisely, most vividly described "fact" would really occur factually in the future; or, again, as to how far Philo held this or that past "fact," something certainly described by him as we should now describe a thing held by us to have phenomenally occurred

43

(e.g. the moving of the rock in the wake of the Israelites' march through the Desert), to have factually happened; and the answer will, or certainly ought to, be that we are but artificially forcing certain distinctions, which are elementary for our minds, upon intelligences in which those lines of demarcation were very vague and floating.

We cannot, then, take the mere emphasis, clearness, and schematic presentation of apparently phenomenal happenings as guarantees of their real "factualness." For, as we see in the Priestly Code and in Ezekiel, religious history and prophecy actually tend to become *more* clear, emphatic, and, as it were, mathematically balanced, as they get further away from the original phenomenal happenings or concrete hopes. And the necessary suspense of judgment and slow approximation to a probable solution, as to the factual or non-factual character of this or that part of the narratives thus handed down to us, will be specially trying to one who feeds his faith upon at least a certain nucleus of the histories thus expanded, especially if he further feels and holds that a certain amount of such phenomenal "factualness" is simply essential to this his religious faith.

2. Now the second point which I would urge, at first adds to, but in the end takes away from, the difficulty which springs from that haze of phenomenal and factual-seeming affirmations, which ever plays, as a margin, around the downright factual occasions and the vital spiritual interpretations of every creed and of every at all complex conviction. I am thinking of the ambiguity, at first sight closely akin to the floating uncertainty just considered, which characterises the appeal to concrete phenomenal events and to their documentary attestation—the appeal, I mean, as ordinarily practised by the historical religions. For, on the one hand, every theology, which is not content with a piecemeal illuminism or with moving in an obvious vicious circle, finds itself constrained to appeal to the witness of historical docu-

ments of various kinds; to invite the historical and critical examination of their contents and evidence; and to admit that, should there be no fairly cogent historical proof for, still more should there be conclusive historical proof against, the phenomenal factualness of a certain central nucleus of events (for, at this stage, there is as yet no question as to the spiritual substance and meaning of these events), then its faith would either have to go altogether, or to find its immediate occasion and material in another set of phenomenal happenings.

Kant's objection, if at all pressed or extended, does not really hold. For religion—above all, the Christian religion—cannot but require the aid of every side of man's essential nature, even at the cost of a certain apparent dependence upon things and functions not directly religious at all. And, indeed, it is only by treating a certain useful division of labour, and a certain ultimate hierarchy and organisation of ends, as though that division meant ultimate and absolute separation, and as though this hierarchy meant the sacrifice of their specific character, on the part of the relatively lower functions, to the special nature of the higher ones, that we can come to consider religion and theology as not, in proportion to their fullness, requiring the aid of certain immediately non-religious activities of the mind. God is as truly the God of Nature as the God of Grace: of "that which" bravely "questioneth and that which" humbly "kneels": the immediately religious functions and objects cannot be, as a matter of fact never are, properly exercised and attained, if limited to exclusively or directly religious occasions, means, or ends. If religion cannot be the leaven in the flour, the salt of the earth, the light of the world, unless itself is truly leaven, salt, and light: neither can it be these things, unless there exist, unless it acknowledges, respects, and comes into close contact with, flour and earth and world. And all this is, surely, no wonder. For, in so far as these materials and elements stimulate and are permeable by those preservative and ennobling forces, it is God who has made the one set as truly as the other, and has made the one for the other—or, rather, for an ideally previous but executively consequent whole—a whole which is greater than, which alone gives its ultimate place and function to, even the leaven and the salt and the light.

3. But, on the other hand, the average practice of every theology tends to appeal to historical criticism, as long as the criticism supports it, or attacks one of its rivals; and to ignore or to oppose criticism, of precisely the same type and cogency, as soon as the criticism concludes against the phenomenal factualness assumed to underlie of necessity this or that doctrine of this theology. And thus theology appears to be as incapable of renouncing the appeal to historical tests as of abiding by them.

Theologians, indeed, are generally perfectly willing that historical criticism should establish, or even should reject, this or that phenomenal happening, as such, in accordance with the critical principles accepted by all the world when they are applied to any other kind of historical evidence; but on condition that, the critic's work being concluded, they should be able to come forward, and to proclaim the factual character of those impugned phenomenal happenings, on, I take it, one or more of three grounds.

Historical Criticism is declared to be mere surface work. It is Faith that sees deeply; and the faith of ages in this or that doctrine, including belief in its phenomenally factual base, and in an intrinsic, necessary connection between that faith and this belief, sees and knows here with authority, where criticism is out of its depth.

Again, the connection between the doctrines built upon these challenged phenomenal happenings and the doctrines which are built upon unchallenged factual events, is too close and intrinsic, for the former doctrines, and with them their phenomenally factual base, not to be reasonably unchallengeable by criticism, in the mind of one prepared to accept, or who has accepted, the truth of these latter doctrines and phenomenal happenings.

Or, finally, the ethical and spiritual fruits of belief in, and of practical dependence upon, the doctrines built upon those challenged phenomenal happenings, are too clear and deep (to one who accepts such a test, and holds it to be affirmatively met in the case of the other doctrines based upon the unchallenged happenings), for confidence in the factual character of the phenomenal happenings underlying the former doctrines not to be well-placed.

4. Now I take it that only the following general position will combine the elements of truth present in such contentions. This position would distinguish sharply between belief in the strict necessity, for a particular historical religion and theology, of a centre of factual phenomenal happenings; and belief in the strict necessity for factual phenomenal happenings to lie at the bottom of each separate article of that religion and theology. It would affirm the former belief, and would deny the second. It would, again, distinguish sharply, and everywhere, between the phenomenal happenings with the critical evidences for them, and the spiritual substance of those happenings and its penetration; and would treat the former as the necessary and divinely-willed, yet "secular" and natural *prolegomena*, and the latter as the true gift and work of religious experience, grace, and faith. And it would, finally, distinguish sharply between hesitation or non-acceptance, in regard to the factualness of this or that phenomenal happening, belief in which may have hitherto been the part-occasion of, and may have given a vivid presentation to, some one point or application of the Christian Faith, and denial of any kind or degree of spiritual and moral truth and fruitfulness in that point or application. We all make an analogous distinction in reference to the relations between the spiritual soul and the material body. The necessity for that soul's functioning, during this

life, of having a physical body in and through which to function, does not involve a corresponding necessity for that functioning being strictly limited to the range of that physical body: as a matter of fact, the spirit's range seems to be distinctly wider than that of its physical yoke-fellow and instrument.

IV

But the last and greatest problem still confronts us. Is then Reality at its deepest, is God Himself, or at least is the Spirit of Man, to be conceived as essentially and purely successive—as an unending process; as involving, if not juxtaposition in space, at least succession in time?

1. If Renan, in this a kind of rabid Hegelian of the Left, is wrong in maintaining that God Himself is but in process of becoming, are not at least Leibnitz and Robert Browning right in conceiving man's spirit as so essentially successive in its operations, that Heaven itself is held to be unthinkable, indeed undesirable for man, except as an unending succession of knowings, feelings, strugglings, willings, achievings by the spirit of man, in and with the help of the Spirit of God? Or is not the Mysticism of all times and places right precisely on one point, in holding the opposite view? and is not man able, even here and now, vividly to conceive, is he not continuously and necessarily implying, and in some moments and in some degree and form experiencing, however indirectly, the essentially spaceless and timeless character of ultimate Reality, of all Normative Beauty, Truth, and Goodness, indeed of his own spirit and its fundamental experience of that Reality, in proportion as this spirit bears within it the deepest characteristics of humanity?

2. Now, as Professor H. J. Holtzmann puts it, "we can indeed know about ourselves only in so far as we arrange the content of our interior experience under the form of a something perceived in time; and as, in this way, we

become ourselves so many phenomena to our own selves. Yet we can as little, whilst so doing, keep ourselves from considering this form of cognition as, somehow, in strange contradiction to its object. If we would recognise this form as truly adequate to its object, our whole being would have to be resolved into a pure flux of succession, so that we ourselves would, in proportion to the temporal distance of the Now from the Then, have gradually to become a vanishing point, a sheer myth to our own selves. . . . And yet we undoubtedly become more sure of the supertemporal unity of our being in proportion to the deepening of our personality. As this our personality becomes established, we cease to know whether the years are flying or are crawling past us, and we become indifferent to such ravages as Time can execute against us. . . . Indeed, psychology is showing us how instantaneously our time-perception is modified, by even slight changes in our physical organisation. . . . We cannot, then, accept objective Time otherwise than as a useful convention; and must continuously bear in mind the fact, as certain as it is permanently incomprehensible by our understanding, that the white light of Reality, which fills our consciousness with its real content, is, as it were, broken up and spread out for us, as though by a prism, into a colour-spectrum; so that what, in itself, exists in an immediate unity becomes understandable to us only as a juxtaposition and succession. Beyond that prism there is neither juxtaposition, Space, nor succession, Time."

3. One chief point and important distinction in this whole position has been considered and, I think, satisfactorily met, by Aristotle; hence, as far back as about 340 B.C. As Mr. Schiller, in the finest of his essays in *Humanism*, has admirably argued, we are in sore want of some such conception as the great Stageirite's doctrine of "Unmoving Energy." As Mr. Schiller well puts it: "Instead of classifying Energeia under Kinesis, 'function' under 'process,' Aristotle simply makes Energeia the

wider and supremer notion, and subsumes Kinesis under it as a peculiar species, viz., an *imperfect* Energeia. Kinesis, that is, arises from the longing of the imperfect for the perfect, of the 'matter' for the 'form'; it is simply the process whereby it reaches whatever degree of perfection the inherent limitations of its nature concede to it." And hence God, the All-perfect, is considered as pure Function, Energy, without a touch of Process. He is thus the "Actus Purus" of Aquinas, and of all the Christian Scholastics ever since.

It is clear that we thus get in Aristotle the earliest, and even to this moment the most satisfactory and scientific, description and explanation of that great stream of experience and conception which runs throughout all the fuller and saner Christian Mysticism—the experience and conception of "Action"—the full Functioning of the Spirit and Personality, in which all its Potentiality is actualised, and where the very fullness, richness, and harmony of the Action produces an overflowing joy and peace, an equilibrium of the profoundest, purest Energising; and all this in contrast to "Activity," which is but a restless, intermittent, feverish, self-occupied moving to and fro of some ineffectual wishings, imperfect willings and the like, in the midst of numerous unactualised capabilities. And the human being in becoming more and more Spirit and Personality—more and more Function and Action, and less and less mere Process and Activity—becomes more and more like to God, the ceaseless, utter realisation of all His nature's possibilities.

4. Now it is only Emptiness, not Action, and Unity of mere Oneness, and not Unity in Diversity, which are in ultimate antagonism with History: indeed, History is both achieved and perceived only if we believe and will more than mere Succession, more than sheer Process. There is no ultimate conflict between History and Simultaneity, as long as we recognise three things. We must grant the real variety-in-unity of this simultaneity; we

have to admit that the worth of this variety springs from
an already immanentally extant and operative scheme by
which each differing constituent finds a unique meaning
and happiness in developing itself in a non-interchangeable position within, and as a non-replaceable contribution to, the larger whole; and we have to hold that the work,
pain, and joy required for, and following upon, the effective
constitution of these "cultural" organisms, are deeply
real also, and are somehow directly connected with, are
already somehow represented, and will become equi-
valently apparent, in the ultimate non-successive Reality.
Thus neither any particular individual nor any particular
age has to wait, with regard to the whole of its meaning
and effectiveness, for other individuals or for other ages.
For we each of us already form, at our best, one particular
link in but one great chain from earth to heaven; yet each
little link is also, severally, already linked directly to
Heaven itself.

5. Indeed, there are ever two respects in which History,
in the full sense of the word, in its practice denies, and in
its theory should repudiate, the ultimacy of all mere
clock-time.

History is obliged, for clearness' sake, to project its
objects and their life, as it were, on to the screen of clock-
time succession. Yet M. Henry Bergson has shown, with
wonderful delicacy and penetration, that, in the process
of this projection, certain profound modifications in what
we know to be the true nature of the History thus pro-
jected are necessarily introduced. The purely *quantita-
tive* character of spatial concepts, and of the spatial motion
of an atom (at an equal or measurably different rate of
progress) from one spatial point to another and another
ever equidistant one, is made to replace, by way of
"explaining," the purely *qualitative* spiritual forces and
experiences, such and such mental apprehensions, emotions, volitions, and their deeper effects, all which things
occur in every conceivable variation of rapidity or slow-

ness. And, above all, the fixity and *mutual exclusiveness* of those pieces of clock-time—for these characteristics also have been taken over from the spatial concept—get forced again, as a would-be explanation, upon the quite different, because essentially overlapping *interpenetrative*, mutually modifying forces and experiences of man's inner life. Now this kind of varyingly rapid or slow succession of qualitatively various, mutually interpenetrative, forces and experiences, M. Bergson calls "Duration," as against (clock-) "Time"; and he shows this clock-Time to be a compromise, the joint product of Duration, which alone is truly experienced, and of Space, which alone is clearly picturable. And since all the characteristically human values and ideals, indeed the very notion of worth, are developed, captured, and maintained, not in Time, but in Duration, History is busy with realities which, at bottom, even here and now, are not in "Time" at all.

But even further. If, with Professor Rickert, we insist that History essentially involves a judgment of worth, and hence necessarily lays the emphasis not upon Becoming as such, but upon the worth of this Becoming and of the Being that thus becomes: we find that History ever postulates and involves, as its background and foundation, not even Duration, but, at least, as an imperative measure and ideal, a pure Simultaneity, where all Process, even every worthy Process, ends in pure Function of the most varied and the most unified, the noblest and the most fruitful kind.

6. Now it is because of these, its two super-temporal characteristics, that History is not in any real antagonism with Religion. And more than this should be affirmed. For History is essentially necessary to Religion if only as a corrective, probably the sole efficient corrective, against the delusions of a false Mysticism. For false Mysticism has not been satisfied with denying mere Clock-time and proclaiming Simultaneity and Action as

E

what ultimate Reality already fully is, and as what we ourselves may hope, in a future form of existence, to possess, according to our creaturely degree, in predominance and with clearness. But it has generally ignored or denied the profoundly important element of Duration; and, still worse, has attempted to reduce the Simultaneity to a mere empty point of blank Unity.

Now these two errors are inter-related; and History, and the acceptance of History as necessary to Religion, effectually suppresses them both. *Because* there is so rich a variety of constituents to harmonise, with every constituent, as far as possible, itself again an organism deriving its fuller self-expression from its function in that larger organisation; *therefore* we poor little human organisers require Duration, till our organising task be fulfilled. And *because* this harmonisation and integration —not of dead things into a dead mosaic, but of living forces into a great equilibrium of, at least preponderatingly, simultaneous action of the richest, most unified and efficacious kind—is our end and ideal; *therefore* has History got a true final meaning, and therefore will that Simultaneity in no way abolish even the least of the valuable resultants of the Succession in History, or be in any sharp antagonism with what now looks like mere Process, but which, to be truly Historical, is even now something more than such mere succession.

Simultaneity and Eternity would be as worthless as Process, if they were mere empty forms; the profound worth of what is held, of what the holder is, thus simultaneously, has to be there, for the simultaneous presence of it all to matter truly. But given the profound worth and reality of what we then have and are, and hence the maximum unity in variety and variety in unity possible to our natures: then Simultaneity, which even now we cannot but apprehend to be the true form of full Reality, and to be involved even in our own present spiritual life at its deepest, will indeed add to, for it will be the adequate expression of, Abiding Beauty, Truth and Goodness. The Spirit's little melody in Duration would then become a mighty harmony, a *Totum Simul*, in Eternity: that Eternity the sense of which underlies and accompanies all our deepest denials, all our deepest affirmations, hence all our History, even here and now.

III

ON THE PLACE AND FUNCTION, WITHIN RELIGION, OF THE BODY, OF HISTORY, AND OF INSTITUTIONS

III

ON THE PLACE AND FUNCTION, WITHIN RELIGION, OF THE BODY, OF HISTORY, AND OF INSTITUTIONS [1]

1. IN my address to you this evening I will everywhere presuppose the following seven great principles so nobly taught you by your distinguished President:

(i.) Religion, in proportion to its depth and self-knowledge, is never a means, is always an end, *the* end.

(ii.) Religion, in proportion to its genuine religiousness, always affirms more and other than laws of the mind or impressions of the soul. It ever affirms Reality, a Reality, *the* Reality distinct from ourselves, the self-subsistent Spirit, God. It is, essentially, affirmation of Fact, of what *is*, what aboriginally, supremely *is*. It is, in this sense and degree, ontological, metaphysical: it is this, or it is nothing.

(iii.) Religion presupposes, and reveals, man as inevitably moved by, and in travail with, this sense of, and thirst after, truth, *the* truth, reality, *the* Reality. Man cannot renounce this sense and thirst as an illusion; the very dignity and passion that accompany or foster, at any time, his declaration of such illusion, ever imply such ontology—that there somehow exists a more than merely human truth and reality, and that man somehow really experiences it.

(iv.) Religion requires the actuation of *all* man's faculties; it is in relation with *all* the other levels and ranges of man's experience. The sense of Beauty, the

[1] An Address delivered to the Religious Thought Society, under the presidency of Dean Inge, July 1913.

sense of Truth, the sense of Goodness—above all, the sense of the inadequacy of all our purely human expressions of them all, and yet that these senses are not vain or merely subjective and simply human: all these finally imply, all are necessary to, all are in relation with, the full and healthy life of religion.

(v.) Religion is not a refuge, *the* refuge from scepticism, and not a substitute, *the* substitute for non-religious thought and reality; it positively requires, and it reveals, the truth and well-groundedness of the fundamental, also the non-religious needs, virtues, aspirations of every human mind and soul.

(vi.) Religion cannot be taken as essentially and everywhere separate from, and indifferent to, History. Whatever may be the difficulties and obscurities of their inter-relation—*that* is too *simpliste* and too sceptical a solution.

(vii.) And, finally, man attains in religion, as truly as elsewhere—once given his wholehearted striving—in proportion as he seeks not too directly, not feverishly and strainingly, but in a largely subconscious, waiting, genial, expansive, endlessly patient, sunny manner. This is indeed the "gütliche nicht grimmige Ernst" of the great German mediæval mystics.

2. I now proceed to invite you to help me in building upon, and in protecting, these foundations common to the Dean and myself. The further convictions now to be developed cannot claim to be thus common to us; yet they have come to be felt and to be found by me, during and after forty years and more of thought, action and suffering in these matters, to be true applications and protections of those foundations.

I have chosen my special subject-matter, because I can assume you to be all more or less historically and institutionally nurtured and inclined, indeed to be, predominantly, practising members of the Church of England, and yet to be all more or less beset—as who is not, in these our times and troubles?—with the inclination to have done with any and all contingent, temporal and local, audible and visible things—with the Bodily, the Historical, the Institutional in Religion. For Religion has, surely, only to do with the Absolute, the Spiritual, the Eternal and Omnipresent: with the simple pure human spirit in its spiritual relation with the one Spirit of Spirits, God.

And I have taken George Fox's *Journal* as my spring-board, sample-book, and test. For it is English, and it is, in its complete and fully authentic text, still new as a publication (end of 1911). Again, we get in the Quaker position, especially as thus practised and proclaimed by Fox, probably the sanest and richest of such purely spiritualist religious attempts that are sufficiently within our own time, place, race and experience, to be really, perhaps readily, understood by us. And, finally, I personally owe much to Quakers, and I sincerely care for many an ingredient of the Quaker habits and convictions: I thus have a good chance of understanding because I love.

I propose, then, first roughly to sketch what I believe Psychology to teach concerning the operation of man's mind and the awakening and awareness of man's spirit; and what I think History teaches as to the action and interaction of man's body and spirit, of History and the Non-successive, of Institutions and the Omnipresent, within Religion in general.

I intend next to quote and describe George Fox's attitude towards all these things, and to bring out his spiritual nobility and the striking measure of abiding truth and fruitfulness to be found in his life and teaching.

And I will finally return to modern Psychology with greater detail, and to recent study of Christian origins with some precision; and will try to indicate where they agree with Fox, and where and why we require something more inclusive, something possessed of more range, tension and justice, if we would leave and give to religion its full balance, sanity, depth and appeal.

I

If we look back or around with some insight amongst human lives, or if we at all adequately analyse our own selves, we everywhere find an interaction, a tension, a giving and a taking, an hostility and a friendship, a bridging and a breaking, between the bodily and the mental, the present and the past, the individual and the social. I thus find the claims of my body upon or even against my mind, and the claims of my mind upon or even against my body; the claims of the past—the past of other personalities or of my own personality—upon my own, or my nation's, or my race's present condition and disposition, upon my *hic et nunc*, and the claims of this, my own, or my country's, or my race's present upon that past; and, finally, the claims of my own individuality upon the family, or society, or nation, race, or Church to which I belong—as those organisms are now, contemporaneously with myself—and the claims of these various complexes upon this my individuality.

1. As a matter of simple fact we nowhere find, as a constituent of our own human life and nature (except we ourselves make abstractions), *pure* spirit, or *pure* body, or a *purely* spiritual or a *purely* bodily act. But everywhere we only find spirit awakened by, and in its turn awakening, checking, impelling, spiritualising body; and body furnishing such awakening, material, friction, medium of expression and of appeal, yet also obstruction and deflection, to spirit. Thus those interesting cases of Laura Bridgman (1829–89), and of Helen Keller (born 1880), the two blind deaf-mutes born and educated in the United States of America, show us, as Professor Jastrow, their careful student, writes, that "the mental training and culture resulting from the assimilation and elaboration of ideas is measurably" (i.e. to some appreciable extent) "independent of the sensory means by which the mate-

rials for these are furnished." But he has promptly to add: "Yet this is but moderately true: our senses are more than a scaffolding to knowledge. . . . The mental canvas, though conveying a similar impression, is not suffused with the glow of vivid life-likeness, with the warm and rich reality of experience. The normality of the intellectual life of a gifted blind-deaf person"—such as it is—"is largely the resultant of the community of expression with that of the seeing and hearing." But "the richness of the verbal associations must inevitably be paler and more meagre, and, in certain directions, defective or false. This 'literary' tone of thought and memory, of imagination and application, is unmistakably reflected in the writings and conversation of Helen Keller." [1]

Now all this cannot fail to apply not only to the mind's and spirit's apprehension of historical events and personalities, but also to their sense of and search after God, the Infinite. For this sense and this search of the Infinite —especially the Religious Infinite, the simultaneous, complete Perfection—springs up, for us men, in contrast with, hence on occasion of, our consciousness of the Finite. Augustine's "Thou hast made us for Thyself, and our heart is without rest until it rests in Thee," doubtless requires primarily, to be experienced, God and the human soul; yet it also requires this human soul to be awake to, and to be solicited by, the endless variety of sensible things and of their sensible impressions, furnished by the sensible world.

But, indeed, even the simple awareness of our minds with respect to these our own minds, or to other fellow-minds, or to the Supreme Mind, God, appears (at least in its inception and within this earthly life of ours) to be tied to the stimulation of the senses belonging to the bodies conjoined to these our minds. Thus those two blind deaf-mutes will have been simply without any awareness

[1] *Dictionary of Philosophy and Psychology*, ed. J. M. Baldwin, 1911, under Bridgman.

of their own minds or of other minds, or of God, before *some* awakening of some sense perception.

The same lesson of the pathetic dependence of spirit upon body is exhibited in cases of hysteria, where the swiftness, fullness, balance and truth of the soul's emotional response appears closely linked with the all-round and harmonious awakeness of the psycho-physical organism, the nervous health of the body connected with this soul. Dr. Pierre Janet's books especially are full of cases to the point. And, indeed, any one of us can all but continually observe cases, which fall short of such marked abnormality, yet which nevertheless indicate, plainly enough, the close connection between nervous health and emotional range, depth and balance.

2. And History is penetrated, from one end to the other, with a similar polarity — an interdependence, a tension and hostility, a mutual incapacity to do without or to cohabit peacefully, of Past and Present. Each twin would often willingly kill the other; neither twin can, for one instant, really exist without the other.

And here, although the contrast and conflict is often as acute as ever is or can be that between body and spirit, we find, on analysis, that the two constituents are partly nearer to, partly further from, each other than are the body and the soul. For here we have in the Past something that was the Present; whereas in the Body we have (*pace* the Idealist Philosophers) something that never was spirit. On the other hand, we have, in the Past as contrasted with the Present, something often, perhaps mostly, quite detached — seeming to be quite detached — from the Present, something dead and opaque, in contrast to the Present, which thus appears living and transparent; whereas the Body is a concomitant of the Spirit, not detached from it, and alive even when apparently living a life in conflict with that of the Spirit.

Nevertheless this detachedness and deadness of the Past obtains, in reality and not in seeming, only for single individuals and groups who cannot, need not, must not, try to penetrate, discriminate and assimilate the entire past even of themselves, still less the past of humanity at large, but who at best do so only in so far as they can utilise, interpret, absorb and eliminate it. Yet, although, thus, *much* of humanity's total past remains detached and dead—at least to our consciousness—from any one of us, or even from any group and age, *some* of that Past can be, ought to be, attached and made alive to any and every soul, and no human soul lives deeply and fruitfully in and by the Present, except it be profoundly and affectionately rooted in the Past.

As a matter of fact, the human soul can only aim at this or that attitude towards the Past, since the Past is *there*—is operatively present, for good or for evil, generally for both, in the Present. The soul can attempt to ignore, forget, do without the Past. But thus it inevitably contracts its own powers and possibilities. For man's Present is as certainly awakened, and, to a great extent, as only awakened, by the Past, as his spirit is awakened by his body. And, again, the Past being so largely a principle, action or personality which once was present but incomplete, and which now is past indeed but complete, we can there see, as we never can in the Present, the bearing, effect and hidden nature of principles, actions, personalities, which are always in part still present—in this our day's approximations to them. And, indeed, that Past is, in different degrees and ways, actually present, through its effects, with us now; and hence we shall never know this our *now*, with full vividness and fruitfulness, unless we know this now's *then*, its past. And, finally, we are personalities; and such personalities, planned in view of our becoming, can only be achieved in time, across helps and obstacles, joys, sorrows, actions, productions, graces, temptations, victories—all demanding time, succession. And they are achieved not in a mere succession, but in a succession more and more interpenetrative, ever nearer to Simultaneity, ever increasingly the expression of a spirit itself more and more penetrated by, and aware of, God, the purely Simultaneous and All Present.

Hence the immense importance of History in all human endeavour and experience; hence its supreme importance in Religion. For Religion deals indeed, centrally, with God, and He is not successive but Simultaneous; but, then, Religion is man's apprehension and experience of God, and man can as little vividly apprehend Eternity, the All Present, out of Time and Succession, as he can vividly apprehend Spirit out of all relation to Body. But, if History and the records of History are important in Religion, we cannot simply eliminate learning, tradition, Doctors, Rabbis. These may have their abuses, and may require check, supplementation, renovation by intuition, inspiration, Prophets; but they cannot simply be supplanted by the latter.

Let us vividly realise that the conflict here is not necessarily between Priests and Prophets. The Rabbis and Pharisees, whom our Lord and St. Paul denounced, were not Priests; the strictest Literalists amongst Protestants have been even vehemently opposed to all Priesthood. There is, indeed, a certain wider margin for conflict between Prophets and Professors than there is between Prophets and Priests. For Prophets and Professors both essentially claim to be teachers, the one by Inspiration, the other by Tradition; whereas Prophets claim to teach, and Priests (strictly) claim to sacrifice, to perform cultural acts—an activity in itself simply different from teaching, and which need not come into conflict with such teaching.

But, indeed, even the frequent conflict between Doctors (whether Priests or not) and Prophets does not mean that the former are always wrong and the latter always right; or that mankind could do with one group or tendency alone; or that Prophets and Inspiration could really flourish without Doctors and Tradition; or that Doctors

and Tradition could beneficently flourish without renovation by further fresh light and life and love. The conflict
between the two looks as though it meant these things,
because the Prophet has the immense advantage, as
regards the immediate appearances, of attack, of movement, of concentration upon particular abuses, of fresh-
ness, presentness, direct, readily understandable appeal.
Yet, upon close examination, we always discover that, be
the abuses or errors on Tradition's side ever so heavy,
some Tradition not only remains necessary, but is operating
most powerfully, as a positive ingredient and shaping
power, within even the most independent-seeming, the
most anti-traditional utterances of any Prophet that
ever lived.

3. And, finally, the sense of Omnipresence attains to
full vividness only by means of a keen sense of spatial
difference. *Here* in space is, for man in this life, never the
same as *there* in space. Abolish, if you can, this difference,
the sense of this difference, and you abolish for man, at
least in this life, the sense of Omnipresence, of the not
simply here and not there, of the not simply there and
not here, the sense of the contrary to our spatial instinct
and category.

And, in Religion in particular, it is useless to argue that,
God being everywhere, what need have we of special
places for His worship? It is man who worships, not God;
but man, here below at least, experiences in space as he
does in time; one place is not the same to him as another
place, any more than one time is the same to him as
another time. Cease to worship God in particular places,
and your worship will become less vivid, less concentrated. And particular places are necessary for worship,
if worship is to be social. Yet the history of Religion
teaches us that it, as indeed all the larger and deeper
complexes of man's life, requires to be developed *socially*—
also socially. And this social worship will—for a creature
sensible-spiritual as is man—not be fully normal and

complete, unless it contains a central element of action as well as of saying and of teaching. A simple mental cultus is too brainy for mere man, and involves too hazardous, too uncharitable and intolerant an attitude towards all the religions of the world, with the sole exception of the religion of the Synagogue and of the pointedly Protestant Sects.

Here, indeed, we do get Priests and Symbolic Cultus and Sacraments; and here we can have conflict of Priests with Prophets and Professors. Yet here, again, the conflict does not reach as deep as it appears to do, not to the substance, as distinct from abuses and exaggerations. And here, again, the Prophets are full of conceptions and emotions derived from Symbolic and Sacramental Cultus. Thus, once more, man is a complex creature; he will do well not to mutilate himself, but, instead, to check, supplement, purify, ever anew, each constituent and range of his religion by the others.

II

What admirable, helpful, touching experiences, teachings, inspirations, but, also, what impressive warnings are to be collected from the life, sayings and influence of George Fox (1624–91)! The man who can read his *Journal*, especially as we have it published now in Mr. Norman Penney's beautiful edition,[1] without deep respect and much profit, is certainly to be pitied.

There is the splendidly stirring contemporary background to these naïve self-chroniclings; the Battle of Worcester, four interviews with Oliver Protector, travels in New England, and the like, are vividly present before the reader.

[1] *The Journal of George Fox*, edited from the MSS. by Norman Penney, with an introduction by Edmund Harvey (two vols., Cambridge University Press, 1911).

Indications of Fox's own heroic vagabondage, and of men's involuntary apprehension of his virility, show from out these pages as freshly as when they were written or as when they occurred. "I sat amongst the furzebushes, being weary with travelling, till it was day. And at break of day I got up and passed on in the fields, and there came a man with a great pike and went along with me to a town; and he raised the town, before the sun was up; and so I declared God's everlasting truth amongst them" (I. p. 30). And when, after much uproar in Ulverston Market, he came up again through them, "there meets me a man with a sword, a soldier. 'Sir,' said he, 'I am ashamed that you should be thus abused, for you are a man,' said he" (I. p. 59). Indeed Fox was just that—a man.

And then there are deep and delicate spiritual experiences, and wonderfully happy combinations and applications of Scripture texts. Thus he can tell souls: "There was their first step to peace, to stand still in the light that showed their sin and transgressions" (I. p. 50). And: "Friends, though you may have tasted of the power and been convinced and have felt the light, yet afterwards you may feel a winter storm, tempest, hail, frost and cold, and a wilderness and temptations. Be patient and still in the power and still in the light that doth convince you, keep your minds unto God, in that be quiet that you may come to the summer, that your flight be not in the winter" (I. p. 224). And when once he is struck down and recovers consciousness, "I lay a little still, and the power of the Lord sprang through me, and the eternal refreshings refreshed me, that I stood up again in the eternal power of God and stretched out my arms amongst them all and said again with a loud voice: 'Strike again, here is my arms, my head and my cheeks.' . . . And I was in the love of God to them all that had persecuted me" (I. p. 58). And as to combinations of texts, we find in a vehement denunciation of "Priest" Lampitt, "that Christ

F

which died at Jerusalem cried woe against such as thou art, and Christ, the same to-day, yesterday and forever, the woe remains upon thee eternally" (I. p. 88). And, in a more general appeal: "To the light which Christ Jesus hath enlightened you withal in your consciences I speak . . . to that in your conscience I speak which never changes. . . . If you did love the light, you would come to abide in the Vine, which is Christ, and sit under the Vine" (I. p. 87). And he prays "that you may all see Christ, and come to witness the unchangeable priesthood" (I. p. 94). There is a nobly sensitive sense of the difference between living Spirit and its more or less dead literary expression, and an impressive, however excessive, demand for present inspiration. "The Scriptures are the Words of God, but not Christ the Word" (I. p. 105); and "the Scriptures was given forth by the Spirit of God; and all people must first come to the Spirit of God in themselves, by which they may know God and Christ . . . and the Holy Scriptures, and the Spirit which was in them that gave them forth" (I. p. 70). Hence a continual insistence upon how "God" Himself "was come to teach His people by His Spirit and to bring them off all their old ways, religions, churches and worships: for all their religions and worships and ways was but talking of other men's words, but they was out of the life and spirit that they was in that gave them forth" (I. p. 48).

Fox is very sure that he himself has learnt directly and exclusively from Christ—by pure, sheer inspiration. "The Lord opened to me by His invisible power that every man was enlightened by the divine light of Christ." True, already the year before "he often took his Bible, and went and sat in lonesome places till night came on." And the "opening" just referred to—how often must he not have read its very words in the Prologue of St. John's Gospel. Yet "this" opening "I saw . . . without the help of any man; neither did I then know where to find it in the Scriptures; though afterwards searching the Scrip-

tures, I found it" (George Fox's *Journal*, abridged by
P. L. Parker, 1903, pp. 11, 28, 29). And the simple admission on the part of a Jesuit, who "utterly denied" that
they, the Papists, "had the same pouring out of the Holy
Ghost as the Apostles had," settles the question of Popery
for Fox (*Journal*, ed. Penney, Vol. I. pp. 323, 324). And
similarly, when Fox asks certain "priests" "whether any
of them could say they ever had a word from the Lord
to go and speak to such or such a people," and "none of
them durst say so": Fox remains utterly unsatisfied when
one of the priests declares that "he could speak his experiences as well as I." Indeed Fox tells him that "the
false prophets and false Apostles, that never knew or
heard the voice of God and Christ, might get the good
words and experience of others" (I. pp. 54, 55).

And Fox finds that precisely this pure, sheer inspira-
tionism and direct divine mission, and this alone, escapes
the denunciations of the entire line of the true Old Testament prophets, and their culmination in Jesus Christ.
Everything else is Priests and Scribes, Types and Hire-
lings, steeplehouses, Jeroboam's calves' houses, the natural
man, the man of sin, spiritual adultery, the Whore, Baby-
lon, the Beast of St. Paul and of the Book of Revelation (I. pp. 153–8). "Of all the world's ways to Christ,
the way is the Lord bringing His people to Himself, and
from all the world's churches to the church which is God.
. . . All those images and crosses and shapes are amongst
them that are apostated from the image of God, the power
of God which is the cross of Christ. . . . Let this go to
the Kings of France, Spain and Pope." "He that feeleth
the light that Christ hath enlightened him withal, he
feeleth Christ in his mind, which is the power of God,
the Cross of Christ, and shall not need to have a Cross
of wood or stone to put him in the mind of Christ or His
Cross," Fox adds, in a disposition of soul not unlike
St. John of the Cross (I. pp. 174, 175).

A fine instinct is ever alert in Fox against religious

persecution. But this persecuting spirit is noticed by him only in the Churches and groups of mediæval and modern times, and is found there as an essential constituent of every institutional religion, and as a flagrant self-confession of these Churches of their incapacity freely to gain and freely to retain adherents. Nor does all this at all blunt his keen appetite for divine judgments upon his, Fox's and the Quakers', adversaries (I. pp. 332, 333, and *passim* throughout both volumes). Indeed, already the differences and mutually exclusive claims of these many visible Churches are considered as transparently destructive of the appeal of any one of them, and as showing how only a purely spiritual communion can be one, universal, tolerant and yet freely constraining. "Unto all" these visible Churches "I answered: 'If we could own any outward City or place to be the Mother Church, or any outward profession, we would own outward Jerusalem, where Christ and the Apostles preached and suffered, . . . where Christ commanded His disciples to wait until they was endowed with power from on high, and where was the types and figures and altar which Christ ended. But the Apostle saith (Gal. iv. 25, 26): 'Jerusalem now is in bondage with her children, but Jerusalem which is above is free, which is the mother of us all.' . . . So they are not Jerusalem's children that is free and above, that gives the title of 'mother' either to outward Jerusalem or to Rome or to any other place or sect of people." All such "be like Jerusalem below, in profession without possession" (II. pp. 130, 131).

Thus he everywhere contrasts "the state of the Church in the Apostles' days and the Apostacy since" (I. p. 37). These temples and steeplehouses have the Pope's name "marked on the top or the end of them yet with the Cross" (I. p. 130). Fox is evidently turned physically sick by a "steeplehouse" which "was very much painted" like Jezebel, the harlot queen. And at forty-six years of age, "I lost my hearing and sight, as a sign to such as would

not see and such as would not hear"; and "all that winter
I could not endure the smell of any flesh meat, and saw
all the religions and people that lived in them, and the
priests that held them up, as a company of men-eaters."
"At this time there was great persecutions" of Friends;
and "as the persecution ceased, I came from under my
travails and sufferings" (II. pp. 165, 167, 169).

And there is, finally, a vehement antipathy to all learning
and syllogistic reasoning. Thus at Durham a man comes
to set up a College "to make ministers of Christ"; and
Fox "let him see that was not the way to make them
Christ's ministers—by Hebrew, Greek and Latin and the
seven arts, which all was but the teachings of the natural
man. For the many languages began at Babel. . . . And
Pilate could set Hebrew, Greek and Latin atop of Christ
when he crucified Him . . . Christ Jesus which was in
the beginning before Babel was" (I. pp. 311, 312).

And yet, as against all this intense Puritanism which
indeed predominates on Fox's surface, there are inter-
connected convictions and insistences of magnificent delicacy and breadth which certainly constitute Fox's true
depth, moving force and grand appeal.

There is, for one thing, his insistence upon the possibility, the fact, of *real*, not simply imputed *holiness*,
attained by the redeemed soul even here below—as against
both Luther and Calvin and, indeed, the Protestant
Reformers generally. "Who come to the Church that is
in God, and Christ, they must come, out of the state that
Adam is in the Fall, driven from God, to know the state
that he was in before he fell"; "He who was perfect comes
to make man and woman perfect again" (I. pp. 224, 351).
Indeed he is in constant conflict with those who "plead
against perfection," and insists upon how "the seed of
God in all," "the Spring," "the plant," "the spark in
every soul sins not" (I. pp. 136, 223), and holds that
"Job stood for perfection and his integrity" (I. p. 136).

Here Fox doubtless seems to insist upon a literal

faultlessness here below. And, indeed, the doctrine of the in-dwelling Christ somewhat readily lends itself to such grave abuses as that into which Fox's own convert, James Nayler, fell, to whom a band of followers rendered homage in imitation of that given to Christ (see Penney's note, *Journal*, I. p. 398, and compare in the *Journal* Nayler's own words). Yet I take Moehler to be right in holding that Fox's intention was substantially identical with the doctrine of the Council of Trent; and that his *animus* was directed against the limitation of God's grace to a hiding of man's persistent corruption—to a change in God's estimate of man, whilst man himself remains essentially the same. Certainly the same reproaches have pursued Fox in this matter as those which have been persistently levelled against Rome; he and the Friends generally are "will-worshippers" (II. pp. 317–19).

And, as the second spacious conviction of Fox, there is his constant insistence upon *the universality of God's grace and of Christ's redemption*—this against Calvinist predestinarianism. Thus Fox asks a certain Dr. Wittie: "What sort of men those were that Christ had not enlightened and His grace had not appeared to them, and to whom Christ's grace did not appear, and that He had not died for?" (II. p. 96). And against certain Irish Presbyterians, who said that "God hath ordained the greatest part of men for Hell," Fox declares: "Christ sayeth to His disciples, 'Go, teach all nations.'" "God would have all men to be saved: mark all men, then, the stock of Esau and of Ham also" (II. p. 149).

Let us leave this strong, deep, tender soul upon this its noblest, truest, sweetest note.

III

It is pathetic, yet highly instructive work, to follow this deeply candid, rarely religious spirit, so nobly flushed with enthusiasm for Christ our Lord, for the element and germ of good in all men, for the free givenness of all we have and are, for the need and fruit of recollection and silence, the Prayer of Quiet, and for detachment from money and persecution, into his extreme spiritualist positions—into the strange general psychological prejudices, the historical misconceptions, and the sterilising and unjust practical consequences of this "pure" spirituality.

1. As to the Psychology here revealed, we have a strange general misconception as to its actual functioning, and a strange general misjudgment as to the range of its religious character and worth. We can take these two strangenesses which, after all, are most understandable, together.

Everywhere Fox feels and speaks as though man does and can understand something new without the presence and operation within him of something old—he is unaware, that is, of the universal fact and law of *apperception*, by which it is, as it were, with the tentacles, the mouth, the digestive apparatus of what I already know, hold, and am, that I can and do seize, swallow, and assimilate what I do not yet know and have, and what as yet I am not. Professor William James's small boy who, under the great Horseshoe Fall of Niagara, stood dazed with the thought, with the appearance, of such thundering masses of the stuff which his mother, a week before, had blown up his nose, as a cure for some little trouble: there you have the mighty new thing offered, and the tiny sole means of incorporation in the perceiving mind. And, similarly, everywhere my newest insight, my most vivid intuition, my richest present and my most exalted inspiration require, largely depend upon, are impossible without my previous insight, my memory, my past, my tradition. All these latter things, taken generally, are no less worthy of God than are the former. And everywhere Fox feels and speaks as though the stimulation, food, growth, offered even to the entirety of this my memory-intuition, my past-present, by the literary precipitates, the artistic expressions and the historical incorporations of the memory-intuitions, the past-present of other spirits, other ages, were always of secondary importance, were indeed never essential, indispensable. True, it is Christ Who is held by Fox to enlighten all men, and the character of this Christ is, as a matter of fact, derived by Fox from the New Testament documents. But this Christ enlightens all men so entirely to the same degree, in the same manner before as after His earthly life, and without as with personal knowledge of Him during His earthly career, or even the historical knowledge of this His earthly life, that, at bottom, only an omnipresent illumination, independent of all time and place, of history, of tradition and institutions, is thus proclaimed. The transition from this to the cold secularism of Benjamin Franklin—to the holding simply of a universal rational endowment of man, a reasonable insight into and within sublunar economics, politics, etc.—has been shown by events to be very easy and most natural.

It is this, his ignoring of apperception, of the need of the past, of memory, of tradition, of history and of its precipitates, that forces Fox to insist so vehemently upon the need of every soul—at least every religious teacher—to have literally the same degree and kind of inspiration as was possessed by the Biblical seers and writers; as though no artist is more than an impostor who does not possess, and does not know and does not avow that he possesses, the very same amount and kind of artistic genius as that which produced the Parthenon Sculptures of Pheidias or the Madonna di San Sisto of Raphael.

Again, it is his one-sidedness which gives Fox his continuous undervaluing (in his analysis and theory and in his criticism of others, though not at all in his own practice and utilisation) of literature, records of the past, as dead things and as inferior to all present living spirituality. Fox's theory here is wrong, for these records are, really, and especially in his own practice, as it were, roses of Jericho; they are only apparently dead; and, upon revival within and by our minds, they promptly turn out to proceed doubtless from the same source as our own lights and powers of truly spiritual interpretation, yet to proceed from it with a volume, momentum and purity utterly beyond our own attainments, either actual or possible. If this fuller and fullest life, as it reveals itself to us as thus fuller and fullest, simultaneously awakens our own to greater fullness, even to all such fullness as our life is made for—why and where is this fuller life's greater fullness an irritant and depression for us? Star differeth from star, and yet star transmits light to star, rose differs from daisy, yet rose unfolding awakens daisy: where is the harm, the annoyance or tyranny in all this?

And, finally, this radical incompleteness of his general analysis explains also Fox's fantastic misconception as to the sources and occasions of his own ideas and convictions, and as to where other preachers ought to seek and find them. Thus, that "Christ is the light of every man that cometh into the world," was *not*, as Fox will have it, simply a direct inspiration of the living God to the living Fox, discovered later on, by this same Fox, to have also been vouchsafed to the writer of St. John's Prologue fifteen centuries before; but it was an instruction derived by the willing, grace-impelled mind and soul of Fox, together with Papists and other "letter" worshippers, from that "dead" Scripture. And that the clerics of the various Churches admitted to Fox that they did not possess the very same amount and kind of inspiration as the Apostles, does not stamp them, even as teachers, as impostors or as simply useless; for not only single man, but also humanity at large, requires moments, whole periods and contributions, of antiquity and tradition, apperception, memory, precipitate, *status quo*, "letter." And that such clerics admit they never felt the call directly from God to testify directly to such and such individuals and groups, again decides nothing final against them, unless mankind does not require general testimonies and appeals — unless Pheidias's Sculptures and Raphael's Madonna cease to be of use as soon as they are not, or do not remain, or do not become anew, addressed consciously by one person to another person.

2. As to Fox's conception of History—his reading of the New Testament record—he is one-sided as to facts comparatively of detail; and he remains strangely unaware of the consequences which necessarily follow from a central peculiarity of prophetic temper and teaching, as found also in this New Testament.

(i.) As to the main details, if we move from the more recent, more developed types of historical representation and of doctrinal conviction to the more ancient and less articulate, we find them as follows. St. John's Gospel furnishes Fox with practically all his images and ideas of light, life and love, and it doubtless really does contain a magnificent Universalism, a soaring Spirituality, and an impressive insistence upon the Here and Now, the Present and Presence of Eternity and full Redemption. But its Institutionalism, its Sacramentalism, its rigorous delimitation is profound, all-pervading, and yet explicit also. "Verily, verily, I say unto thee, Except a man be born again of water and of the Spirit, he cannot enter into the kingdom of God," Christ Himself here affirms to Nicodemus (iii. 5). And "Verily, verily, I say unto you, Except ye eat the flesh of the Son of Man, and drink His blood, ye have no life in you"; "If any man eat of this bread, he shall live for ever," Christ Himself here proclaims in the Synagogue of Capernaum (vi. 53, 51). In both cases a visible, sensible element—water and bread and wine—is emphatically included, and the insistence upon the visible, sensible contact with or feeding upon them; the necessity of these rites is so intensely emphasised, that Rome itself has here done nothing but variously to soften this stringency. On the Cross Jesus' side is here pierced, "and forthwith came there out blood and water" (xix. 34), as the very certain indication that Jesus is the source of the two great Sacraments—the Holy Eucharist and Baptism. And, indeed, throughout the Johannine writings, "the brethren" are exclusively the members of the Christian Church thus washed and fed by the Sacraments of Christ. Thus we find here a striking example of the law, so contrary to Quakerism, that Universalism and Ecclesiasticism, Spiritualism and Sacramentalism can go, indeed have gone and do go together, each in and through the other.

As to St. Paul, from whose pneumatic teaching so much of Fox's daring spiritualism is derived, nothing can be more certain than that Baptism and the Holy Eucharist are for him sensible-spiritual, and not purely spiritual, and that these sensible-spiritual acts form, for him, the very basis and centre of the Christian religious life and worship. Thus, here again, a spirituality so rarefied as almost to break away altogether from the earthly, historical Jesus, is stimulated, saturated and steadied by certain sensible symbols, vehicles, acts; and the practice of, and command to practise, these sensible-spiritual acts is found within the earthly career and orders of Jesus Christ Himself.

And, finally, as to the Synoptists. If we take them as we have them, we find that at least their more recent con-stituents are clearly against "pure" spirituality. For, in Luke, Jesus, after giving the bread to the disciples at the Last Supper, adds the command "Do this"—this sen-sible-spiritual act—"in remembrance of Me" (xxii. 19). Matthew concludes his entire Gospel with the great scene where Jesus, once more upon a mountain, solemnly proclaims "All power is given Me in heaven and in earth," and immediately adds: "Go ye, therefore, and make disciples of all nations by baptizing them in the name of the Father, and of the Son, and of the Holy Ghost" (xxviii. 18, 19)—where, beyond doubt, a visible immersion in physical water is meant. And, in Mark, Jesus, immediately before His Ascension, declares to His Apostles: "He that believeth and is baptized shall be saved" (xvi. 16), where again an immersion in water is most undoubtedly intended. But, even if we restrict ourselves to the most ancient constituents of the Synoptists, we still find not pure, but mixed spirituality. Thus there is nothing more primitive, explicit and vivid in Mark than the Baptism of Jesus in the Jordan by the Baptist; how, as soon as He emerged from His immersion in the water, "He saw the heavens opened, and the Spirit like a dove descending upon Him; and there came a voice from heaven, 'Thou art my beloved Son, in whom I am well pleased.' And immediately the spirit driveth Him into the wilderness" (i. 9–12). A genuine spiritual experience and growth in Jesus' own soul, which operates continuously up to His death upon the Cross and beyond, is here occasioned, not by Spirit only but also by sense, by physical contact with physical water. Mark, too, with Matthew and Luke, gives us that most primitive account of the woman with an issue of blood, who came behind Jesus and touched the hem of His garment—doubtless one of the four tassels of the sky-blue zizith worn by all devout Jews. Straightway she is cured and Jesus feels that virtue has gone out from Him; and He reassures the trembling woman: "Thy faith hath made thee whole; go in peace, and be whole of thy plague" (v. 25, 34). Yes: her faith, but her faith aroused on occasion of, and manifesting itself by, physical contact.

And, finally, in Mark the disciples, when sent out by Jesus, "anointed with oil many that were sick and healed them"—quite unrebuked by their Master (vi. 13); as, indeed, St. James's Epistle invites "the presbyters of the Church" thus "to anoint the sick with oil in the name of the Lord," and this "prayer of faith shall save the sick, and the Lord shall raise him up; and, if he have committed sins, they shall be forgiven him" (v. 14, 15). Thus, here again, we have a sensible-spiritual act productive, not only of sensible, but also of spiritual effects.

(ii.) But a much more general, indeed an immensely far-reaching fact and condition has now been fully disclosed by biblical criticism, a fact and condition operative especially in the last half of Our Lord's short public ministry, and which, if it raises formidable problems for Christology and all Church orthodoxy, very certainly ruins the basis for acute hostility to all and every historical development and supplementation of Our Lord's actual teachings by theology, law and institutions derived largely from Jewish and heathen sources.

We find, then, that the first Apostles, and even still— predominantly—St. Paul also, really believed that Our Lord would promptly, during the lifetime of some of them, appear again upon earth, and make all human conditions radically new; and we find that, in Our Lord's own teaching also, the shortness of the persistence of our visible world's present order is implied, taught, solemnly insisted upon. His Proximate Second Coming, with its profound change and conclusion of all earthly conditions, becomes especially emphasised from the great scene with Peter at Cæsarea Philippi onwards. Even if we could explain away certain central affirmations of the utmost solemnity and clearness, there would still remain all those generous, most authentic parables, from after that scene, which so markedly insist upon the abrupt, proximate, purely God-given end and renovation of all things in His Second Coming, and upon, on our own part, utter detachment and strenuous watchfulness. These parables of storm, stress, suddenness and transcendence, are certainly authentic, but not more so than are the parables of the first joyous, expansive period, which emphasise the slow growth, the successive development, the immanent ethical work and enjoyment of the soul upon and within itself, in this beautiful world of physical sunshine, air, wind and rain, flowers, birds and children.

It is clear that we can either concentrate upon the relatively immanent, ethical, continuous, out-going, joyous movement, or upon the exclusively transcendent, religious, abrupt, incoming, heroic movement, or upon both. And only the last concentration—the fructifying, alternating of one movement by and with the other—gives us the complete Jesus, the true genius of Christianity. And thus we get this genius to consist, essentially, not in a list of things absolutely wrong, and in another list of things absolutely right—but, even more than in a small list of things always and simply wrong, in the continuous sense that the very things we, men, are to love and seek are also the same things which we are to be detached from, and from which we are to flee. Attachment and cultivation, and detachment and renouncement will thus each gain and keep a splendid spaciousness of occasions and materials. There will be no fanaticism, but a profound earnestness; there will be no worldliness, but an immense variety of interest and expansion towards all things in their specific kinds and degrees of goodness, truth and beauty. Fox can truly be said to possess something of this combination, as against the Puritan concentration upon the movement of detachment and abruptness only.

And yet he remains profoundly unfair to the historical and institutional developments all around him, and scolds them as corruptly Jewish or Pagan, or both, or worse, because he does not realise how all the great prophets, including even the King and Crown of the Prophets, have appeared in the history of the world as so many great stormy petrels, as warning voices, calling man back to God, the Eternal, on occasion of some national break-up and coming change. They all of them have uttered truths, and have awakened instincts and apprehensions of priceless worth and potency; especially does Our Lord's religious and moral teaching, temper, example and power remain the full expression of God's truth, love and life. Yet they all teach with this intense sense of God's Eternity and of the Proximate End of man's earthly career. Hence they all do much to purify and spiritualise man, but they do little or nothing towards helping him to organise and develop his earthly life and his social duties—all which have not come to an end, but have, on the contrary, grown fairly continuously into ever greater complexity, tension and difficulty. And hence those spirits that have aimed at an organisation of Society have all been driven to borrow largely from the Old Testament legal codes and Jewish arrangements, if they wanted this organisation to be directly religious, and from Stoic principles and Græco-Roman orderings. Savonarola did so, Calvin did so, Cromwell did so; there was, here at least, an intensely religious motive, and to talk of decadence or apostasy because of these inevitable, unsought supplementations would be childish. But, if so, then also Rome and the other Christian organised Churches cannot, straight away and on prin-ciple, be condemned as apostate, because they have done what they could not, in the very interests of the persistence of religion, help doing—because they have organised Christian thought, Christian Society, Christian Ethics, Christian worship, with Christ and His life and teaching in the centre indeed, but with large supplementations from Jewish and heathen sources. In all these things there doubtless lurk dangers; and abuses have existed and do exist; protests against these, by all means, are to be applauded; but the principle in itself is inevitable.

We should, of course, be unfair did we forget that Fox and the Quakers were only drawing the logical conse-quences, with much insight and courage, of two inter-connected reactions common, in various degrees, to the Protestant Reformers. Luther's earlier Protestantism, with its appeal, away from all constraint and conformity, the visible and the social, to the free, the various, the

invisible and the individual, which he, and still more his
successors, so largely abandoned later on, is regained and
retained by Fox with a fuller consistency and assurance
of step. And Zwingli's and Calvin's profound antagonism
to every cultural sacrifice, to all sacerdotalism, has here,
in Fox, become fully consistent. And these two antipathies
limit Fox to the elements of worship inherited by Christians
from the Jewish Synagogue—Praise, Prayer, Reading,
Instruction. He can and does flush all this with Intuition
and Emotion, or he can reduce even all of this to silence.
But nowhere is there any remnant of the much-hated
opus operatum, of any reminiscence of the Jewish Temple
or of Pagan sacrifices: a distinctly thin, brainy, where not
emotional, worship remains; *opus operantis* alone abides,
or alone is supposed to do so.

3. As to the effects of thus taking religion as complete
in pure prophetism, let me insist upon three, which, I take
it, indicate most conclusively that we have thus an important criticism, a precious constituent, but not the whole
of religion, still less the whole of life. These effects concern,
successively, the recruiting and staying power of religion,
its tolerance and comprehension of the positions of
mankind at large, and the special conditions and cost of
the religious, the Christian temper, and of its transmission
from soul to soul.

(i.) It is, surely, a most striking fact that the Society
of Friends (in this respect like unto the Unitarian Body)
—with its indifference or hostility to all formal Creeds and
Confessions, and with its constant insistence upon the
universal light of Christ and love of God towards men,
and upon man's supreme duty of a similar love towards
God and Man—has not spread, does not spread, indeed
does not even simply keep pace with the growth of the
population. It is strange, for these two bodies, the one more
affectively, the other more rationalistically, surely appear
thus to have concentrated upon what all men hold or could
hold, and to have dropped whatever divides or need divide

men from each other. And it is a precarious thing to find
the cause of this strange sterility of appeal in the too great
purity, the too great elevation of these beliefs for the
multitude, or in the traditional averseness of these bodies
to propaganda. For both bodies are especially enthusiastic concerning the universality of the light of grace and
of the power of reason; and—let Quakers and Unitarians
preach and print or not—men, if these beliefs be really
sufficient and supreme in furnishing the aids and in
excluding dead-weights of the spiritual life, will of
themselves discover and adopt these beliefs and the men
who already hold them. This same stand-still is occurring
with the Brahma Samaj body, so high and pure, so
universalist and loving, in India. And Board School
religion offers the same promises and brings the same
disappointments. We will, we must, if we possibly conscientiously can, escape from this sterility, which, let
us note, does not affect the great Institutional Churches
to the same degree. These are either at least holding
their own proportionately to the growth of the population, or, at least, are lagging behind less markedly than
are those two bodies.

(ii.) It is, again, a most impressive fact that these various
attempts at discovery of, and restriction to, a certain
already universally active minimum, this Puritan averseness to the physical, the sensuous, the dispersive, the
"natural" in all its degrees and kinds, develop and
involve an objectively wider intolerance than do any of
the historic, institutional creeds. Even a Spanish In-
quisitor entirely understands and respects the traditional,
cultural, sensible, particular element—the presence and
prizing of such—in Judaism or Protestantism; he only
objects to this or that form, here offered, of such element
—especially to the deliberate preference of these forms
to that of the Roman Church. But the Quaker and the
Unitarian, as such, are far more "superior" people; they
treat, in all cases, these historical, institutional creeds

G

and acts as superfetations, as things that had everywhere better be away. Nevertheless all intensely live religion keenly feels its own organic unity, and that its strength lies precisely in such incarnations, explicitations of its spirit. And hence those abstractive persons appear to concrete religionists to be like Delilah shearing off Samson's locks—absurd hair, mere hair—a thing for barbers to haggle about; as the martyrisers of St. Agatha who cut off her breasts—mere excrescences—which henceforth robbed her of nothing but the sweet glory of nursing motherhood; and as Heracles lifting Antæus up from the ground, which this giant had to touch if he would keep and renew his strength—silly muck, subject-matter fit only for dung-beetles and mudlarks. And, indeed, the historical-institutional religions, especially Christianity, necessarily involve the recognition of stages and degrees of mental and spiritual illumination, each, however, always clothed in, stimulated and propagated by, sense impressions and concretions: such Christianity cannot be intolerant all round except by forgetting its own links with Jewish History and Scriptures and with Græco-Roman heathen philosophy and law. There is here no search for a minimum, but there are various approximations to a maximum; no one abstraction, but various concretions; no braininess, but a large subconsciousness; no aloofness from the poor, "but here the poor have the Gospel preached unto them." Here also intolerance, even fanaticism, are ever to be watched against, and here superstition is never very far away; yet we do not here begin, we do not even end with, the elimination or the slighting of the Particular, the Bodily, the Historical, the Institutional—that is, the universal human occasions, means and expressions, of the Universal, the Spiritual, the Eternal, the Omnipresent.

(iii.) And the last striking circumstance is that the abstractive religions do not give us the recognition, the practice, the poignancy, of the Cross, of self-renunciation, as essential to religion and its propagation, in the

fullest depth and delicacy, the widest freedom and
fertility of both. If, as we grow older, we watch—say
from some high vehicle—the crowd of a great city,
what an amazing thought, fact, it is, if we realise even
the central conditions thus here before us. For, see, this
crowd of swiftly dying men, these streams of beings
who, singly, live but some thirty years of adult, fully
effective life, they transmit, each generation to the other,
the torch of life. And note the marvel of it. The construc-
tion of the most delicate microscopical and astronomical
machinery, the chemical finding of Radium, the decipher-
ing of Assyrian and Egyptian texts, the mastery of the
human voice, of complex musical instruments and of
mighty orchestras: all this, quite apart from anything
more creative, is taught and learnt, is acquired, in hand
and eye and ear and brain-cell, by one generation to
another, by one generation from another. And yet reflect:
the fullest marvel lies not there. All this would instantly
cease, were it not variously but really penetrated by what
expresses itself most fully and clearly elsewhere than in
these arts and sciences. The goodwill, self-mastery, self-
renunciation, the Cross—these, too, are handed on, these,
too, do not die, even though the runners in this, the
noblest torch-race, fall, each, after a little stretch of the
narrow path that leadeth upward unto life. And remark,
especially, that the appeal from one man of such goodwill
to another whom he would win to it, is nobly, particularly
crucifying for him who appeals, because the appealer
reveals, and should reveal, this goodwill in its concrete,
historical, spiritual-sensible, personal form. Precisely thus
the appeal is at its strongest. And yet, if offered thus, it
must be, it ought to be, in part rejected. The combination which has cost him who offers so much, which he
loves so dearly, will—even if the appeal be accepted—have
to be resolved by him who accepts it into its constituent
elements; some elements can and will be accepted, other
elements will be, ought to be, ignored or dropped. And

the appealer will have to find his joy in this death of himself, which thus can and does become, at best, the life of another soul. But he will, of course, have to be prepared also for the other fate—of his appeal not being answered—not even in the long, the very long run. The very fact of the incurable particularity, in part, of even the most universal of what we do and are, gives a ready excuse and escape to the will that is not "good," not yet "good." For the individual appealed to can always, however much the fact may be irrelevant, dwell upon the appealer being different—hopelessly different—in degree or kind of character, devotedness, etc., from him who is thus appealed to; and he can refuse to find and accept in the appeal a certain substance which *does* suit him and which it is for him to adapt to his own uses. Thus there is in every offer, and in every acceptance, of one soul to another and by another, an element of noblest generosity and death, and this element is, obviously, recognised and fostered fully, not by the abstractive and purely spiritual religions, but by the concretionist, historical-institutional, incarnational Churches. The criticism of St. Augustine, which possibly was not fully just as against Plotinus—that he could, in the pages of the Platonists, find indeed that God was the Word, but not that the Word became flesh (*Conf.* VII. ix. 1, 2)—remains deeply important for us all. In our relations between one generation and the other, one sex and the other, one individual and the other, we will ever remember the need, the cost, the glory of this element of incarnation and of death in life, of life through death. Especially will we gain and keep an endless love and restraint, patience and joyous trust in our relations with the young, still necessarily so full of the "confusions," the largely dim, distracting tumult of the senses and of the visible life—and this is, surely, the supreme test of the worth of our religious outlook—by such a constant sense and practice of the Place and Function in Religion of the Body, of History and of Institutions.

IV

ON CERTAIN CENTRAL NEEDS OF
RELIGION, AND THE DIFFICULTIES
OF LIBERAL MOVEMENTS IN FACE
OF THE NEEDS : AS EXPERIENCED
WITHiN THE ROMAN CATHOLIC
CHURCH DURING THE LAST FORTY
YEARS

IV

ON CERTAIN CENTRAL NEEDS OF RELIGION, AND THE DIFFICULTIES OF LIBERAL MOVE-MENTS IN FACE OF THE NEEDS: AS EX-PERIENCED WITHIN THE ROMAN CATHOLIC CHURCH DURING THE LAST FORTY YEARS [1]

IT is a great honour, may I say so frankly, the best kind of bracing, because an unusually rousing incentive humbly to attempt my very best, thus to find myself permitted to address a meeting of Scotsmen—men of my own blood on my mother's side—men who on the average always somehow seem, so far more spontaneously than the English, to require and to rejoice in thought and con-templation—ardent attempts to reach the root principles and the ultimate laws in the life of things. And here I am privileged to speak, not only to a chosen band of Scotch scholars, thinkers, pastors; but fearlessly, hence respect-fully, to articulate my most intimate thoughts, convictions and hopes, under the presidency of a man, whom most of you here present doubtless know far more fully than myself, but whom none of you can more deeply reverence and admire than, with many a co-religionist and fellow-worker of mine, I myself admire and revere.

Do you love rivers, those moving masses coming from, leading to, far away, those nobly suggestive symbols of our little fleeting lives in what they have of expansive and aspiring, of fruitful and of nobly great? There is one such river scene and symbol dear to me since early manhood onwards. It is close by to where the lovely Moselle joins the majestic Rhine—where, in Coblenz, stands the noble

[1] Address delivered at Edinburgh, 7 July, 1914.

twin-towered Romanesque Church of St. Florinus. There
my uncle, Clemens von Hügel, was baptized; there, above
all, some three and a half centuries before, in 1431,
Nicolas, son of a poor Moselle fisherman in the near-by
village of Kues, was Dean. Thus *Confluentia*, the Roman
centre at the confluence of waters draining and enriching
wide countries varied and fruitful, but vigorous and
hospitable, has long stood before my imagination as a
symbol of the ever necessary, the ever difficult, the ever
noble harmonies achievable by man, and actually attained
by that capacious soul—a mind, heart, will and character
so rich and far-reaching, so deep and delicate, so virile
and so true. Christianity, Neo-Platonism, the Teutonic
spirit, the early Renaissance; authority and liberty, Society
and the individual; the depths of faith, the clarities of
reason, the vigour of action, the warm, life-welcoming
and life-giving expansion and embrace of love: all these
even individually great and difficult things met, in a
rarely full and perfect degree and manner, in this noble
precursor and adumbrator of the modern spirit at its
very best and deepest.

I want now to invite your full attention, for a little,
to certain permanent elements and requirements of
religion, which we can never, for long or very largely,
neglect or affront without damage to ourselves or to others,
and which, nevertheless, are easily overlooked or affronted
by us if and when, pricked on or oppressed by the abuses
special to religion and these its elements and requirements,
we attempt the reform of these abuses.

I find chiefly five such complexes of abiding need, of
ready abuse, of easy yet impoverishing or even fatal
misconception and opposition. Let us take them in an
order ascending from the more readily perceptible to the
least visible and most central of such needs, abuses,
misconceptions, oppositions. Yet they are really—these
five complexes—all interdependent; and they all five
contribute their irreplaceable quota to the special force,

flower and flavour of the Christian spirit; and hence even the first complex will be properly understood only after the due apprehension of the last, and within the world and life constituted by, and penetrating all the five with the most varied cross-currents and interstimulations.

I

When my future wife, at that time still a vigorous Protestant, was in the summer of 1872 on a visit to her much admired friend, the very spiritual and very anti-Roman Broad Church Dr. Alexander Ewing, Bishop of Argyll and the Isles, she, one morning at breakfast, found her host greatly depressed and perturbed. Some hours later he took her for a walk, and explained how that certain strong central hopes of his had just—he was sure of it—been quite finally dashed to the ground. That he had had the greatest confidence in the power towards the reform of Roman Catholicism possessed by Père Hyacinthe Loyson, the French Carmelite; and that none of that man's troubles—not his expulsion from his Order, nor his excommunication by the Pope—had, in any degree, weakened his, the Bishop's, faith in Loyson's capacity for this difficult, supremely important work. But that, by this post, he had learnt of M. Loyson's marriage. Well, Loyson might, after this, continue his activity as though nothing had happened; many outside the Roman Church might even believe that nothing had occurred to hinder his work: but he, the Bishop, knew that this act of Loyson had blotted him out, for good and all, as any really effective agent and weapon for the work the Bishop had so longed to see him accomplish.

Now, even before then, and very much more since then, and especially during the years of peculiar stress and strain of this Pontificate, have I wondered at the insensibility of many, even otherwise highly gifted and sincerely

religious persons—of course chiefly amongst Protestants—
with respect to this, surely not very abstruse or very difficult point. For Christianity is—is it not?—centrally a
religion of renunciation, of heroism. The application of
such things, even where we may consider it, even where
it may really be, unwise or excessive or perfunctory,
demands (does it not?) a cautious criticism, since at least
the original spirit of self-denial was present there, and self-
denial—not necessarily your sort, even if you have the
grace to practise a self-denial—has an inalienable right
to the respect of every Christian; indeed, of every at all
generous and noble soul.

Assuredly the question of life-long, obligatory celibacy
is a grave one; certain modifications of the discipline now
required by the Roman Catholic Church in its Latin Rite
may be seriously desirable—say, in the spirit and to the
degree proposed in a fine petition by certain High Lutheran
Theologians submitted to the Vatican Council in 1869;
as we all know, the discipline of the Roman Catholic
Church itself still varies in the different Rites within its
borders. Especially may one well wish that clerics who,
under the present discipline, find themselves very gravely
strained or tempted, might, as in the Græco-Russian
Church, be allowed to marry, even after ordination,
sinking then back into the ranks, yet still into a specially
honoured position amongst the lay communicants of the
Church. Thus the Church would not lose such men; and,
above all, such men would not lose the Church. In all
such matters there is room for reform.

But all this has, surely, nothing to do with the point
so well seized by Bishop Ewing. I like to believe that the
Bishop saw even further than into the bare fact that
Roman Catholics, those strange creatures, feel very
finally as they do upon this matter. I trust that he had
sufficient delicacy and generosity of imagination to realise
vividly that here was not simply a strong prejudice which
wise men would not unnecessarily affront, but a high

aspiration, a heart of nobility, which good men ought to respect. That, in a word, we have here one of the forms—crude, artificial, inopportune though you may hold it to be—of that renunciation, that asceticism, which, in some kind and degree or other, every religion, indeed every philosophy, at all deep and delicate, must, and indeed does and will, revere, inculcate or at least imply.

Romolo Murri, the Christian Democratic Roman Catholic priest, whom I know fairly well—a keen and vigorous, at all times a more ethical and social than a specifically religious or mystical spirit—has, as you doubtless know, married an able, cultivated and wealthy American lady; and both he and she, and many of their well-wishers amongst non-Catholics, appear to believe that this act will actually help on such reform work as Murri has been now so long engaged upon within the Roman Catholic Church. Need I say how glad I am that he still cares for Christianity and for Church? I think of another Italian cleric who also has married, and who—at least so far—seems quite to have ceased to care for either. Yet events are proving the truth of my special contention. One of the chiefs of the very League founded by Murri, a highly respected lay Catholic, promptly after the announcement of Murri's determination to marry, issued a most dignified, firm and yet generous declaration. This document expressed the Leaguers' deep appreciation of the rare qualities, services, sufferings of the vigorous Christian Democrat, and their unalterable gratitude to Murri, and their abstention from every judgment as to the quality of this action of Murri with respect to his own conscience and intrinsic obligations; but it then insisted that, if Christianity, the religion of heroism, is to be solidly sustained, still more if it is to be seriously renovated, this can be done only by maintaining, indeed increasing, the heroism present at the time of the attempt at reform within the body to be thus reformed. Hence, that they wished Murri all peace of conscience in his present circumstances, and the sincere gratitude of all men for what he had done and suffered; but that Murri had no further place in their organisation; that, for them, he had lapsed into private life, into the non-leading ranks.

A little scene, of the most authentic kind, is often, in this matter, vividly before my mind. There was the Abbé Huvelin—a rich and deep, a cultivated, above all an heroic soul, to whom I owe incalculably much. A man full of vitality, the strongest passions and the deepest affections, the life of deliberate, irrevocable life-long celibacy, entered upon by him in full manhood and with the clearest understanding of its meaning and range, was, I am very sure, profoundly costly. Yet he willed, used and loved this renunciation as an instrument, condition and price of the tenderest love of souls in God and of God in souls, right on to his end, in the seventies of his age. And yet if, in 1872, the strongly Protestant Bishop Ewing could clearly see the mistake—at least, if he would still remain a leader in reform—of M. Loyson's marriage, this saintly Roman Catholic cleric could in 1909, when M. Loyson was broken-hearted at the death of his wife, see and feel the pathos of the old man's bereavement, and could fly to him with all the tenderness and consolation which this rich heart knew so well how to find and to impart. Yet little as the Scotch Protestant would, even in face of M. Loyson's trouble, have retracted his opinion as to the tactical ruinousness of that marriage, so little did the French Catholic relax his sense of the heroic spirit of Christianity, and his deep regret that a priest and a friar had not somehow been able, or been willing, to hold out in the particular kind and degree of heroism he had at first undertaken, and to which the very best instincts in the best Roman Catholics rise in reverent respect and profound trust.

II

When as a boy, of an early impressionable and reflective nature and mind, I was beginning to grow up under the strong influence of a very thorough teacher, and a good moral man, my German Lutheran tutor, now long dead, I used to feel myself affected in a curious, not precisely docile manner, by his glowing references to the special merit of Luther's life-work. The braininess of the thing, the doctrinaire character—not, of course, of many of Luther's protests against abuses, of his desire for greater sobriety and simplicity, of his humorous peasant force, of his deep mystical sense, or of the heroic elements in his personality and life, but of his famous "Paulinism" (surely, his more than Pauline Paulinism)—this is what surprised me. The surprise remains. Only some four years ago, a most winning and devoted young Swedish Lutheran student of theology was, on the Malvern hills, looking down with me upon that noble battlefield of England, the wide Worcestershire plain, still bathed in the evening sunshine, the tall great Malvern Priory Church already in the shadows at our feet. And we were speaking of Piers Plowman, and of his vision of the judgment to come—of the Dissolution of the Monasteries. And I was saying how strangely up and down, and flecked with light and shadow, is our poor human history; for that, though in Langland's time this Malvern Priory was certainly corrupt, and though, some two hundred or so years later, many of the monasteries were truly dissolute and deserved their dissolution which then came, yet this particular Priory had, by that time, become again so fervent and beneficent that even that ferocious monk-hater, the strenuously Protestant Bishop Latimer, implored Henry VIII. to spare that monastery. I added how much I longed that at least the great majority of the monasteries, when Wolsey and Henry began their suppression, had been in a similar state of fervour; and especially that the reforms desired and the spirit represented by Nicolas of Kues, and then by Erasmus and especially the saintly Thomas More, had been more general and had been accepted by Rome. But here again, as in my boyhood, I had before me a man who, though certainly endowed with a body and its senses, appeared to be addressing a disembodied spirit. I knew and know, of course, how considerable remained, as a matter of fact, from the very beginning of his reform period in Luther, the range of the body-and-sense element in his religion, and how increasingly these things became again recognised, in this and that, after his first, often beautiful, spiritualist period had passed. Yet I have experienced once more how little this recognition is characteristic of Lutheranism—perhaps even of Protestantism generally as such; how little there is here of any, however inarticulate, philosophy of such things; how much, on the contrary, principles and prejudices of anti-body, anti-senses kind prevail—I mean, of course, as to the body and its senses as occasions and vehicles of the awakening of spirit. My fine young friend, then, promptly brushed all my quite inapplicable admissions and wishes aside; and insisted with unhesitating discrimination upon how religion, in its inception and principle, has nothing to do really with anything but the mind, with certain thoughts instilled into this mind by the other mind, God—thoughts, too, not as to the world at large, or as to even my own general dependence upon God, but thoughts as to my sinfulness and my already accomplished redemption from it by Christ. Faith without, or abstracted from, works; mind without, or previous to, the energisings of the body; my one mind abstracted from other minds, and driven in upon its own state with regard to one single issue: my friend found this entrancingly simple, spiritual, northern, modern; and I found it unassimilably thin, abstract, doctrinaire, inhuman, driving me into endless self-occupation and scruples instead of unto God, our liberty and home.

After all, I had already found up on Alpine heights, some thirty years before, that pure glacier water cannot be retained by the human body—at least, not by my own; and, similarly, this teaching would not do for my own poor soul, *that* I saw and felt most clearly.

It has here, again, been the Scotch who have, even quite recently, reconfirmed me in this attitude. I have, these last months, had a pressing occasion to study more carefully than ever before David Hume's *Treatise*—the epistemological parts; Thomas Reid's still most instructive, at times, indeed, truly masterly analyses and arguments; and the truly admirable, if I may say so, the exactly right positions and elucidations of Professor Andrew Seth (Pringle-Pattison), in his *Scottish Philosophy*, a book of delightful sanity and balance. True, together with Reid and Seth, my attention, in the study of Hume, was chiefly directed to the proofs that the mind and its intimations and certainties are *not* the senses and their impressions, are not distillations or concentrations of the sensible impressions in so far as these impressions are purely sensible, but that the mental intimations and certainties are something essentially distinct and different. The Sensualist Philosophy is thus fundamentally erroneous. Yes, but neither Reid nor Seth, nor—in our times at least —any other competent psychologist, would maintain that those mental intimations and certainties arise, within us men, in this our earthly life—the only life we directly know at all—except, at least in the first instance, and more or less up to the end, on occasion of the stimulations suffered by our senses and the impressions then conveyed by them—by these and by our memory of them. The intimations and certainties of my mind as to hardness and softness, as to space and as to time, are indeed distinct and different from the stimulations and impressions of my senses which suggest them, which call them forth;

nevertheless those intimations and certainties are very really suggested and called forth by those stimulations and impressions.

I doubt whether, even still, the general reading public is vividly aware of the deeply interesting cases of those two deaf-dumb-blind girls, Laura Bridgman and Helen Keller—of how their minds and souls were found to be empty of ideas or ideals except in proportion as substitutes for the sense impressions of which they were bereft had, with endless patience and trouble, been devised and set going within their psycho-physical mechanism. There appears to have been no trace within them, otherwise and before, of an idea of God, of the soul, of their own identity and personality. These ideas and convictions are not abstractions from, or concretions of, the sense impressions; but even these ideas and convictions, concerning non-sensible, spiritual realities, are actually thought and experienced by our human minds and souls—at least in this our earthly life—on occasion of, in contrast to, by means of, the stimulations of our senses and the images and memories awakened by them.

Now I know well, of course, the causes, so many and so ancient, largely so plausible, indeed so worthy of respect, that have operated and still operate against the frank and full, the deliberate and fundamental recognition of an inalienable place and function of the body and senses, of symbols and sacraments, in religion. Nevertheless, here also, a noble and generous imagination ought not, one would think, to be incapable of realising and respecting the belief in, and the practice of, such things in forms or sides or stages of religion other than our own. Especially ought such a liberality of sympathy not to be so very difficult, since it stands an admitted principle of all the deeper teaching and training within, say, the Roman Catholic Church, that a movement away from, a self-denial in, those things is also most truly necessary, since only in the rhythm of action and reaction, of the going out to these things to the verge of abiding distraction, and of the coming back from these things to the verge of persistent emptiness, is the soul's full normality and development attained.

I do not know that, amongst present day Roman Catholic reformers, the fashionable mania of everywhere finding magic in such recognitions and practices is particularly frequent or malignant. Yet the influence of at least one of those Protestants who have most actively sympathised with the movement—viz. M. Paul Sabatier—has been doubtless in the direction of, at least, attributing no importance to these things, except where they are found as very obvious excesses or abuses. And, of course, the critical historical studies of the religious, especially of the Christian origins—which have had, most rightly, to be busy, which, perhaps, of themselves will have to continue busy, over the historical provenance of this sensible-sacramental current, which have traced it back to various Hellenistic, largely unwholesome or even clearly immoral, mystery cults and doctrines—have, so far, greatly encouraged such a hostility or, at least, indifference amongst scholars possessed of little or no personal experience or traditional training in such things as part and parcel of their religion.

Yet three wide-reaching, deep-rooted facts are, I believe, powerfully at work to gain a full and final re-recognition and practice, with wise and practical safeguards, of these things.

These things are in the New Testament itself, strongly, operatively, undeniably. Whether or no they be already in the oldest layer of the Synoptic Gospels, whether or no they be imported, at least in their raw materials, from Hellenistic sources, these convictions and practices are emphatically, ardently preached, they are carefully organised, by St. Paul; and the Johannine writings presuppose, and are coloured by, these practices, convictions, ideas, feelings, even where these writings appear

H

to be most purely ethical or spiritual. To accept the development of Christianity, as it actually took place within even its first half-century alone, is to accept at least the general principle and substance of these things.

Again, these things will have eventually to be judged, not by whence they came, but by whither they go; not by their historical provenance, but by their truth, that is, their fruitfulness. I do not here take "fruitfulness" in a simply pragmatist sense, in the sense of practical utility only; I mean quite as much that the wise acceptance and practice of these things is rich in suggestion, explanation, completion of the theory of religion, indeed of the analysis and system of our life generally, and of its apprehension of realities in proportion to their depth. Men will thus, after a while, turn from the question as to who first taught these things, and as to where he found them more or less already in operation, to the question of what they are worth and effect—as to whether, yes or no, they are led up to and surrounded by similar needs and helps at the other stages of our many-levelled lives, and whether they do or do not, at their best, preserve or develop certain characteristics of the full Christian temper and expansiveness which cannot ordinarily be cultivated otherwise.

And, finally, these things have been abandoned or opposed, at all extensively and earnestly, from motives not intrinsic but extrinsic—as a reaction against certain complications and abuses brought in their train. Not, I submit, anything intrinsically absurd in the sense-symbol-sacrament conception, not any consequence necessary or universal in the practice of such things, has caused the bitter hostility to them; but simply the fact that sacraments have meant priests to administer them, and have meant *that* which has made it possible for priests to be oppressive in life generally—especially in science, philosophy, politics. But if so, and the case of Wycliffe especially is most instructive in this direction, then not these things in their essence, but the misuse of such things will have to be guarded against; and such misuse will (in the very long run and on a very large scale) be best —at least, be not too costingly — avoided by the deliberate recognition of the danger, the use, the need of such things and by their wise and careful practice. I love, as prophetic with regard especially to the political objections and prejudices against these things, to remember Mrs. Hamilton King—yet amongst us, that still ardent admirer and disciple of Mazzini, a woman who, under the influence of that vehement hater of all oppression, became a devoted member of the Roman Catholic Church, and whom even so pronounced an ultramontane as was Cardinal Manning —I am thinking of the Cardinal in his earlier and middle Catholic years—befriended from her reception onwards, and whose great panegyric on Mazzini, her long poem, *The Disciples*, has been allowed to stand unmolested to this hour, precisely as she wrote it before she joined the Roman Catholic Church. True, Mrs. King is no historical critic, no metaphysician; but she is a deeply intuitive and mystically attempered, an ardently, explosively social and reforming spirit; and all this has fully and happily found its home within the sensible-symbolical-sacramental conviction and practice of the Roman Catholic Church.

III

A further point on which men specially busy with the adaptation of the Christian doctrine and practice to what appears to be best, or at least most abiding and most growing amongst the new conditions of mankind, are likely — especially, I think, in Latin countries — pretty readily to cease seeing things steadily and whole, is History. I mean, in particular, the difficulty, function, need within the religious life of Factual Happenings and of belief in their happenedness.

When, during the last nine years of Pope Leo XIII.'s

life, I regularly spent half—more than half—of my existence in Rome, and the question of Biblical Criticism was beginning, increasingly, to occupy and to alarm the authorities, I used fairly often to visit Cardinal Rampolla, recently deceased, then Papal Secretary of State; and his Eminence would invite my impressions and opinion upon this great subject-matter. The Old Testament was then to the front; and I ventured to suggest how fortunate, upon the whole, was still, at that time, the position of the Roman Catholic Church in this field. For it could, with perfect truth, claim to have laid, through its priest, Richard Simon, and its layman, Jean Astruc, the foundations of the criticism of the Pentateuch; and it could also assert that so far it had not committed itself to any solemn or final acts against it. Would it not be well, even in precise and solemn theological condemnations of the results of specialist studies, science or scholarship, to rest satisfied with the condemnation of Heliocentrism and Galileo, as the share, in such acts, of the Roman Church? Why not leave to the Presbyterian Churches *their* share of such proceedings, in their solemn trials and condemnations of Pentateuchal criticism in the persons of my valiant friends, William Robertson Smith and Charles Augustus Briggs? If the situation were left thus, a pretty fair division of praise, if not of blame, would remain apportioned between the Roman Catholic and the most anti-Roman of the Christian Churches.

Criticism moved on, especially after Pope Leo's death, from the Old Testament to the New; and a devotedly good, but quite differently tempered bishop came to sit in St. Peter's Chair, fronted thus by questions of the deepest delicacy and difficulty, and of the widest range and alternatives. And, under the rapid succession of almost numberless condemnations and restrictions of every kind and of almost every degree of solemnity and precision, it is no wonder if (especially in cases where the critical, or even hypercritical, acumen and activity of men is greater than their philosophical training, self-discipline and insight, or, especially, than the depth, delicacy and urgency of the spiritual life within their souls) certain extreme effects are now traceable, within the Roman Catholic Church, as truly in the direction towards the left as in that towards the right.

I am not, here, thinking of M. Loisy, the dignity of whose life, the abiding fineness of so much of whose critical commentaries, whose admirable defence, in these last few years, of the original character and abiding worth of religion, as against Sir J. G. Frazer and M. Salomon Reinach, and of the historical reality of Jesus against Arthur Drews, and especially whose many troubles and sufferings added on to his immense laboriousness keep me still his devoted grateful friend, and hold me aloof from examination and criticism of the faults which doubtless cannot fail, here also, to limit and obscure his great lights and merits. But I am thinking of more than one other man known to me as, in intention and doubtless in the eyes of God, still active members of the Roman Catholic Church, and whom, again, I am not disposed to criticise as characters, but only in one of their ideas or convictions.

I find then, here, sometimes even a considerable conservatism as to the degree to which, *as a matter of fact*, historical happenings have become, or are becoming, untenable as such, or in this or that form of happenedness. But what has here disappeared, what indeed is recognised as having gone from out of these minds, is any belief in the abiding necessity, the irreplaceable function of historical happenings within the spiritual life. Such men may be, I believe they are, more conservative than M. Loisy was to what they hold to stand disproved; but they are fully, explicitly radical, in their negation as to any intrinsic necessity for the survival of any factual happenings whatsoever. They may still actually hold the Virgin Birth and the Bodily Resurrection in the ordinary sense and degree of factual happenings; but not only could these happenings, as such, but also the Sermon on the Mount and the Parables, the Cures and the Conversions, the Passion, indeed the very Person of Jesus, as so many actual happenednesses and at one time visible and audible facts, go, and nevertheless Christianity and Catholicism could and would remain. For that Christianity and Catholicism are essentially a system of principles and laws, for and in all the deeper and deepest human life and conduct, are ideals and incentives all the more operative because they take a visible, pictorial form. These things, these ideas, would remain true, even if every one of the alleged happenings and historical facts turned out to be pure creations of the imagination, incorporating, not what is nor what was, but what ought to be, and the deepest note in the human soul, this oughtness.

But this degree and kind of "safety," of emancipation from the complications and uncertainties of contingency, turns out, I submit, impossible and ruinous, under the combined pressure of general experience, whether individual or social, of psychology and epistemology, especially as applied to religion, and especially of the analysis of Christianity's deepest characteristics.

Certainly, in general psychology and epistemology, we have already found a great twin fact to be fundamental— the difference, indeed, between sense-stimulations and impressions on the one hand, and mental presentations and convictions on the other hand; and yet also the need we men have—yes, we men, not any abstract system, nor beings of a higher order than our own—of those sense-stimulations, for the awakening within our souls of these mental presentations and convictions. Thus, at the very basis and beginning of our rational, characteristically human life, lies this mysterious incommensuration between the apparent nature of its constituents and the close interconnection of their action; what seems the sheerest, the most fleeting of contingencies is strictly necessary for the awakening of even the simplest idea and assurance of something profoundly different, of persistent being, of space and time, of Eternity, of God Himself. At the higher or profounder ethical level we find again a somewhat similar, but still richer and more wonderful twin fact: the deep difference between sense and soul, and yet the need that the soul has of sense, even, especially, for its purity; for the purity of man should ever be conceived with reference to his body, it is the virtue of the spiritualisation of sense—you can no more have it without sense than you can have it without spirit. And, above all, at the religious level and within religion's characteristic world, do we get, increasingly with the increasing richness, hence truth and vitality of the religion, an again similar twin fact of difference and dependence. Certainly Christianity stands for the deeply fruitful fact, conviction, practice and achievement—Incarnation, in the widest and most varied, as well as in the most precise and deepest, sense of the word. For Christianity, surely, is not simply a doctrine—however true—of certain laws and principles of the spiritual life, with vivid pictures of apparently historical scenes and personages, not one of which need have any factual, happened reality. But precisely the central conviction and doctrine of Christianity is the real prevenience and condescension of the real God— is the penetration of spirit into sense, of the spaceless into space, of the eternal into time, of God into man. Here, again, incommensurables are in close relations of effect, of need. The lower is here the occasion—for us poor men, in this our little dispensation, the necessary occasion —is the nidus, springboard, material, vehicle of the higher and the highest. The higher bends down to, attracts, the lower; the lower rises on tip-toe towards, thirsts after, and finds and wills the higher.

This condescension and ascension, this union, is doubtless achieved in unspeakably different degrees, and even kinds, of fullness and perfection. Yet it is not a simple idea, but a solid fact; not something that so universally *ought* to happen, that in fact it never happens at all; not something, again, that we can, or even must, assume to have happened at some time, in some place, with profoundest fullness, but in this its happenedness is known to God alone. No: even though historical tradition everywhere brings with it certain difficulties and obscurities of its own, it can and does, still outside of our ethical or religious interpretations of it, also furnish us with a certain kind and degree of reasonable assurance that such and such scenes, words, persons—whatsoever their worth and meaning—have really happened. And psychology and epistemology, still more ethics, and, above all, religion, in particular Christianity, cannot really do without this most humble seeming assurance of sheer happenedness, even though they all—religion especially—rightly and promptly find on occasion of and in these happenings meanings, truths, realities, and motives, beyond what the non-philosophical, the non-ethical, particularly the non-religious man will discover in them.

The special difficulty here will, I believe, eventually turn out to lie, not in the apparent paradox of the general position—here Christianity is very certainly anchored in the imperishable reality of things and of man's essential position and make—but in the complexity and delicacy of the practical application and working of this general position and principle within the organised religions and for the average man. And this means, ultimately, the difficulty of creating, and still more of maintaining, amongst more than a picked few, a sufficiently high level of intellectual patience, and of faith in God and in the fundamental position — the major premiss — of those organised religions themselves.

For it is evident that we can take this need, on the part of every full and popular religion, of historical happenednesses, of factualness, in one of two ways: a difficult and slow, but, in the long run, thoroughly safe and fruitful way, which specially affirms the major premiss of the position underlying the historical religions; or an easy and prompt, but, in the long run, unsafe and sterilising or revolt-producing way, which specially affirms the minor premiss of that same position. In the first way, we mean that a nucleus of historically assured and historically testable factual happenings is indeed necessary; and that, believing as we do in God, and in His slow and mysterious, yet most real, in the long run irresistible, working within man's struggles and labours, especially where these are sincere, sensitively docile to the teachings of their own science and of its history, and disinterested and costly, we feel assured that, through and in this our human toil, He will see to the persistence of this nucleus; but that, just as He alone can sufficiently maintain this nucleus throughout and beyond our best endeavours, so also He alone knows with entire finality the precise delimitation of this range of happenedness. What we religionists thus affirm is much like what all spiritualists affirm concerning the reality of body and soul, and of their mutual relation and need: the body requires the soul, the soul requires the body; there is a real and necessary interdependence between the two, yet they are not simply co-extensive; the soul ranges further than the body. And this way would still leave considerable duties to the official Church authorities. They would have to discountenance all views that inculcate or imply the non-necessity of a factual nucleus; to exhort to, better still to help in the development of, cautious and courageous, deeply scholarly and sensitively spiritual veracity in such studies; and to keep carefully alive the sense and practice of the religious life, of the soul's relations to the great realities of God and of other souls, and of the Creeds as standing for this great system of truth and reality, possessed also of a nucleus of historical happenedness. The Creeds would thus remain true, even if this or that of their articles would have slowly, cautiously, to be re-interpreted as true in not a factual sense or in a factual sense somewhat different from the old one. In this way nothing would here conflict, on principle and in the long run, with the reasonable claims of historical criticism, or with the major premiss of the Church's fundamental position itself—that her religion is in part based upon historical facts ascertainable by the usual historical methods, and is emphatically not a simple intuitionism or *fideism* of any kind.

But if the question be answered the other way—which assuredly is the more obvious, the more clear, the more consonant with, and comforting to, human impatience —the Church authorities, and, indeed, the ordinary believer with them, are called upon to defend (and this quite finally, as the last ditch in the protection of the Christian citadel) not only the major premiss, but the minor as well; indeed not so much the major as the minor. Here the anxiety is not to keep the Church from fideism —to retain history as history—that is to allow, indeed to encourage, historical tests and conclusions to be applied and to obtain as regards the historical happenings, real or apparent, present within the Christian tradition and Creed. The anxiety here is to retain at any cost, even at the cost of the ruin of this major premiss, the minor premiss in exactly the extension, detailed applications, and kind and degree of meaning in which it has for very long been held. Not only, thus, does the Creed possess an abiding nucleus of happenedness, not only does it remain abidingly true, in the traditional sense of this truth, if the Creed be taken as a whole, and not only can even its several articles all continue to be held true in very real senses of the word "truth"; but each article, in so far as ever held to state an historical happenedness at all, is taken as of strictest necessity abidingly true and binding in that precise kind and degree of happenedness. Taken thus, the claim to history, to happenedness, cannot fail, more or less, sooner or later, to find itself in conflict with the historical workers and their conclusions. For even though the Christian faith arose on occasion of, and around, and concerning certain factual happenings, which it penetrated and interpreted, but has transmitted to us also as so many happenings credible even by those who do not thus penetrate and interpret them; yet this same faith also early developed certain fact-like pictures and symbols of this its belief; it is impossible carefully and sincerely now to study the Pentateuch or the Johannine writings, without the admission of this much. Such pictures and symbols are not necessarily false, but their truth will be not that of happenedness.

Now it is doubtless because of the strong insistence by the official authorities upon taking factualness in this second very wide extension and absolutely fixed application, that so appreciable a number of the finer minds even amongst men sincerely anxious to be, sincerely believing themselves to remain, sincere Christians, indeed Catholics, have allowed themselves to fly to the other extreme—to the denial of any and all necessary, abiding connection between factual happenings in general and religious faith. Yet this latter negation is even more "simple," i.e. less adequate to life and the real situation, than is the affirmation of those who have occasioned it. And this "simple" negation then reacts back upon the "simple" affirmation; not all the scholarship, good faith and sufferings of such doctrinaire reformers can prevent their "simple" negative from still further confirming their official opponents in the conviction that only in their own extension and precision of absolute factualness can the health and security of religious faith be found.

IV

Our fourth complex which deals with the needs and laws of institutional, social religion, and with the special difficulties here of wise and fruitful reform-movements, will be found, I believe, to have, at bottom, particularly close connections with our fifth and last, busy with the needs, laws and difficulties concerning God and a deep and fruitful faith in Him. But let us keep each complex as distinct here as possible from the other.

How engrossingly interesting are the facts and conceptions of liberty and equality as these have grown under the stress of the richness of the human life and destiny, especially as these have been revealed, and immensely enhanced, by Christianity in the most various ways and stages! And how especially instructive is this study if taken in comparison with those "simplifications," abstract theories and doctrinaire battle-cries produced, in these matters, by the abuses of human institutions civil and clerical, and by the impatience and counter-injustice of the sufferers from them!

The chief upshot for our fourth complex here is that liberty especially, yet also equality, has received its profoundest growth and propagation in the world of thought and emotion at the hands of Christianity, and that Christianity promptly utilised and deepened certain Greek philosophical, especially Stoic, conceptions for the articulation of these its convictions; but that certain parts and tendencies of these same Stoic conceptions were and are unassimilable by Christianity, and that it is precisely these parts and tendencies which the doctrinaires of the Enlightenment and of the French Revolution developed into a difference and recalcitrance of the most far-reaching importance and effect.

According to the characteristically Christian conception, we start with human society as an organism—a body composing, and composed of, its members, each various although constituting only one body; each powerful, but powerful to give because also powerful to get, because actually first receiving much and very much; each necessary with a certain uniqueness, but this within an organism larger than itself. Already here, at the start, each individual member is necessary, is various, is unique; their liberty

is not *in vacuo* or without aim or end; and their equality
is not atomistic or interchangeable. All have duties, all
have rights, all have service within and for the one body.
And of such organic bodies there is not only one, but
there are many: the family, the commune, the Church,
human society at large, the State; these are all organic,
all give to the individual as well as they receive from him;
they are none simply the sum-total of their constituent
parts. And the individuals composing these complexes
are themselves organic, a little world within themselves;
and they can and do grow from relatively unarticulated
or chaotic entities into being richly articulated, harmonious persons. A body with its members, not a sand-
heap with its grains of sand. And further, in the Christian
conception and conviction, the individual is indeed not
merely a part of a whole, in the sense that he has no worth
in himself; he, the individual soul, has an infinite worth;
yet—let us mark it carefully—upon *three conditions*, which
indeed are each equivalent to the other. The individual
here, prized thus infinitely, is not the empirical, un-
spiritualised, predominantly animal individual, as we find
him on the street or in many of our own moments—
in and as predominant in all except the saints of God;
but the individual here meant is the person, the spiritualised, the God-seeking, the God-sought soul. And if
even those individuals on the street and in our own many
moments can also be treated as thus precious, this is only
because, and in so far as, they are capable of becoming
such a person and moments in such a personality. Again,
the individual thus prized develops into a person within
one, or rather several wider complexes, the family, society,
the State, and (religiously) within, and through service
for, the Kingdom of God. None of these complexes are
simply the sum-total of the individuals who enter them,
or even of the persons who become persons within them;
they all are more and other than such a bare sum; they
all give as well as get: they all possess a quasi-personal

spirit, influence, formative power. And, finally, the individual thus personalised is solicited, sustained, completed and crowned by God, the great prevenient Spirit Who works within and through this His kingdom of spirits, yet Who is not (any more than the created spirits composing this kingdom) simply a part of, or even simply the totality of, this spirit-complex. This last condition must stand over for our last complex. Now against this apprehension, rich, concrete, organic, various in unity—where the individual gets before he gives, and where he becomes a person, no doubt in conflict as well as in conformity with his environment, itself never simply perfect since composed of fellow-mortals—yet, still, becomes a person never simply through and by himself, and never as a unit interchangeable with other units—stands the thin, abstract, atomic conception of the doctrinaire Enlightenment. Here there is, strictly, no complex, for there is no whole consisting of differing, mutually supplementary, mutually necessary parts. And, strictly, there is only one legitimate sum-total—the State. And this State is the clearly understood and deliberately willed contractual creation of the originally independent individuals; they were equal, and they remain equal, and the contract aimed, and aims, above all, at securing this equality. The individual thus is here before the totality, and the individual no more becomes a person than the sum-total becomes an organism. The types of the body, of the family, of the Kingdom of God have here no place.

It appears fairly clear, too, that this inorganic, repetitive, uncompensatory, monotonously equalitarian system readily suggests an equality—an interchangeableness of quality and worth—also between different stages of society, and different contemporaneous bodies, schools, Churches: an equality really abstract, unreal, doctrinaire. And here, again, through an impatient forcing of facts, and a violent clarifying of the rich obscurities of life, we end, not in levelling up as far as may be, but in levelling down as ought not to be. We want to be equally just, and we become uniformly undiscriminating, incapable of loving, hence of understanding any one thing, from sheer determination not to allow it to be, in its degree and kind, unique, irreplaceable.

Now it is plain, not only that the abstract, atomistic conception of liberty and equality, and the forcing of life into these moulds, is the easier view, at least for abstractly-thinking races and movements, such as the Latin mostly are, but also that religious reformers will everywhere pretty readily sink from the organic to the atomic conception, at least as regards the Churches, or the particular Church to which they belong. For such reforming movements are inevitably the work of individuals, or at least of small groups of men, in conflict with the average and the routine of the general body, the Church complex to which they belong. Hence, even simply to preserve the sense of the need of such a complex, whilst working hard, and amidst often violent opposition from the *hic et nunc* mouthpieces and organs of this complex, for its reform is of necessity both difficult and rare.

I take it that, in the recent movements within the Roman Catholic Church, there has been less lost in the way of a diminution of the sense that a religious organism, a Church, is needed, than in the way of a diminution of the sense that the various religious bodies and Churches are of most diverse idiosyncrasies, strength and weakness, of very different stages of spirituality and experience, resourcefulness of help, degree of truth, life, love, reality. And yet, if these differences are facts, they should be remembered, should they not? After all, amongst animals the ox is strong in his neck and horns: do not deprive him of these "mere accidents," these "non-essentials." Insects fly at random and drop down helpless if you deprive them of even one of their feelers—those small, insignificant-looking etceteras of their structure. The union of the Lutheran and Calvinist Churches of Germany has largely helped on the dreary non-Church-going, the vague religiosity in place of definite religion, of the greater part of Protestant Germany.

The recognition of these differences will be able to become both vivid and elastic, patient and articulate, in proportion as Christians of all sorts and degrees come to recognise—as, if they grow in the historic sense, they inevitably will—the two great ranges of variety, successive and simultaneous, to be found in those great collections of classical religious writings, the Old and the New Testaments, which still feed and stimulate them all. For there is the divinely permitted, the divinely willed variety and growing worth of the Old Testament on to the New: what a blessing, what a ferment of wide and wise ideas concerning God's education of our race is thus the Christian Church's splendid breadth of action when it solemnly included the Old Testament in the Christian Canon of Scripture! This inclusion, and again the presence in the New Testament of a strong Church current—I am thinking especially of one great element in St. Paul, and of the presuppositions of the Johannine writings—a current which does not prevent the Synoptists representing more the smaller groups of Christians all bent upon heroic holiness, and St. Paul and the Johannine writings containing also a strongly mystical, enthusiastic current: all this remains, amongst every Church, Sect and isolated individual of an at all Christian type, an admirable ferment and incentive to the conception and conviction of Givenness, Prevenience, Objectivity, Universality, the Church; those of Initiative, subjective striving, small groups of heroic souls, the "Sect"; and those of the Circle, the dimmer yearnings, the immediacies too, of thought and of feelings, of the mystics. We thus see that these latter two movements and dispositions have also their deep roots already in the New Testament itself; and that the first—the Church movement—is no more, in its essence, a corruption of, or a deflection from the other two movements, than are the second two movements, in their essence, a corruption or deflection from the first. All three movements are, in their essence, legitimate and ineradicable. But the Church movement is the more massive, and the one most capable of the breadth, patience, sympathy necessary for the inclusion, the encouragement of the other two. And certainly only in proportion as it can, and actually does so, is the Church type justified, theoretically and practically, in claiming a strictly sole rule. This type, in such a case, becomes so inclusive as to deserve, in this its inclusiveness, to be recognised as all-sufficing.

V

The Rev. Dr. J. N. Figgis, in the last of those of his books which I believe to show him at his best—his studies in Canon Law and in the growth of modern political ideas — gives us vivid sketches of the practically identical doctrine, and crisp, stimulating applications of the doctrine, of three men great in his eyes, and certainly considerable in themselves: Bishop Creighton, Professor Frederick Maitland, Lord Acton; respectively Anglican, Agnostic, Roman Catholic. The social and juridical foundations of this doctrine have been, and are still being, most impressively elaborated by that astonishingly erudite, sensitively human, magnificently inclusive and synthetic mind and soul, Professor von Gierke of Breslau University. Von Gierke finds, as we have just done, those two conceptions of liberty, the concrete, rich and organic, the abstract, thin and atomic, in conflict with each other, especially since the introduction of Roman Law into the Teutonic Corporations and their laws, and, more tangibly, since the later, doctrinaire stage of the great French Revolution, and of the domination, more or less throughout Western

I

Continental Europe, of its assumptions and temper. And von Gierke finds the problem of liberty to lie precisely in the question as to whether there exist, and, if so, where are situated, training-grounds and formative bodies of experience, affection, influence within which the crude individual can achieve his development into a person. The Family, the Guild, the Commune, the Church, the State, are all found to be such bodies, because none of them simply the sum-total of the individuals composing them, because all possessed, as according to the old Teutonic traditions, of a true personality, not, as according to the more doctrinaire current in Stoicism and in the late mediæval Canon Law, simply a fictitious personality. So little here does individual liberty necessarily conflict with groups larger than the individual, that true liberty, because true personality, can only be achieved within and in service of such larger groups; what does conflict with personal liberty and its growth is the refusal of full recognition as legitimate to any but one group—the State —and the conception of it (the two things go together) as simply the sum-total of the individuals composing it. Here, on the contrary, the general conception is so richly organic, that the State itself is an organism holding within it other social organisms, each distinct from the other, and with another range, and at another level, and these minor social organisms, again, composed of individuals growing into persons, hence again of beings of an organic trend, more and more actually articulated into rich organisms.

Now this general conception, traced with magnificent *maestria* by von Gierke, throughout West European history, gets specially elaborated by Creighton, Maitland, and Acton in the realm of the Church. Here too, here especially, this conception appears as the one true view. We get again a rich organism, a body requiring all its members, with none of these interchangeable, with each of these requiring all the others. St. Paul's splendid re-statement of the Stoic image of the body and its members, Nicolas of Kues's grandly rich and elastic system in his *Catholic Concordance*, appear thus as the last word of insight and of wisdom; and Ultramontanism of all kinds, from Gregory VII. to Pius X., turns out both foolish and criminal. *Huc usque eruditi viri.*

I was glad to be able gratefully to thank Dr. Figgis for the stimulation afforded us by his books on Canon Law and Political Ideas. Yet I had to add some words of misgiving, of query, of reference to other thinkers, of personal history. And his answer was thoroughly frank and modest—he evidently himself feels the point I want now to urge. It is, then, not urged against himself—it is only here put forward as, I think, explaining clearly the last, the most central of the needs of religion and of the difficulties in the way, if not of liberal Religion, yet at least of liberal Reformers, to meet and satisfy these needs.

If we look at the more characteristically modern movements and attitudes around us concerning the inner life, we shall, I think, have to admit that they are, consciously or unconsciously, full of Pantheism and Subjectivism— not of these alone, or irremediably, but preponderantly, and for the time being. I do not say that this Pantheism and this Subjectivism really fit or require, or have sprung from, each other; I only mean that each of these attitudes here preponderates in these souls generally with more or less of interconnection. A thirst for a totality, where everything is necessary to all the rest; but a totality, and *that* is all. A totality which, if we like, we may call God; and which some are even bold enough to think, or to seem to think, we could adore. A totality to which, within ourselves, corresponds "Cosmic Emotion"—also a synthesis of feelings, with no one feeling given to anything, but just to this synthesis and to the object of this synthesis, the organised universe. This is very certainly a kind of Pantheism. And the Subjectivism would, I think, if pressed, make short work of even this "God." For the Subjectivism still very common (perhaps more as a temper of mind than as a philosophical position, recognised as such) is a careful restriction to the processes of the senses, the imagination, the mind, the feelings, the will of man— a proud enumeration of his various microscopical and telescopic instruments; a cautious evasion of the questions as to whether, with all these ingenious instruments, he sees anything but the insides; or even a delighted, or truculent, proclamation that the vision of these insides is indeed all we attain, but that the vision is indeed lovely, and worthy of all the portentous trouble, wrangling and pain it has cost mankind. Professor Vaihinger manages to repose at the point where he concludes that the mind has an innate necessity to postulate what it knows, what at least it can know, what we now know, to be false. The philosophy of the "Als Ob" reveals everywhere as the strongest and the most fruitful, and yet as the most demonstrably false postulates, God, Freedom, Immortality; men have to act as though such things were. But others, especially Feuerbach, have pushed home, at this point, and have declared war everywhere upon this poor dear "Als Ob."

Now I take it to be certain that neither that Pantheism nor this Subjectivism will permanently satisfy the spirit and the mind of man. Not that Pantheism: for religion, in proportion as it has risen above the animistic and other earlier levels into the great personalist conceptions, and has penetrated all our assumptions and thinkings with them, has found not Nature to be God, but God to be distinct from, indeed contrasted to, Nature, however truly Nature may come from Him and He may be in Nature also. And, if we have our difficulties in finding an all-wise, all-powerful, all-loving God in a world which also contains the disasters of Messina and of the *Titanic* and the *Empress of Ireland*, at least we do not directly worship, we do not adore that world; nor will superstitious scientists ever succeed in popularising such a double-dyed unreality of mind. And not that Subjectivism: for religion, again, has too much taught and trained us to find the dignity of our nature in our reason and conscience indeed, but this because our reason and our conscience intimate and reveal realities other and more than themselves—the various infra-human and human worlds, and God within and beyond these various worlds.

But pray note. If religion really and rightly has for its object, not directly the world, even as a totality, but God as distinct from, although sustaining the world, if its object is not only immanent but also transcendent, is an immanent transcendence, something that we do not make but find, then the specific social organisation of religion cannot just simply and completely be the Creighton-Maitland-Acton synthesis. As, with regard to the general relation of God and the World, religion will have to resist their simple identification—will have to resist Pantheism and must demand Theism; so, with regard to God and Christ in the Church, religion will have somehow not to conceive and practise the Kingdom of God and the Church as something simply built up by their human constituents, as something growing up, coral-reef like, from below, but as something also, indeed primarily, *given* by the Divine generosity, as something descending from above. "You have not chosen Me, but I have chosen you," says Christ to His Apostles.

Now it is not only I, the Roman Catholic, who, in the midst of these problems and their difficulties, still see this, see this, indeed, with a (for me) quite fresh keenness and poignancy. Professor Ernst Troeltsch, that strongly Protestant, that sensitively anti-magic and anti-Rome Christian of amazing competence and knowledge, sees this too. Indeed I think A. L. Smith, of Balliol, in his fine lectures on Church and State also perceives this. But, if this is true, it is of profound importance. For it would mean that the conception and practice of authorities in the Church—whether the authorities be men, or rites, or books, or all three—as givennesses, as descending down upon the individual and even upon the sum of individuals

—that all this is not necessarily and always corruption, superstition, man-worship, that indeed something of the kind is true and necessary. It is deeply interesting to note, especially in Troeltsch, how this sense that a movement from above downwards, and, as it were, from outside inwards, is essential to full, forceful religion at least as truly as is the movement from below upwards and from within outwards—how this sense softens in him the now still ordinary Protestant judgments as to such Popes as Gregory VII. and Innocent III., and especially as to the whole Thomistic doctrine as to Nature and Supernature. Not only (on this latter point especially) do we get clean away in Troeltsch from the painful patronage, or even contempt, still so common in writers strongly influenced by the Enlightenment, but we find a penetration of and sympathy with, not only the truth and nobility, but the relative very real originality—on a large scale—of Aquinas, which the Erasmus-More-Colet and, in recent years, the Creighton-Acton school never, I believe, for very simple reasons, at all achieved. Indeed, it is difficult for a reform-Catholic to keep, still more to acquire, such a sense; for it is but human nature to tend to reject *en bloc* what is forced upon you *en bloc*, and not to discriminate, and not to be just, above all not to be generous, with an interpretative rich imagination, towards what is being used from day to day to crush all movement, all growth, especially of the historical temper and criticism, within you and all around you. Yet the reaction against the reactionaries can go much further still; it can coalesce with, and give edge to, the other objections against Theism. And then we can find men—some of them of clean, indeed noble character, and of competence and insight on other points—ending at last in enthusiasm for that strangest of truncations and abstractions — religion, a universal religion, without God. Already, in Lessing's *Nathan der Weise*, we have Nathan exclaiming — in demonstrable excess of the formal intention of the play, which is merely busy with the equality in value of the three great Theistic faiths, Christianity, Judaism, Mohammedanism: " Ah, wenn ich einen mehr in Euch gefunden hätte, dem es g'nügt, ein Mensch zu heissen!" And, similarly, we can now actually find men, who have suffered much at the hands of theologians, who always seek and find the justification of their censures and prohibitions in the transcendent, the absolute, the ontological; men who were doubtless already previously over-impressed with the purely immanental, deliberately subjectivist arguments and writers in modern philosophy — we can find these men thirsting after, vehemently or angrily proclaiming that they have found, a religion which is satisfied with being purely human. Here men do not merely believe in the objects of religion with human obscurities and limitations; no, what they believe is just purely human, is known to be purely such, is revelled in because admittedly, proclaimedly, such alone. And Roman Catholicism is by such men held to be the most apt for such a transformation of all the extant Churches, since it has had the largest and longest series of contacts and interchanges with the arts, philosophies, sciences, policies of every degree and kind of civilisation and race. The position is not unlike Comte's, but it is suppler and subtler, softer and more sentimental; and, instead of loving and emphasising the external, compulsory, police, hierarchical, mechanical and blind obedience element and temper—instead, indeed, of largely springing from the admiration of these things —this temper shrinks and escapes from such things altogether, and is, indeed, driven, in its dread and fear of them, even away from and beyond the convictions which alone can efficaciously combat these excesses. For, here again, we have to retain a firm hold of those elements of truth and of life which the abuses caricature or misapply, if we would conquer the abuses.

Of those who have taken up the position here considered, M. Marcel Hébert, of Paris, is, doubtless, amongst former Roman Catholic priests, or indeed former Roman Catholics generally, the most persistent and explicit. His influence has been perhaps not very extensive, but it has been very real, in the case of some distinguished minds. And amongst men who have never been Roman Catholics, but who have sympathised with the reform movement within the Roman Church, M. Paul Sabatier has, in the last two years or so, declared himself in print enthusiastically at one with M. Hébert. Much as I respect the fine, pure, unselfish characters and motives of both these men, and great and pressing as I know the abuses to be under which they thus react, I cannot but feel sadly confident that this position would spell ruin to religion and the Church, indeed would reduce both to a gigantic "much ado about nothing"—or, at least, a much ado about something utterly different from what religion has ever claimed to be, and from what man seeks and wants when he turns to religion. And very certainly such a position confirms, as nothing else could, the opponents of all reform in their conviction as to the inevitably atheist goal of all and every discrimination or change; and thus calls forth a recrudescence of the very abuses it began by attempting to cure.

We have now rapidly gone through the five complexes where religious needs clamour for one thing, and where the abuses incidental to this thing tend to make the reform movements ignore or oppose this thing, or substitute another for it.

For Religion, in its deepest orientation and need, requires Asceticism, in some form or other; it requires touch with the senses as well as with the spirit; it requires factual happenings, apparently pure contingencies in time; it requires associations, institutions in space; and, above all, it requires a central affirmation of a Reality other and deeper than the single soul, however rich, than Humanity, however complete, than the totality of all finite intelligences and lives, however superior to man.

Whereas reform—I mean also good, necessary, Christian and Catholic reform—readily tends to discover so many dangerous abuses, so much of convention and excess of form and defect of spirit in the asceticism professedly before it, as to treat the extant discipline as, if not contemptible, yet as negligible; to become irritated with the difficulties and complications in the way of the historical evidences for historical happenings, to the degree of attempting to base religion solely upon experiences capable of being equally acquired at every time and in every place; to react against the inevitable oppressions and superstitions which incrust associations and institutions, even into sinking back upon the quite lonely, individual life of the soul, upon a Plotinian *solus cum solo* habit and practice; and, finally, even tending to evaporate the objectivity of religion, to minimise, or to shift away from the centre of interest and devotion the more than human object of religion, to make religion from ontological subjective, from affirmation of and life in Fact, a simmering in sentiment—this, in great part, to escape from, to cut at the roots of, the sanction to all the oppression—the transcendent God Who backs and needs the autocratic Pope.

In each case, I submit, the escape and remedy lie not in yielding to such, most natural, contractions to the narrowness of the *status quæstionis* presented by the sheer conventionalists, but, on the contrary, in a deepening and widening of the *status quæstionis* itself—in a further deepening and a more heroic living of these requirements of religion itself, and in a more fearless prosecution of the laws and activities intrinsic to the other levels and ranges of our human life. This will inevitably still further complicate, or seem to complicate, religion and life; but, in the long run, the congenital, fundamental, interrelatedness of things, the fact that there is God in the world and that the most antagonistic-seeming movements, wherever genuine and sincere, do, in the long run, secretly seek, secretly supplement each other, will and does assert itself. Without God all our best arrangements and apologetics are but chaff before the wind; with God—and there *is* God—even our fiercest feuds, even our wildest whirlwinds of human passion, reveal, sooner or later, the deeper and deepest foundations and interdependencies of our bewilderingly manifold needs and apprehensions.

Let us conclude with an episode within the lives of certain present-day souls—a fact and experience which have remained vividly in my mind ever since they were brought home to me. These things will, I believe, powerfully illustrate the main contentions of this our study.

The late Dr. James Martineau, the well-known Unitarian preacher and philosopher, had allowed me to come and see him, for the first time and the last, in his rarely tidy study in his house in Gordon Square. He was then over ninety years of age; yet bolt upright he sat, slim of figure, faultlessly neat, clean-shaven, clear-eyed, keen of speech, vivid in mind, utterly youthful and ardent of soul, there—the fine, aspiring man—before me. And, as the finish of our long talk, he told me the following experience of his:

"In that chair in which you sit, there sat, not many weeks ago, a man whose case will, surely, interest you as much as it has interested myself. Not much over a year ago I was first visited by this man, then quite unknown to me, even by name, and who came, without presentation of any kind, and simply asked to be allowed to see me. The man was an American, in his middle thirties" (I think Dr. Martineau said), "of vigorous health, spirits and will, of university training and considerable culture—a man of wealth and leisure. He sat in your chair there, and, that first time, said he had long known me in America by repute and from my writings as an honest man—as a believer, it is true, but as a believer in not over-much. And since he was now perplexed and in want of sound advice, he had just come straight from America to Europe and this room in order to consult me, and, if possible, to act on my suggestions. That, after taking his degree, he had found himself free to do with his life whatsoever he might think most useful and pressing for himself and others. That he was at that time, not only without any religious belief, but full of the most complete, contemptuous conviction that religion is utterly illusionist and thoroughly mischievous. Hence he decided to devote all his time and strength to the systematic eradication of religion. He had now a record of ten years behind him, during which the weekdays had been spent in preparing the unhesitating assaults of his Sunday lay-sermons. That he had had, from first to last, very great success—at least of the more tangible kinds: wherever he went there were crowded meetings, cordial receptions, apparently unhesitating acceptance. And nothing that he could trace or name had happened within his own personal life to make himself hesitate at all. And yet, he knew not how or why, he had now for some months become pursued by the suggestions, as of so many whispers: 'Is it not possible that, after all, you are mistaken? How can you be so utterly sure that all the various religions, also in what they all jointly affirm, are purely, foolishly, demonstrably deluded? Why not suspend your propaganda for a little? Why not re-study the whole question in a more leisurely, a wider, a new frame of mind? Why not at least get away to Europe—procure an opinion as to what to do and how to act?' And so there he now had come to me, and he would ask me: 'What would you, Dr. Martineau, yourself do in such a case as mine?'"

And Dr. Martineau then proceeded: "I told him, after careful reflection" (I suppose Dr. Martineau asked the American to return after some days), "that the following is what I myself would do. Let him give twice six months to the following double experiment and analysis. Let both half-years be spent by himself each time exclusively amongst members of one and the same race: the first

six months amongst the most traditionally and still
unbrokenly believing and practising persons of this
race, bereft of all the charm of intellectual culture, quick-
wittedness, breadth of sympathy, modern elasticity; the
second six months amongst the persons most emancipated
from all such religious traditions and convictions, but full
of all the charms of intellectual culture, quick-wittedness,
breadth of outlook, ceaseless mobility and elasticity of
mind. The first six months will best be spent in a West-
phalian peasant family—Roman Catholic unbrokenly for
well a thousand years; and the second six months shall
be spent, equally exclusively, amidst the medical students
of Berlin, full of the flux of our day. Thus the difference
of race will be eliminated, and also the possibility of, on
either side, being bribed against his better judgment.
And, when he had quite finished his twice six months'
immersions, let him ask himself sincerely, whether either
group, and if one of them, then which, possessed that
deep mysterious thing, the secret, the wisdom of life—
which group knew, operatively, the meaning of birth, of
suffering, of passion, of sin, of joy, of death. And let
him come and report the upshot to him, Dr. Martineau,
in this same room.

"Well, the American carried out this entire programme,
and there, in your chair, he sat again quite recently, and
reported his conclusions to me. He had lived long enough
immersed in the atmosphere and experiences of each
group, to have lived with each through a birth, a death,
a grave moral lapse—troubles, sufferings, successes of
various sudden or sullen kinds. The Catholic peasant
group had been rough and clumsy, narrow in its sympathies, full of prejudice even against orthodox Protestants, and quite incapable of conceiving a modern doubt
or difficulty as anything but so much pride or impurity.
They were always treading on his corns, and were full of
little practices, superstition, magic. The sceptical medical
group had been polished and supple, open to anything

provided it were but new or spelt revolt, full of encouragement to every scepticism, sure everywhere that it was
manly and true. These men were always soothing and
anticipating all his tastes and fancies; and as to religious
practices or scruples, they had, of course, simply none.
And yet, and yet! When face to face with those grim
realities of life, those clumsy, 'superstitious,' narrow
Popish peasants possessed a depth of insight, an assurance
of action, an at-homeness of conviction, of a magnificent
swiftness, purity and massiveness. And, when face to face
with these same realities, the nimble 'enlightened'
materialist students were utterly helpless, without insight,
action, conviction of any kind. The contrast and difference
was clear, decisive. Should he ever again lose this sense of
the unspeakable superiority possessed, in what supremely
matters, by those traditional believing Westphalians over
these individualist sceptical Berliners?"

And Dr. Martineau finished by telling me how he said
to this young man: "Now, look you—you have received
a great grace from God, a light which you must carefully
guard and conscientiously follow, or it will dwindle and
go out. Return to America now, but courageously re-start,
reform your life to the degree and the kind which your
experiences may now tell your conscience clearly that you
ought thus to change. You know well that I am no Roman
Catholic. I shall be glad if you shall find yourself not
obliged, in conscience, to identify, for your own self, a
deep faith in God and a devoted life in Him and for Him
with Roman Catholicism. But pray understand me well:
did I find myself in my conscience forced to choose
between God and the Pope, and no Pope, indeed, but
also no God—no fervent, devoted service of God, of
Christ, of souls—then, without a moment's hesitation,
I would choose, as I would in such a case wish yourself
to choose, not no God and no Pope, but Pope—even
Pope—and God."

You will remember how David Hume, in that *Natural*

History of Religion of his, which combines so much fruitful originality of insight with so much of strange delusion and violent injustice, keeps solemnly doffing his eighteenth-century hat to the immaculate structure of philosophy—to its demonstrations, so beautiful, simple, tolerant, as to the absolute uniformity of Nature, the existence and complete self-expression of God in this quite general providence; and how he gives even more numerous vigorous kicks with those fine buckle-shoes of his to the beliefs—the muddy, fantastic, bloody superstitions—of the popular religion, with their particular providence, their prayer, their miracle. Yet even Hume has to admit that, somehow, those sublime convictions have little hold upon the great mass of mankind, whereas these grovelling superstitions possess the most appalling range, depth, tenacity and effects.

Now what especially Hume here fails utterly to see, is the dependence of philosophy, for its materials and experiences, indirectly also for its estimates and graduations of religion, upon the historical and social religions, upon the various cults and Churches. Any one, all of these complexes may demand criticism, checks, completion from other levels and activities of man—especially also from philosophy; philosophy may be a useful, possibly an irreplaceable aid in more and more completely arriving at what in the religions is most specifically religious, and how and where they should stand in a classification of them. But philosophy no more makes religion than botany makes plants or astronomy suns and moons; and criticism of all sorts is—in these deep matters especially—worse than useless unless it is inspired by a genuine experience and love of religion. Hence we must here always have our nails before we pare them; we must pare them, not in order to make them or to have them, but in order to keep them in as nearly as possible the size, shape and other conditions in which, from long and manifold experience, we find nails ought to be.

Thus love—love of religion, and love of the other kinds, levels, ranges of life—is here the fundamental need—a standing within these living complexes and necessities. The concrete has here always to come first, and to be reached last; the criticism, the aloofness, the negation has everywhere to remain a means, not the end, a pain, not a pleasure.

V

THE IDEA OF GOD

K

V

THE IDEA OF GOD [1]

It is with a sense of deep and humble gratitude that I here venture to appear before you—gratitude for the grand subject given me, and gratitude for the kind of audience before which I am to make my attempt. For the subject is in very truth the deepest, widest, richest, the most fundamental and perennial of all subjects actual or conceivable. And the audience is definitely religious and knit together by appurtenance to one of the large historical and institutional Christian bodies. I can, and will, thus treat my subject according to its own deepest nature—that is, as a subject primarily religious and even theological and only secondarily philosophical. I shall throughout attempt always to keep the discussion in close touch with the most abiding, though not of necessity the immediately patent, intimations and requirements of the religious sense, as these are most fully revealed to us by Christianity, and especially as they have been practised and theorised across the ages and the races in the great historic Churches. But what, even as thus restricted, is to be the more precise range of our study, and what are to be the tests which I myself shall apply to my conclusions, and which I shall invite you to apply to them yourselves?

As to the range, it will, I think, be the more useful course if I explicitly renounce any attempt at even superficially covering the immense ground of the entire subject. I take the great rival systems and tendencies which (in

[1] September 1918. An Address to the Anglican Fellowship, delivered at Oxford, August 1918.

varying degrees, ways and combinations) obstruct or
obscure, deflect or distort Theism to be four, each system
or tendency representing an over-emphasis, or mistaken
extension, or misinterpretation, always plausible and
mostly nearly true, of certain great facts or laws, and of
certain moods and cravings present in the wide, rich,
complex world around us, and in the many-levelled
soul-life within us. There is Materialism, always by far
the clearest and simplest, apparently the most certain of
all possible outlooks, with its intense sense of the reality
of our bodies extant, here and now, amidst the real rocks
and trees, the real dogs and cats, the real other human
bodies, and amidst the real tables and chairs, spoons and
forks, bludgeons and rapiers. Mind, soul, spirit, will,
character, person: all this here remains more or less
derivative, shadowy, evanescent. There is Pluralism, next
in degree of clearness, which holds the ultimate Reality
to consist of at least two distinct substances or wills or
persons, each limiting the others, and each essentially
finite in nature and capacity. And, indeed, actual life
does furnish, at least at first sight, much evidence for such
check and countercheck wheresoever we may look. There
is Pantheism, with its thirst for Oneness and for the
Whole, and its tendency to resolve all things, however
different seeming, into but so many mere, more or less
transitory appearances, or into parts requiring essential
transmutation, of a single Reality, an Absolute which is
itself free from all spatial or temporal, indeed from all
ethical and spiritual, determinations whatsoever. And,
indeed, Art, and Science, and Philosophy cannot other
than seek after certain unities and wholenesses, as their
respective subject-matters; and is Religion itself really
in quite other case? And there is Agnosticism, which rests
upon the obvious truths of the manifold limitations and
infirmities of the human mind; of the apparently endless
and always inconclusive battles, actions and reactions,
the short-lived triumphs of all the constructive general

outlooks; and of the inexhaustibleness of the realities which still baffle as they confront us.

Now had I been speaking on the Idea of God, say, between 1850 and 1900, I should have had specially to consider Materialism and Agnosticism, as indeed was done, with admirable, most successful penetration, by Professor James Ward, as late as 1896-8. But the twentieth century has seen, amongst leading thinkers, a marked retrocession—for a while—of Materialism and Agnosticism, and as real a return of Pluralism and especially of Pantheism. It is, then, various forms and degrees of these two systems, and especially of Pantheism, which I propose particularly to consider in this short address.

Now, Professor Pringle-Pattison's *The Idea of God* is, to my mind, splendidly satisfactory concerning all Materialism and Agnosticism—in certain respects more satisfactory than is Professor James Ward in his last fine book, *The Realm of Ends*, 1911, 1912. But this same book of Professor Pattison's, whilst, for my thinking, still fully satisfactory concerning Pluralism, somehow or somewhat fails, in certain important respects, adequately to meet what I believe to be fundamental intimations and requirements of the religious facts and experiences. I should not know where to find a more reverent and religious tempered, a more highly competent exponent, even on the points where I find traces of a semi-Pantheism; indeed, even in this same book I find, as I believe, all the elements and motives which press for a modification of the positions in question. I will, then, confine my philosophic discriminations almost entirely to the statements and references of Dr. Pattison's *The Idea of God*.

As to our tests, long happy conversations come back vividly to my mind, which Father Tyrrell and I kept up so happily in summer rambles around beautiful Yorkshire Richmond. Tyrrell would put it that we could and would consider ourselves as in touch with reality and truth whenever our conclusion, however indirectly, continued or resumed the most pertinacious (even if now forgotten or unpopular) work and results of the past ages; when the same conclusion turned out, unforcedly again, more or less unexpectedly to meet and to explain difficulties and obscurities as these obtruded themselves upon us in the course of our own work and fortunes; and when, finally, the same conclusion also elucidated the precise root, range and reason of the error thus rejected in the opposite view, and when it did so leaving such a view in possession of much truth in other, often closely-connected, points. And Tyrrell would warmly agree that we should guard against too much tidying-up—against all shrinking from leaving many a problem open. He would consider ourselves to have already achieved much if, without any definite counter-theory of our own, we succeeded in formulating the facts and the problems more completely and more adequately, and in showing why and where the contrary solution failed fully to meet these facts and adequately to solve these problems, even though we had no precise other answer to offer as a substitute. It is in such a spirit that I would wish to offer my criticism of thinkers to whom I owe so very much. To agree is always sweet; to differ is bitter, except with regard to writers too little sympathetic to one's mind for oneself to have much prospect of learning much from them. In the case of Professor Pringle-Pattison, I have some thirty years of happy assimilation for which to thank him; it is, indeed, the very facts and truths so largely learnt from himself which have fed and fanned the difficulties and objections to other parts of his teaching—parts which, brought clearly forward here, will, I hope, at least give fuller point and fruitfulness to my attempt at articulation of the deepest intimations of Theism.

I will divide my study into two parts. The first part shall consist of an analysis of our human consciousness at any given moment—hence in the present, and of what it furnishes of religious implication or evidence.

This part shall consist chiefly of quotations from, and comments on, the positions found acceptable or problematic, of the *Idea of God*, wherever these positions specially concern the similarities or differences between Pantheism and Theism. And the second part shall carry the discriminations thus gained concerning the Present, back to questions concerning the Past, and forward to questions concerning the Future—all this now more largely in my own words, especially in my return, in conclusion, to what I hope to have increasingly shown, as we went along, to be the innermost requirement, the delicate, difficult paradox, persistently operative in all living and untamed Theism.

I

Let us, then, attempt a vivid description and a clear analysis of the central religious evidences or implications operative within our normal present human experience. I take them to be essentially four, and to be most conveniently taken in the following order of increasing religious significance.

1. There is the experience of the reality, and of the need, of Eternity in and through the experience of real Time.

Professor James Ward had pointed out in 1886: "There is an element in our concrete time-perception which has no place in our abstract conception of time. In time, conceived as physical, there is no trace of intensity; in time, as psychically experienced, duration is primarily an intensive magnitude." Then, in 1889, Professor Bergson gave us his exquisite analysis of our experience of concrete Time as Duration—as constituted by various overlapping, interpenetrating moments, in contrast with the sheer succession of Abstract Time where each moment is absolutely equal to every other, and where each moment is entirely self-complete and impervious to every other moment. Then the late Professor William James, in 1891, gave us his wondrously vivid presentment of our actual experience of Time, as "not a present thin as a knife edge, but with a certain breadth of its own—a saddle-back on which we sit perched and whence we look in two directions into time. We experience *duration*; and only as parts of this duration-block is the relation of succession of one end to the other perceived. The experience is from the outset a synthetic datum, not a simple one. We seem to feel the interval of time, as a whole, with its two ends embedded in it." And now (1918) Professor Norman Kemp Smith, in his finely probing *Commentary to Kant's "Critique of Pure Reason,"* drives home for us the utter certainty and the primary significance of this, our concrete Time-consciousness. We possess three ultimate-seeming forms of experience—experience of Self, experience of Objects, experience of Time. Hume could argue that the two first experiences were illusory. But "consciousness of time is a fact whose actuality, however problematic in its conditions, and however mysterious in its intrinsic nature, cannot, even by the most metaphysical of subtleties, be in any manner or degree challenged." Among the conditions indispensably necessary to the possibility of this our consciousness of time are both "consciousness of self and consciousness of an objective order of existence" (pp. 241, 242). But, further back, Lotze had impressively urged: "We readily utter the words: Past is past! But are we fully aware of their gravity? The rich past—is it indeed nothing? And is the history of the world merely the infinitely thin, continually changing, strip of light which constitutes the Present—a strip of light marching between a darkness of the Past, which is no longer anything at all, and a darkness of the Future, which is also nothing?" We have here, in reality, as Professor Pringle-Pattison points out, an unconquerable demand; we instinctively treat Past, Present and Future as organic each to the others, and we thus "in an important sense transcend the temporal aspect of the time-sequence." Professor Royce elaborated this point very finely in his *The World and the Individual* —this dim but deep sense, this keen need of Altogetherness, of Eternity operative within our consciousness of concrete Time. Yet it is St. Augustine who, already and more richly, more poignantly, more religiously than anyone else to this our day, unfolds the soul's need of, the soul's home in Eternity. This Eternity, which we thus most really imply, which we most profoundly need, our religious sense can and does find, because of our own little strip of Simultaneity; yet the Altogetherness which this our religious sense seeks and apprehends is not its own, but that of a Reality not all unlike yet distinct from itself, in which, in Whom it is rooted—in Whom it lives and moves and has its being. "Thy years neither go nor come; but these our own years both go and come, that they may all come. All Thy years stand together, because they stand. Thy years are but a single day; and this Thy day is not every day, but To-day; Thy To-day is Eternity" (*Confessions*, XI. xiii. 2). And the great African already elaborately studies the soul's experiences of a melody or of a poem, in which the series of sounds is not a simple succession, however much conceived together, "but is," as demands Dr. Pattison, "significant, and in a proper sense a whole."

I do not doubt that we should follow St. Augustine and St. Thomas, and Professors Royce and Pattison, in holding the Divine consciousness to be in itself thus significantly simultaneous, rather than Professor James Ward (*The Realm of Ends*, ed. 1912, pp. 472-4), in considering even the Divine consciousness to possess a certain successiveness. Yet Dr. Ward's reason for clinging to such a successiveness is a very profound one—a difficulty entirely overlooked by Professor Pattison; and we shall have to try to meet it, even though differently, in our second section.

2. There is, again, our very vivid, indelible impression

of the Reality of the External World and its appearances
—not only of the organic world of plant, animal, man,
but also of the inorganic world of crystals and of rocks,
of the air, rivers, oceans, and of the stars. And this impression of reality extends also to the secondary qualities
of all these organisms and things—to the particular tone
and inflection of my brother's voice, the leaping of my
dog in the grass, the scent of that apricot on the old red-
brick, sun-baked wall, the iridescence of this opal, the
sound of the grinding of the pebbles on yonder sea-shore.

Here I believe Professor Pringle-Pattison to be profoundly right in maintaining three points as against a
now long and illustrious tradition, from Berkeley and
Locke down to Ferrier, and, indeed, also Professor James
Ward. That not only the various stages of organic life—
plant, animal, man, and whatever other organic finite
beings may inhabit the other stars—but also the physical
universe and the various physical things, here and there;
that they each presuppose the lower stages of reality,
organic and inorganic, and are explained in their inner
meaning and ultimate end by the higher stages of that
same reality—the crystal, by the plant; the plant, by the
animal; the animal, by man. Thus man is organic not only
to the world of organisms, but also, with them all, to the
inorganic world. Again, that the existence of the physical
world is thoroughly distinct from our apprehension of it
—that only as a subject-matter for human knowledge can
it be known by man, can he affirm its existence. And,
finally, that such a full integration of the inorganic, as
real and as part of the world and as necessary to this
world's organic stages, is most important and wholesome
as giving its due place to the truth lurking in Materialism,
and as furnishing most appropriate material, occasion,
friction, discipline for the various consolidations of life
and mind. We thus reach a closely interrelated, most
variously knit whole. And, thus far, not only Professor
Pattison, but also Professor Bosanquet, indeed also

Dr. Bradley in his less illusionist moods, appear to meet man's thirst for the Whole in a thoroughly satisfactory, bracingly wholesome manner. Certainly Theism will never escape fully all ultimate Dualism, or final Pluralism, or essential Agnosticism, without some similar insistence upon Wholeness, Unity, and Knowableness of the World. Indeed, Theism cannot be true, if such insistence be false; for if the Universe, in all its essential qualities and relations, expresses the mind of God—God the very standard and perfection of Unity and Wholeness—we cannot but expect this universe to constitute thus a whole, in which matter and spirit, crystal, plant, animal and man, the various levels of richness to be known and of consciousness with which to know, will all variously but most really each require, stimulate, aid, check and fulfil all the others.

It is, however, precisely at this point that I reluctantly still find Hegelianism, in some of its more or less Pantheistic tendencies, at work even within Professor Pringle-Pattison's outlook. For the moment I shall treat these tendencies as though they were something special to Dr. Pattison, yet as, there also, in conflict with his own deepest religious requirements and tests. But it will conduce to ultimate clearness, if I here pass on to my remaining two religious intimations, taking them more or less together.

3. Man's dim, but deep, his "confused" sense of God is awakened and sustained only on occasion of, together with, in contrast to, well inside this same man's many-levelled, manifold impressions and stimulations—physical, vegetative, psychical, mental, spiritual—as these proceed from physical, vegetative, psychical, mental, spiritual realities distinct from himself, but none entirely unlike certain elements of his nature, and all operating as parts and parcels of the Whole—a Whole within which the whole Man is organic. This dim but deep sense does not, of itself or directly, furnish any definite, clear, stable conception, or even image, of a Perfect Being: it is a

sense both more and less than it is a sense different from
such a conception or image. This sense gives a vague
yet also vivid, unbounded impulsion and unrest—a search
for the clarity of something already obscurely possessed.
We have something, in appearance, purely dynamic, not
static; obscure, not transparent; something which, did it
remain at this stage, might—though without full satisfaction—be "explained" as purely immanental in its
origin and end. But—4—this dim sense is met, in real life,
by the clear conceptions, the historic incorporations, the
traditional training schools, the visible institutions of
the great world-religions. And, in this meeting, the dim
demand is satisfied by the clear supply, the immense
movement is discovered grounded in an immense Abiding-
ness, and all pure Immanence, however masked, however
subtle, becomes and remains impossible in the long run,
as a would-be adequate philosophical explanation of this
great religious fact, when applied, not merely to the middle,
but also to the beginning and the end of the fact; not
only to the various occasions and conditions of the soul's
experience, but to the central subject-matter—to the
Ultimate Cause and Final End of this experience.

I propose, then, now to show why I feel Dr. Pattison
to be still profoundly satisfactory as to 3; and how I find
him self-contradictory as to 4. That adequacy and this
insufficiency are, I think, in some ways interconnected
as cause and effect, in ways admirably laid bare by
Dr. Pattison himself, when dealing with largely similar
confusions committed by other philosophers in other
subject-matters. For this momentary purpose, then, our
3 and our 4 shall be taken together.

Professor Pringle-Pattison, then, insists, at starting,
upon how "No supposed result of speculative theory
can override a certainty based on direct experience";
and that "in no sphere of our experience is the implication of objectivity—the 'truth-claim'—more insistent, one
might say, more overwhelming, than just in the moral

and religious life. . . . The fundamental presuppositions of any experience must be accepted from the experience itself; they may be explained, but not explained away" (pp. 288, 252).

We next find that among these data is "the certainty that it is *we* who act and we who think"—"no theoretic difficulties in conceiving how we can be free should prevent us from recognising that we are free" (pp. 288, 293). Among these same data, again, is "the unity and centrality" or "the centrality or focalised unity which is the essential characteristic of a self" (pp. 283, 271). "The formal distinctness of selves is not affected at all by the extent of the knowledge they have in common, or of the sympathies they share. Finite centres may 'overlap' indefinitely in content, but, *ex vi termini*, they cannot overlap at all in existence; their very *raison d'être* is to be distinct and, in that sense, separate and exclusive focalisations of a common universe" (pp. 263, 264).

Further, Professor Pattison scathingly rebukes all idea that man himself makes values or reality, and refuses to worship Man as such. He denounces "Comte's foolish phrase about the heavens declaring the glory, not of God, but of Kepler and Newton"; and Swinburne's "Glory to Man in the highest! for Man is the master of things" (p. 238).

Indeed, Man and God do not form one centre, consciousness, selfhood, but two. "I appeal confidently to the same great experiences," which require the individual to find his full life in service of other individuals and of the whole, "to prove the absolute necessity of what I will call 'otherness,' if they are to exist at all. It takes two not only to make a bargain" at the level of the legalistic world; "it takes two to love and to be loved, two to worship and to be worshipped" in the depths of the religious life. "The most perfect *alter ego* must remain an *alter* if the joy of an intensified life is to be tasted at all. Selfhood is not selfishness" (p. 289). "The unification of conscious-

ness in a single Self is fatal to the real selfhood either of
God or man" (p. 390). "The integrity of the self-conscious
being is involved in the very perfection of the divine
nature" (p. 320).

And, further, these two centres, consciousnesses, self-
hoods, are assuredly not on a parity—indeed God holds
more than any primacy of honour. Thus the Professor
sarcastically rejects ravings such as "the desire and
determination of modern humanity to have a voice and
vote in the cosmic councils," and such again as "the
Democratic Conception of God which can brook no
such class distinctions as the effete European contrast
between God and man" (p. 238). And he most truly
insists: "The reality of the ideal and its infinite transcendence of finite attainment is the very note of moral and
religious experience" (p. 382). Hence, "to treat God as
no more than *primus inter pares* is to lose touch both with
speculation and religion"; and "the relation between the
finite spirit and its inspiring source must be, in the end,
incapable of statement in terms of the relation of one
finite individual to another" (p. 320). "There is surely
a singular impropriety in speaking as if we and God
together constituted the sum-total of existence" (p. 389).

Hence, "we must, of course, distinguish between such
an infinite experience," such as God possesses of the universe as an ultimately harmonious whole, "and the experiences of ourselves and other finite persons" (p. 314).
Hence, too, we must oppose William James's conception
of a finite God, if this God be "conceived as growing
in insight and in moral wisdom through the lessons of
experience"; for, in such case, "one is at a loss to see
why the title of God should be bestowed on an individual
essentially of the human type, though, no doubt, on a
larger scale and at a higher stage of development. . . .
It seems to me impossible to override the testimony of
the religious consciousness on this point" (p. 383). The
intelligence and the freedom of God are different from

those of man. "Although the discursive and scheming
intellect is rightly denied" to God by Spinoza, "intelligence in some larger, directer form—of which we may
have hints and anticipations in our own experience—
must be affirmed." And although Spinoza's protest against
any *voluntas*, conceived as freedom of choice, in God
"must be emphatically sustained," we must insist upon
God's Will "as the inwardly affirmed movement and
rhythm of a concrete experience or life" (pp. 339, 340).

So far we have listened, I feel, to deeply satisfactory
articulations of the most delicate and discriminative
religious consciousness. But unfortunately a second,
certainly different, indeed I believe largely contradictory,
current runs, in places, as strongly and even more clearly,
through Dr. Pattison's thought and trend. I will take
these differing utterances in a somewhat different order;
and I will add to each group my little critical comments
concerning the special point there prominent.

"We must be in earnest with this principle"—with
the refusal to take any one element or moment in a
process and treat it statically as a fact on its own account;
for this principle "applies to God and finite minds, the
apparent beginning and end of the process, just as much
as to nature, the intermediary or connecting term. They
also"—God and finite minds—"cannot be substantiated
as static units apart from the process which constitutes
their life. It is equally essential to be clear on the point,"
in the case of God as it is in the case of the finite conscious
being, "if we are not to involve ourselves in meaningless
speculation" (p. 309). "The universal is no less an abstraction, if it is taken as real, or as possessing substantive
existence, independently of the individuals whose living
tissue it is. They realise themselves through it; it realises
itself in them" (p. 265). And "God has no meaning to us
out of relation to our own lives or to spirits resembling
ourselves in their finite grasp and infinite reach; and, in
the nature of the case, we have absolutely no grounds for

positing His existence out of that reference." In a word,
"the transcendence which must be retained, and which
is intelligible, refers to a distinction of value or of quality,
not to the ontological separateness of one being from
another" (pp. 254, 255).

Dr. Pattison, we saw, repeatedly rejects the *Primus
inter pares* conception of God. Yet here he does not leave
God even simply as *unus inter pares*. For he has strenuously
insisted that "finite centres may 'overlap' indefinitely in
content, but, *ex vi termini*, they cannot overlap at all in
existence; their very *raison d'être* is to be distinct and,
in that sense, separate and exclusive focalisations of a
common universe" (p. 264). God, it is admitted, possesses
a larger content and a higher kind of consciousness than
is possessed by those finite centres. Does, then, the
distinctness, separateness, exclusiveness, unity, centrality
of centres and subjects, diminish to vanishing point, in
proportion to the increase in the depth and range of the
content? Where the content is infinite, does the separate
subject become non-existent? Or, again, if the content of
the divine consciousness be taken as finite, the distinctness of the divine subject would remain, since the content
of the human consciousness is certainly finite, yet the
human subject abides distinct. And that the content of
the divine consciousness is more restricted than is that of
the finite centres would certainly be disallowed by Professor Pattison. And no amount of "overlapping" of the
contents possessed by God and man could involve an
overlapping of existences; at least so it stands as between
man and man—is it not to stand as between man and God?

Again, Professor Pringle-Pattison has most conclusively
demonstrated the "essentially circular" character of Berkeley's argument concerning the non-existence of un-
thinking things. "We cannot conceive," he observes,
"the existence of material things apart from a mind which
perceives or knows them, because, as Berkeley himself
puts it, we are trying to '*conceive* them existing uncon-

ceived or unthought of,' which is a plain contradiction. But," continues with just triumph Dr. Pattison, "that of itself decides nothing as to the existence of things . . . apart from their being known. Berkeley proves that they cannot exist *in the knowledge relation* without implying a mind," also, "that we cannot say anything about them except as known, so that out of that relation they are to us . . . as good as nothing at all. But this . . . cannot prove . . . that being-in-that-relation constitutes their existence. On the contrary, we should all say, *prima facie*, that being known makes no difference to the existence of anything real" (pp. 191, 192). Yet Dr. Pattison's continued insistence that we know, and can know, God only in and through the world, finite spirits and our own minds—an insistence which, indeed, constitutes a most wholesome and valuable method for man's attainment of a valid, full, vivid knowledge of God—is certainly often formulated by him as though this dependence of our knowledge of God upon our knowledge of the world were decisive as to the dependence of God's existence upon the existence of the world. A condition of man's knowledge becomes unperceivedly a condition of God's existence. Thus, when the Professor affirms that, "in the nature of the case, we have absolutely no grounds for positing God's existence out of reference to our own lives or to similar spirits" (p. 254), he is certainly right if he means no more than that we could not affirm God's existence, were we bereft of these circumstances and references for our cognition. But he is certainly wrong in so far as he in any way holds or implies that this cognitive situation of man is of itself decisive as to the possibility or actuality of God's existence outside of this situation. Yet the solemn tone in which he urges his point makes it fairly incredible that he means by it no more than such a jejune epistemological reminder, as would be his words if taken in the first sense. And such an unconscious confusion of thought would be most natural to a mind steeped for a lifetime in

L

Hegelian thinking, even though it has finally overcome, in other points, the weaknesses special to this school.

The existence of finite centres of consciousness "is a fact as true and important 'from the side of the Absolute' as from the point of view of the finite beings themselves"; "only for and in such individual finite beings does the Absolute take on the lineaments of God" (pp. 277, 295). But, if God attains to consciousness of Himself only in and through such finite spirits, God's self-consciousness cannot but grow with the growth of these finite spirits. We thus get a growing God—a conception, as we saw, formally repudiated by Dr. Pattison. In other places Dr. Pattison seems to interrelate the Absolute and the World, as both unchanging, and God and Finite spirits — these spirits at least — as essentially growing. Yet that Absolute, as a matter of fact, has, by the eternal creation of the world, been God all along. If so, then the world, the mean between God and spirits, does not grow; whereas God and spirits, as it were before and after the world, do grow; or, if God is admitted to be the very root and centre of the world, we have a growing root and centre of something that does not grow at all. But, if so, how can progress exist only in the parts, not in the whole, as Dr. Pattison everywhere insists to be the case?

But, above all, this second, more purely Hegelian, current of Dr. Pattison undoubtedly ignores or inhibits or misapprehends one of the two, closely interrelated, crucial and clamorous claims, testimonies and needs of religion—the twin experiences and truths which only together constitute its central paradox—a paradox even richer in range and depth than the "die to live" paradox which is pushed by Hegel to such preposterous lengths. This central paradox teaches, indeed, that God loves man, and is man's friend and *socius*; that God begs man: "My son, give Me thy heart"; that God, very variously but continuously and most truly, reveals His real nature in the world and to man—a revelation at its fullest and purest

in the life, teaching, character, death and living presence
and power of Jesus Christ. But this same paradox simultaneously teaches that this love of God for man, that this
self-revelation of God in nature and in history, is so great
and so wondrous precisely also because there is no parity
of nature or of need, no absolute correlation, between
God and whatsoever is not God; because God has not a
sheer necessity to create, or a sheer need of creatures,
even once they are created. God does not require finite
beings nor the universe to attain to self-consciousness or
self-articulation; whereas all finite beings and the universe
strictly require God for their various degrees of reality
and consciousness. Dr. Pattison is well aware that "most
people might feel it akin to sacrilege to assert the existence
of God in and through man" (p. 254); yet, when in
this current and on this point, even this so largely formidable critic of Hegelianism remains himself strangely
little sensitive to the depth and delicacy of religion's
witness to the self-completeness, the independence,
and the awe-inspiring pre-eminence of God. I take it
that the Scottish Hegelians (on this point including even
Dr. Pattison) and the Hegelian Professor Bernard Bosanquet, of obviously French descent, have been all along
with so little sensitiveness, or have lost so much sensitiveness on this point, almost as largely from an excessive
reaction against Scotch and French Calvinism as from
any excessive fascination by Hegelian Pantheism.

In any case I do not think Dr. Pattison's analysis of the
motives and substance of the Trinitarian doctrine comes
up to his own fine standard for the right appraisement
of such Church definitions, and his own practice when he
discovers two very valuable abiding truths in the Church
definitions of Creation (p. 306). For, in the case of the
Trinitarian doctrine, he allows himself to be carried away
by two, assuredly not central, facts. He sees Hegel so
largely and vainly absorbed in the hypostatising of philosophical reflection, from sheer Unity or Eternal Being on

to this sheer Unity's own self-unfolding, determination, differentiation — as though all this were a historical account of actual successive happenings. And he sees, as Hegel himself saw, this (certainly false) doctrine prefigured in the Church formulations of the Eternal Generation by the Father of the Son. He takes these formulations as really determined by, and at bottom expressive of, the teaching of Philo as to the transcendent Deity, exalted above determination by any predicates known to finite intelligence, and the Logos, the Second God, who is immanent and knowable. Thus the metaphysical creeds are taken by Dr. Pattison to represent, in this idea, "the inveterate tendency of our thought to try to get beyond or behind the ultimate, to project a more abstract God behind the living God, as somehow bringing the latter into being" (p. 313). But this is a most insufficient account of the root motives and deepest substance of the great Trinitarian movement. For can anything be more certain than that its root-causes were the two utterly concrete realities, apprehended in the most realistic ways—the real God of the Jewish prophets, now most completely revealed in His most rich reality by Jesus of Nazareth, and this same real Jesus, so richly real in His life and death, His teaching and His persistent power? The roots of the doctrine were these two realities and the need somehow to co-relate them, as well as possible, with the aid of such (certainly largely inadequate) philosophical systems as were accessible in those ages, and to protect this richness of the life of God as against all absolute co-ordination with the world. Two ages-long currents prove that these were indeed the ultimate needs and motives. The one current never ceased until, as late as A.D. 1215, the absolute identity of each Person with the one "individual essence" of God had been defined, and every vestige of the "second God" suggestions had been entirely removed. And the other current never ceased to oppose such doctrines as those of Meister Eckhart, so much loved by

Hegel when in his full pantheistic moods, condemned by Pope John XXII. in A.D. 1329; "no distinction can exist, or is intelligible, in God Himself," "if I declare God good, it is as though I declared white black." [1] Professor James Ward, in his *Realm of Ends* (p. 190), is far more sympathetic to the Trinitarian doctrine.

And a last point. "The individual," writes Dr. Pattison, "who would find his end in the culture of his own personality . . . suffers the same defeat as the voluptuary who pursues pleasure for pleasure's sake. But although the individual may not make himself his own End, the world of finite individuals may well constitute the End of the Absolute. How can we ascribe to the Absolute the self-centred life, which spells moral death in the creature? More reasonable is it to suppose that the infinite reality reflects itself in the finite nature, and that . . . our souls . . . repeat, in the process of their own experience, the flux and reflux of the cosmic life" (pp. 294, 295). Here again, I submit, we miss the delicate tension of the deepest religious experiences, if we *will* thus force an "absolute correlation" of God and man. If we take so utterly daring a teacher as is St. Catherine of Genoa of man's Pure Love of God as man's perfection, since it alone imitates and reciprocates the Pure Love of God for man, as part and parcel of God's essential nature, we discover that God is found so lovable and so love-impelling, precisely because He who has no essential need to be loved by finite spirits, still less to attain to self-consciousness by their existence and by His love of them, nevertheless does love them far better than ever they can love themselves, and invites their love of Him because it alone is the adequate means and end of their happiness. And if we take Spinoza, so deep and noble in his instincts and intuitions in contrast with his largely ruinous theories, we find him certainly deeply moved, and somehow mysteriously moving, in his insistence that the love with which finite spirits love

[1] Denzinger's *Enchiridion Symbolorum*, ed. 1913, Nos. 523, 528.

God is the very love with which God Himself loves. Doubtless this utter identification is an error, and Dr. Pattison rightly insists on a certain real independence possessed by such finite lovers. Nevertheless, the attraction of such a doctrine for Spinoza and for his readers can hardly spring solely from the intellectual attraction of "the circle," and proves, I think clearly, how far more subtle the true situation concerning the self-loving God is than it appears in certain passages of Dr. Pattison. Surely, it is far from clear that man's seeking of his end in his own personality is wrong, precisely and simply because this personality happens to be his own. I take the essence of the wrongness here to consist in the insistence on a lie in the attempt to make the human personality self-sufficing whilst, by its unchangeable constitution, it is not. But the wrongness of finding His end in His own inner life is assuredly not obvious in the case of God, if, in very truth, that life is self-sufficient. And I submit that one of the two polar facts and truths present in all the deepest religious experiences is that the divine life *is* thus self-sufficing. The scholastic distinction between God's essential glory, as already attained by His own unspeakably rich inner life, and God's accidental glory, as attained in and through finite spirits and their happiness as found by them in Him, may be clumsy, wooden, what not; but it stands for certain fundamental implications and intimations of religion, and philosophy will indeed do yeoman service if and when it succeeds in better "explaining, not explaining away" the twin facts, the dual truth thus aimed at in the past.

VI
MORALS AND RELIGION

VI

MORALS AND RELIGION[1]

I PROPOSE to take Religion here as an apprehension, emotion, volition, life ultimately characterised by its object—as an attitude involving a belief, however inarticulate, in some Superhuman Beings or in One Superhuman Being. I intend to concentrate attention upon certain moral dispositions traceable, more or less, in all deep and delicate thinking and doing, whether such thinkers and doers accept such Religion or reject it, so long at least as a controversial mood does not disturb the simple action and affirmation of their true selves. And I aim at showing how real has been the influence of Religion (taken in the evidential, trans-subjective, realist and personalist sense adopted here) upon the formation of these dispositions; and how irreplaceable, in the long run, is this religious influence for any assured and abiding flourishing of these delightful but difficult, these grandest and humanest of all the human virtues.

I

I take the restriction of the term Religion to belief (whatever may be its other qualities and its quantity) in some Superhuman Beings or Being, to be the most adequate interpretation of the great mass of historical and psychological facts and forces concerning religion, so long as we carefully distinguish these facts and forces from the fancies or wishes, or from the difficulties and scepticisms

[1] An Address delivered at Oxford, September 1920.

of individuals or of times that have been deflected or
arrested, in their naïve religious instincts, by over-civilisa-
tion or the like. It is doubtless tempting, when we are
pressed by the very real theoretical difficulties and practical dangers of Theism, to attempt its explanation in the
past as essentially Cosmic Emotion or some other Pantheistic feeling or outlook; and to insist, for the present
and the future, upon some such emotion or outlook as a
sufficiently operative substitute. Religion, as it has flourished in the past across broad stretches of history, and
as it still subsists amongst average human beings—Religion,
as a sense of the Otherness, the Distinct Reality, the Per-
sonalism of God—thus melts away into a vague religiosity
fearful of any approach to anthropomorphism however
noble. But it is far from easy to succeed in any such
attempted reduction of Religion, even simply as concerns
its past acts and facts. Certainly Buddhism and Confucianism, the two largest apparent exceptions offered
by history, do not, properly analysed, constitute any
final refutation of such a realist view of Religion. For
Primitive Buddhism appears rather as a grand prelude,
an impressive clearing of the stage, for Religion than as
a religion proper; whilst Buddhism, as it has now existed
for many centuries, is admittedly penetrated by belief
in supernatural beings. And Confucianism seems rather
to be an impressively definite, and within its range an
extraordinarily efficient, Moral Code than, in its essence
and centre, a religion properly so called. Both the intense
sense of the mutability and the unsatisfyingness of all
contingent life, which saturates Primitive Buddhism, and
the tenacious practice of order, laboriousness, fidelity and
honesty within human society, which distinguishes Confucianism, are not only great things of their kind, they
are also things variously necessary, as stimulations, checks,
materials, to Religion. Only they are not Religion proper,
not direct parts of Religion itself.

II

As to the virtues, accepted as precious also by circum-spect Agnosticism, virtues which nevertheless appear in reason to involve a Theistic conviction, let us take the following six.

1. Unpretentiousness, littleness in one's own eyes: these habits are doubtless approximately present in some of the moods of an Epictetus and a Marcus Aurelius. Yet *crea-tureliness*, the sense, not of my littleness amidst a huge World Machine, or World Soul, or World Process, but of my weakness and poverty as measured by perfect Spirit —of the Spirit not myself, yet sufficiently like me to humble me whilst sustaining me: this beautifully rich virtue still shines out, in its specifically Theistic colour, in Charles Darwin's touching self-oblivion.

2. Heroism, the holding out against numbers, suffering death: this also appears, on an impressive scale, amongst the Stoics and continues to rejoice us all from amongst men of little or no Theistic belief. Yet Heroism of a homely and happy cast, a disposition and a practice which deliberately sacrifices all things earthly with a genial brightness and assurance that all will be well—a death like that of Sir Thomas More: this appears to require, in the long run, a belief in a Personalist Spirit as the Ultimate Reality. I submit that only the unhappy divorce between head and heart, which so many moderns *will* canonise as though ultimate and indeed attractive, can obscure for us the superiority of this genial over that gigantic heroism.

3. Interdependence, inter-aid between man and man, assuredly requires to be extended beyond Kant's two rules of my continuous respectful non-interference with my neighbour's interior life and of my persistent help of him in all external things and needs. For I have, on the contrary, somehow to love my neighbour affectively

as well as effectively, and I have to bring light and strength
to his interior life. And to do this becomes necessary in
exact proportion as it becomes difficult. A *creative* love
is here required—a love which loves, not in acknowledg-
ment of an already present lovableness, but in order to
render lovable in the future what at present repels love.
But where am I to find a motive sufficiently independent
of my fellow-creature's actual repulsiveness and sufficiently strong to make me love him, the loveless and
unlovable, into lovableness, unless in a love inspired by,
and primarily directed to, a Reality at all times *creatively*
loving, hence supremely lovable—i.e. God?

4. Truthfulness: how immense is our need of it, in
all art and science and philosophy, in all life and character! Yet also how difficult and delicate a virtue it is!
A virtue which (however much many a popular enthusiasm
may obscure the grim fact) depends, in the long run, for
its secure subsistence, upon the worth-while, and upon
the conviction of the worth-while, of all this toil and
trouble. Suppose all our human values to consist, and
to be seen to consist, of but so many passing appearances
of world forces which in themselves are simply mechanical
and material, and will inevitably sink back into what they
really are: how and why are men to continue to strive for
costly accuracy about such mindless happenings, such
trivial disportings? Whereas if we hold our deepest human
ideals and aspirations to be in a real relation to the Ultimate Reality—to be occasioned by the same Reality
which gives to those ideals both their power and our sense
that even they are but approximations: we possess a strong
motive for such delicate truthfulness, even if we had only
to report how poor and fragmentary is all we have and do
and can become.

5. But concreteness, articulation, richness of experience, thought, conviction, and of the many-levelled
world which these our own activities apprehend: how
deep is also the thirst for these, in all fully awake and

unsophisticated souls! Not truthfulness, simply as a formal virtue, but valuable realities reached and served by our veracity—this is what we seek. In vain does Haeckel rejoice that we cannot, according to his calculations, escape the admission that mere ice and snow will be the real end of all realities, however apparently rich may be their endowment. There will, as long as man continues man on this our planet, exist Charles Darwins nobly to express men's general shrinking from such a dreary outlook and from such barbarian joy. Yet it is plain that the said riches, and a thirst for such riches, are but foolish illusions, if there is no abidingness in the higher and highest articulations of reality as apprehended by us. Nor indeed is this thirst, at its deepest, a thirst for sheer Becoming, but, especially in so far as it is specifically religious, it is primarily a thirst for Being—for Being Extant and Realised. The Unmoving *Energeia* of God, the full ocean of His Pure Action, thus affects, and in return is desired by, the feeble river of man's life—a life possessed of so much fretful *activity*, so little fruitfulness and so little peace.

6. A happiness that is not superficial and a depth that is not morbid: this most precious paradoxical combination only Religion (in the strict sense here adopted) appears to produce, and indeed even merely to perceive, with sufficient vividness and power. For the Suffering Serenity, which men have learnt to reverence supremely, springs from the soul's keen perception and peaceful acceptance of its own littleness in contrast, not with more or less abstract laws or problems or with material realities, but with the immense fact of God. The Ideal is here a Self-conscious Real; the Supreme Real is experienced here in and together with other, the contingent lesser realities, and as the ultimate cause both of the existence and worth and of the perennially unsatisfying character of these same lesser realities. Such a suffering of *expansion* mankind will never for very long cease to reverence and

to seek. Yet only a suffering of *contraction*, or, worse still, a deadness to the occasions for either kind of suffering, appears to have any logical place or assured protection in any non-religious scheme of Morals.

III

The affirmation of an essential interconnection between certain moral ideals and habits, esteemed by the finest moral judges as part of the most precious flowering of the ethical life, and the implications of Religion taken in the strict sense of the word, involves no inquisitorial judgment upon any individual, nor the denial of much ethical goodness, even of goodness not entirely without that most precious religious complexion, amongst souls that might be classed, or that would class themselves, as agnostic or even atheist. For what any one of us men really thinks always differs, more or less, from what he thinks he thinks. Again, the most earnest Theist is never quite consistent; the true moral flowering of his religious conviction is always more or less determined—it is deflected or arrested—by causes other than his religion at its best. And, perhaps above all, the moral movement imparted to individuals, or even to entire generations, by definite religious convictions usually persists, more or less, for a considerable time after these religious motives have died out. These three widely operative conditions render impossible any mathematically precise proof or detailed application of the interdependence, here contended for, between Religion and Morality. Yet the very recognition of the existence and widespread operation of these obscuring counter-influences leaves us all the more free to conclude to a conviction, substantially identical, on its epistemological side, with the penultimate of the four or five very distinct positions advocated by Kant in that bewildering mosaic work of his—the *Critique of Pure Reason*. Professor Kemp Smith's masterly commentary makes it now comparatively easy to locate, and to press out the implications of, this richest, critically constructive strain of Kant—so in the *Critique*, B. 436, 525, 673, 678–689. Even here Kant is in part artificial—still a Phenomenalist. But in this, the most constructive of the strains within the limits of his Critical Philosophy, Kant maintains, with great clearness and emphasis, that the "Idea" of the Unconditioned is not just a working hypothesis or useful fiction superadded by the human mind to the experiences of conditional states or existences —experiences which come about, and are thinkable and statable, without any necessary operation of the said "Idea." He here insists that the "Idea" of the Unconditioned is a fundamental condition, a chief producer, of all experience properly human and rational. The notion of the Unconditioned is here found, not as any ambitious and precarious addition to characteristically human experience, complete in itself without any such fantasy of ours; but, by a careful analysis of the conditions strictly involved in all such experience, to be a pre-requisite powerfully operative within, and absolutely necessary to, the very possibility of the said experience. The objective Reality, the Distinctness and Otherness from humanity and all its projections, of the Unconditioned, is here assured within deliberately critical principles. We have here an "Idea," which is not merely a regulative hypothesis, but a genuine intimation and reliable evidence of a more than simply human Reality, of an immensely conditioning, unconditioned Existence. It remains similarly to analyse the Moral experiences, and to find that they include as genuinely evidential a pre-supposition as do the more purely temporal-spatial experiences, and we reach, as a necessary part and parcel of the normal experience of mankind, the objective traces and effects of a Personalist Distinctness and Otherness—a real Personalist God. Thus, even well within strictly Critical principles, we can and do discover the interaction, here advocated, between the *Isness* of Religion, essentially evidential, and the *Oughtness* of Morals, essentially imperative.

VII

SUFFERING AND GOD

VII

SUFFERING AND GOD[1]

A BENEDICTINE Bee-keeper, who has loved and watched the ways of bees for now some thirty years, told me in vivid detail how much circumspection precedes the final straight, bee-line flight to their far-away collecting ground. He has stood, how often! to watch especially the young start their day's work at sunrise. The bee would rise straight up into the air for some fifty feet or so; it there would remain on poise for quite an appreciable time prospecting, circumspecting, taking mysterious bearings all around; and only when it had quite finished this, its leisurely mustering of the situation, would it fly off, but now without the slightest hesitation, intermittence or deflection, to the clover field or heather common or clematis hedgerow some two miles away. Let this little fact and story be to us all a symbol and reminder of the temper and the procedure which, I am very sure, are alone right and promising in the difficult, delicate task before us. Perhaps we may be able to fly straight, to alight plumb upon the solution, the rich system of facts and of reality we are seeking; but, assuredly, we can finish thus only if we begin differently—only if we start, and indeed continue long, in care, poise, and cautious circumspection.

I propose in a First Section to give the chief pronouncements on this question that I have been able to find amongst English and American writers from 1870 to a few months ago—hence during half a century. I will there underline, and if possible still further strengthen,

---

[1] Addressed to the London Society for the Study of Religion, May 1921.

what I believe to be strong and true, or at least thought-compelling in their appeal; and will explain why and to what extent I shall be using one particular writer who, unless we are carefully on our guard as to how we use him, had better, in fairness to the general question and to the other writers quoted, be left out altogether. Then, in a Second Section, I will attempt a short but vivid sketch of the history of the question, in three of its main groups and stages—three contributions which I will strive to show give us the main materials and the stimulating, as yet undiscriminating, "mere" or "block" positions, but not yet the ultimate tests, discriminations and reconciliations. In a Third Section I will give two further groups and stages in the same past history, yet these as containing, not only further materials and stimulations, but also the ultimate tests, discriminations and reconciliations. It is in connection with, and from an analysis and re-interpretation of, these last two groups and stages that I will reconsider the three other groups and stages and indeed the recent pronouncements with which we started. I will pass in brief review the reasons given for suffering in God and the reasons for no suffering in God, and will conclude all by as clear and comprehensive a statement as possible of the actual facts, as I understand them, which are implied or suggested by our deepest experience, and necessities of thought and of action. A second, longer, personal anecdote, giving the conclusions in form of an actual experience and state of soul, shall conclude the whole.

I

In James Hinton, *The Mystery of Pain* (4th Edition, 1870, pp. 39–43), we read:

"If in the only worthy joy, there is necessarily latent the element of pain, so that by an absence it must be felt:

—if in human joy pain is absorbed and taken up, not
merely excluded or set aside, then we at once rise in our
thoughts above ourselves. If this is our joy, then it is
His also in Whose image we were made. The pain that
is latent in man's bliss is latent, too, in God's; in His
(bliss) most as He is highest; and that great life and
death (of Christ) to which the eyes of men are ever turned,
or wandering ever are recalled, reveals it to us. We see
it must be so. If God would show us Himself, He must
show us Himself as a sufferer, as taking what we call
pain and loss. These are His portion; from eternity He
chose them. The life Christ shows us is the eternal life.
He emptied Himself, and the pain became manifest; He
put off His perfection, and the sorrow was hidden and
lost in the fullness of His life no more. It was revealed as
sorrow, becoming visible to human eyes; piercing the
immortal heart before a breathless world which, seeing
Him, sees and knows the Father. Thus our own experience may solve for us the problem, how God is incapable
of suffering, and yet reveals Himself to us as a sufferer.
. . . Seeking for happiness, craving for good, we grasp
at pleasure and turn away from pain. God must teach
us better, and to do so He must show us the root and
basis of His own (happiness). . . . The only happiness
He has, or can bestow, bears martyrdom within it. If He
does not suffer, it is only that His life is perfect; His love
has no hindrance, no shortcoming, and can turn *all*
sacrifice to joy. He stands our great example, not exempt-
ing Himself from toils and sacrifices which He lays on
us. . . . He makes us know with which part of it (our
experience) to link His name. It is sacrifice binds us to
God, and makes us most like Him; sacrifice that to us is
sorrow, wanting (as we are in) life and love; but to Him,
supreme·in both, is joy. And when we say pain is an evil,
we can only mean that *our feeling it to be pain* is an
evil. That marks defect and want, failure of our proper
manhood, shortcoming from our privilege of joy. From

pain we may well seek and pray to be delivered; but by
what deliverance? It may be banished in two ways—by
taking away, or by adding. Pain may be removed passively
by the removal of that which is its cause, letting us relapse
into mere repose, which may seem joy by contrast, or by
the deadening of the sensibility, that shall banish alike
pain and pleasure. But it may also be removed actively,
positively; not by the absence of the cause nor by
diminished feeling, but by a new and added power,
which shall turn it into joy—a joy like God's."

Hinton's scheme is impressive and alluring, not only
by the great eloquence and transparent sincerity which
suffuses it, but because of his admission that in God
Non-Incarnate there is no actual suffering but, actually,
only joy; because of his sensitive perception concerning
the immense fruitfulness of suffering for us mortals,
where and when we succeed in rising to the level of
accepting and utilising it; and because of the directness
with which our own experiences concerning our own
human nature are used in explanation of Joy and Pain
as these are held to exist, not only in Jesus, but in God
as such. We thus get a scheme which does not directly
affront the religious sense, since it holds God as such
to be actually Joy; which fully utilises the apparently
deepest of our own experiences as to ourselves towards
our understanding of Joy and Pain, not only in Christ,
but in God as such; and which greatly simplifies our
deepest insights, and brings their several constituents
into direct interplay, for thus not only Christ as man,
but God as such, God the Unincarnate, is our immediate
exemplar—we are literally only asked to do what He is
always doing.

The detailed objections to this scheme will gradually
appear. But there is one quite preliminary objection—a
difficulty concerning the admission thus of Hinton as a
witness at all, which must already here be briefly met.
If I bring up Hinton thus for respectful, and indeed

sympathetic consideration here, I cannot truthfully avoid, when I come to the full criticism of him, revealing the wild, repulsive antinomianism which he developed later on, as to the most delicate of all moral problems, with the most combative explicitness. I cannot avoid it, for Hinton himself connects that antinomianism in the closest possible way with certain elements—perhaps the chief emotional cause—of the view just expounded by himself. And, indeed, I do not doubt that *in him* the one view really led to the other. Yet how to escape from the cheap, contemptible trick of crushing a view one does not like by the exhibition of certain repulsive consequences drawn from it by the exponent of that view—by an exhibition which leaves aside the question as to the logical connection between the view propounded and the consequences drawn by this, possibly here quite eccentric man? And how avoid the suffusing of the other exponents of the same or of a closely similar view with a disagreeable and unfair repulsiveness which they, at all events, have not deserved by any drawing of similar conclusions? Why, then, not omit Hinton altogether? I find I cannot ignore Hinton because others are not ignoring him. The last of my exponents, as will appear, is a deservedly most highly respected High Anglican cleric of mature years, and late Headmaster of the most famous of all English Public Schools, and this writer of six months ago proposes to us the doctrine and person of Hinton as respectively precisely what our present situation requires and as a saint. I have no right, and still less inclination, to suspect Hinton's motives or character. But the less I suspect his motives and character, the more I am led to suspect his doctrine—the natural affinities and the logical implications of his doctrine, if I find the same man, under the influence of the same ideas and emotions, ending with the enunciation of appalling "moral" appeals, and with the careful deduction of these appeals from certain of his principles as enunciated already here above. Nor

need the discussion of this Hinton affair spread the least
suspicion over the temper and intention of the other
spokesmen. And, if it renders us all additionally careful
in the analysis of the general view and of its implications
and subtler trend, this should not be, I do not believe it
will be, offensive to men of such sincere goodwill as
are the writers I have in view.

Dr. J. Estlin Carpenter, that distinguished Unitarian
authority on Comparative Religion, writes in his *The
Place of Immortality in Religious Belief* (1898), pp. 92–3:

"Nor do I omit the nameless souls in inconspicuous
places who have carried the burden of the world's struggles,
infirmities and sins, mutilated by accident, wasted by
disease—the innumerable multitude of those upon whose
toil the fabric of our civilisation has been reared. Their
sufferings, though hid from men, are known to God;
and, I will add, according to my faith, He shares them
too; for He, in Whom we live and move and have our
being, feels in our nerves and understands our pain, and
the long passion of our humanity is borne in all its multi-
tudinous variety by Him. I do not say that this conception relieves every difficulty, but it lifts the whole process
on to another plane. God is no longer a mere outside
spectator; He is the companion, if He is also (in part
at least) the author, of our woe."

This is, I believe, the most sober of the statements
which I should care to criticise at all—perhaps it does
not really intend to go further than what we shall find
St. Bernard said.

Then there is Mr. C. S. Dinsmore, the American
who, in his *Atonement in Literature and Life* (1906),
pp. 232, 233, tells us:

"In Jesus of Nazareth the Eternal Word felt the pangs
of the cross. . . . As the flash of the volcano discloses for
a few hours the elemental fires at the earth's centre, so
the light on Calvary was the bursting forth through
historical conditions of the very nature of the Everlasting.

There was a cross in the heart of God before there was one planted on the green hill outside of Jerusalem. And now that the cross of wood has been taken down, the one in the heart of God abides, and it will remain so long as there is one sinful soul for whom to suffer."

We shall find the very same thought in the "Patripassian" teaching of the third century, and will there and afterwards attempt its careful appraisement.

That very suggestive, but variously uneven young men's collection of essays, *Foundations* (1912), is in two of its most important papers no less emphatic than is Hinton as to suffering in God. Thus Mr. William Temple (now Bishop of Manchester) writes of God's "self-revelation in Christ":

"God suffers and God conquers. When we suffer, we share the experience of God. . . . The Principle of Reason which governs the world is the eternal victory of Love over selfishness at the cost of sacrifice. But this same Sacrifice is the very Essence and Glory of the Godhead. The life Divine is the Christ-life, the life of utter self-forgetfulness; and, in this period, that means real suffering and sacrifice—until all love is returned. The age-long agony of Redemption is the glory of God" (pp. 220, 222).

And Mr. Walter H. Moberley is as insistent:

"The spectacle of Jesus bearing the sins of His persecutors, and, by so bearing them, initiating their overthrow, is the guarantee that God is bearing the sins of the world; that sin exists only to be caught up and transmuted in the love of God; and that such a heart-subduing, world-conquering sacrifice is an eternal 'moment' in the Divine Life, an essential part of the activity whereby God is God" (p. 315).

Here we have a statement almost as strongly Hegelian as are somewhat similar passages in the writings of that beautiful soul, R. L. Nettleship. Yet Hegel is an uncomfortable ally for Christianity; Christian though he certainly intended to be and thought himself, Pantheist is what his philosophy incurably persists in being. And, finally, we have, in October 1920, an emphatic endorsement, a re-sending out into the world, of James Hinton, "doctor, saint, and seer," and of his teaching as the message precisely required by our times—a message which would train us "to see sin and all evil as a good disguised by our own wrong thinking" (*Hibbert Journal*, xix. pp. 53–60). The article is from the pen of Dr. Edward Lyttelton, late Headmaster of Eton, probably the most definitely High Church cleric, and certainly the oldest in years, amongst the authors here considered by me. Nevertheless he is, with the exception of Hinton, later on in Hinton's life, probably the least cautious of all these writers. Yet the enthusiasm is, in itself, very attractive, and the irritation against the clap-trap optimism of many of the newspapers most refreshing.

II

Let us now, before probing, as far as in a short address is possible, the above deep-seeming and certainly dazzling doctrine, with respect to its implications, affinities and ultimate worth, consider a little the three currents and masses of experience, need and thought, which I take to be the chief as yet undiscriminative and excessive attempts, on the one side or the other, to articulate the facts with which we are here concerned. In Section III. I intend to contrast, with these three variously one-sided and excessive outlooks, the two currents and masses of experience, need and thought, which are the most inclusive and balanced, the most central which we possess.

I take the *three undiscriminative currents* as though they had directly followed each other, each influenced by its predecessor or predecessors, whereas certainly the first and second currents were largely contemporaneous and

appear not to have influenced each other at all, till quite
towards the end of the second current. Also, although
the third current owed much to the second, it owed—
in the special point to be considered—practically nothing
to the first current. We have, instead, three currents of
thought proceeding from different places and times,
races and endowments, but which, at bottom, concern
the same deep experiences and profound realities, and
hence can greatly aid in the full unfolding and clarifying
of our problem.

1. We have, then, first, *the Hellenic and Hellenistic
current,* represented at its noble best by Plato and
Plotinus and, in between, on one point by Aristotle.

True, the Stoics also, with their world-embracing,
world-penetrating Logos, and their conception of human
society as a body with its members, each member perform-
ing a special function within and for the whole body,
largely stimulated and, later on, largely helped to articulate Hellenistic Jewish religion and especially also Christianity, and this in part also with regard to the nature of
God. Yet it is the Platonist and Neo-Platonist current
which, both originally and in its Jewish and Christian
utilisations, is concerned with questions which really
concern the emotions bliss and pain, Joy and Suffering,
or their equivalents, as present or not present in the
Good—in God.

But to seize in Plato, or even in Plotinus, precisely what
concerns us—to seize it, not simply in one or more of
their more or less mythical, popular adaptations, but
within their own fully-meant, deepest affirmation—is far
from easy. For the more we compare and press the several
passages in Plato concerned with his ultimate positions
more or less bearing upon our problem, the more
strangely vague and vacillating do we find him as to the
question of Personality, the more he seems to possess
only two quite frank and really clear positions—the one
directly philosophical and the other pedagogic, and to

satisfy us in neither. In the directly philosophical position there is, in logical strictness, no God, but only the Supreme Idea, the Good; and this Idea, though a live, formative force, is (conformably to the entire system of the Ideas) the most general, abstract and empty of all the Ideas. And, in the pedagogic position, there indeed appear the Gods of the Greek popular belief, with their several, variously limited and morally most imperfect, personalities. But here Plato, at least largely, assumes, for purposes of contact with his non-philosophical fellows and of possible reform, beliefs not his own, and strives to turn them into pictures and myths of the Ideas—with Zeus as the Supreme Idea, the Good. Nevertheless there runs through all Plato's deepest writings an emotion far beyond, indeed other than, what, if we watch it at work and in its concomitants and implications, can, without violence, be sufficiently explained as the joy of the Artist in the statuary-like beauty of the conceptions found or moulded by himself, or again as the joy of the Dialectician in the tested logical interconnection and in the orderly hierarchy of the Ideas. No, the emotion which permeates those deepest passages is stirred by, and given to, a Reality quite otherwise rich, concrete and satisfying for the whole man—for Plato himself is as full of love and awe as ever he is of intellect and system —than are either the Ideas, empty in proportion to their elevation, or the Gods of the populace so divided, so childish, and so largely impure and vindictive. And it is this his warmest, most awed and most rapt emotion, this pressing to what alone can satisfy it and himself thus at his deepest—it is this emotion, never adequately analysed or theorised by himself—this feeling, or rather the Reality thus found—which has thus Itself found and then holds him—which gives to Plato his religious force and pathos, gives him his immense religious influence. It is, then, in such moods and passages of Plato that we can, quite legitimately, watch and see whether

the Ultimate Reality here loved with a supreme love
(a love beyond what could be dictated by the Supreme
Idea—by the Good conceived as strictly general and
impersonal), whether the emotion with which he loves
It suggests in it aught of Suffering or Pain. Indeed, we
can very fairly include in our study the Myths where
these are specially charged with deep emotion. For in
both cases—the dialectical and the mythical—we can
seize the aspirations, the apprehensions, the acquisitions,
of this profoundly religious soul.

In the *Phaedrus* (246, 247 A) the myth of the procession
of winged chariots tells how "Zeus, the mighty Lord,
holding the reins of a winged chariot, leads the way
in heaven, ordering all and caring for all." And Zeus
and the eleven bands of Gods and Demigods who follow
him "see in the interior of heaven many blessed sights;
and there are ways to and fro, along which the happy
Gods are passing, each one fulfilling his own work; and
any one may follow who pleases, for jealousy has no
place in the heavenly choir." An ordering of all, a caring
for all, liberality of soul, no jealousy: and happiness,
happiness—blessedness, no suffering, no pain.

In the *Symposium* (209 D–212 A) there is the great
discourse of Diotima, whose stimulation of the mystical
religious sense and whose various utilisations across the
centuries by this same sense have been truly immeasur-
able. Diotima has described the process by which the
soul can and should begin in youth to "turn to beautiful
forms—to one such form; and then to all such forms of
body; and then to the beauty of the mind; and further
to the beauty of institutions and laws, and on to the
beauty of the sciences—and so drawing on towards the
sea of beauty, until at last the vision is revealed to this
soul of a single science—the science of Beauty everywhere.
For he who has learnt to see the Beautiful in due order
and succession, when he comes towards the end, will
suddenly perceive a nature of wondrous beauty—and

this beauty, Socrates, is that final cause of all our former toils, which, in the first place, is everlasting—not growing and decaying, nor waxing and waning; in the next place, not fair in one point of view and foul in another; but Beauty only, absolute, separate, simple and everlasting, which, without diminution, and without increase, or any change, is imparted to the ever growing and perishing beauties of all other things. What if man had eyes to see the true beauty—the Divine Beauty pure and clear and unalloyed—not clogged with the pollutions of mortality, and all the colours and vanities of human life? Do you not see that, in that communion only, beholding Beauty with the eye of the mind, he will be enabled to bring forth, not images of beauty, but realities (for he has hold, not of an image, but of a Reality), and bringing forth and educating true virtue to become the friend of God and be immortal, if mortal man may." The countless souls, several of them geniuses of the first order, who have utilised this great speech as a vehicle of their deepest union with and joy in God, were, surely, not wrong in feeling that Plato's profound emotion here springs from a religious instinct aroused and nourished by a religious Reality far deeper and far richer than his words and system, taken coldly and strictly, would succeed in justifying. But, assuredly, what he thus apprehends beyond the power of adequate presentation, and what especially draws him onward, is a Reality supremely happy and happy-making, an overflowing peace and joy.

And, in the *Timaeus* (29 E, 30 A), there is the great emphatic declaration concerning the cause why Nature and this All was framed by Him who framed it. "He was good, and in none that is good can there arise jealousy of aught at any time. So, being far from this, He desired that all things should be as like unto Himself as possible. God desired that all things should be good and that, so far as this might be, there should be nought evil. It neither has been, nor is, permitted to the most perfect to do

aught but what is most fair." Even if we cannot press the
Artificer in this great dialogue as expressing, without the
discount of myth, the ultimate thought of Plato, yet this
remains plain here also: all suggestion of even merely
possible pain and suffering remains absent from all the
images and emotions aroused by this Cause or Force,
or Intelligence, or Idea—at bottom really by God, all
this Himself and how much more!

Aristotle is, upon the whole, strangely little religious,
as compared with his great master, Plato. Yet there is
one great doctrine, or rather one great apprehension and
corresponding emotion presented to us by Aristotle, which,
in spite of its own very certain inadequacies, is of deep
and abiding religious significance. This is where, especially in the *Ethics*, he inverts the ordinary view that a
"function" (*Energeia*) is a sort of "process" (*Genesis*), or
even a sort of "motion" (*Kinesis*); and, on the contrary,
makes Function (*Energeia*) the wider and supremer notion,
and subsumes Motion (*Kinesis*) under Function as a
peculiar species—an *imperfect* kind—of Function (*Energeia*). We men cannot be continuously active. But God
is not so hampered—His is a pure and perfect nature.
Hence the divine *Energeia* is kept up inexhaustibly and
ever generates supreme pleasure. (Thus nobly analysed
by Dr. Schiller, *Humanism*, pp. 210, 211). Aristotle certainly presents us here with an impossibly narrow conception of the Divine Life, restricted as it is by him—if we
pin Aristotle to his words and system—to a purely intellectual self-contemplation. Yet here, as in Plato, the
man Aristotle apprehends and thrills to far more than the
philosopher Aristotle succeeds in analysing and systematising; and the witness to God, here again, as Pure
Joy, remains sure and striking. Indeed, in Section III.,
I trust to be able to prove how much we still urgently
require another feature of Aristotle's outlook here.

But by far the most vivid and the most impressive,
because the most sensitively religious, of all non-Jewish

and non-Christian Greek apprehensions of God as Pure
Beatitude and overflowing Beatifier are those stammered
out for us, in touching awe and tremulous delight, by
that great soul Plotinus. Yet here again, indeed even
more than in Plato and Aristotle, we have resolutely to
attend to, and sympathetically to seize, not the logic of
Plotinus's system, but the specific temper and the implications of his emotion, and to trace these back, not
necessarily to that system, but, where necessary, to his
deepest experiences as these may show themselves alongside of and in spite of his own analyses and theories.
Without such a distinction, more or less necessary with
all souls that conjoin great experience with much system-
building, we would indeed be prosecuting an absurd
quest. For, in the systematiser Plotinus, the Highest
Idea, the One of Plato, is neither beautiful nor true nor
good; it is neither Beauty, nor Truth, nor Goodness;
it is neither living nor Life, neither self-conscious nor
Self-Consciousness. It is not to be conceived, even
approximately, with the aid of any of our emotions,
however pure and high; on the contrary, we must negate
them all when we think of the One. Thus to ask whether
the systematiser Plotinus's God is all-happy is a sense-
less question. Not so, not at all so, if we carefully, sympathetically track the experiences, the states of soul of
Plotinus, and if we mark the touching troubledness of
spirit which vibrates through his utterances, a troubledness very certainly, though unbeknown to himself, caused
in great part, not simply by the greatness of the Reality
which he is attempting to seize and to express, but by
the contradiction between his spiritual experiences and his
system's exigencies—between the immensely rich, intensely concrete God, who is touching and drawing his
rarely rich spirit, in the hunger for this boundless Richness and Concretion, and the unpicturable Poverty and
Abstractness of his system which is pressing him down
and dragging him away to sheer Nought. It is that

immensely rich, utterly concrete God who brings the
joy which vibrates so touchingly in this great soul—a joy
so great that its cause, the Joy in God, God as Joy, as
Beatitude Itself, is readily admitted, by the experiencing
to the systematising Plotinus, to be indeed above all
our conceptions. Indeed God *is* beyond even our noblest
and deepest conceptions, yet He is beyond them in their
direction, He is indefinitely nobler and deeper than them all.

The following passages from the immortal Ninth Book
of the *Sixth Ennead* express this tremulous joy at God's
nearness to the human soul and the ecstasy of the soul's
union with Him. "God, says Plato, is not far from
every one of us, but is near to all, without their knowing
it. It is they themselves who flee away from Him, or rather
they flee away from their own true selves. Hence they
cannot seize that from which they have fled, and cannot,
having destroyed their own true self, seek for another;
as a child which has become insane and has become beside
itself, does not recognise its own father. But the man who
has learnt to know himself, will also know whence he
comes." "Bodies are indeed impeded from communion
with other bodies (by intervening bodies); but Things
Bodiless are not separated from each other by (intervening) bodies; such Bodiless Things are not separated
from each other by space, but by Otherness and Difference;
when, then, such Otherness is absent, Bodiless Things are
close to each other. The One, then, having no Otherness,
is always present (to our soul); but we are present only
when we are free from Otherness. And the One does not
strive after us, so as to be around us, but we strive after
It, so as to be around It."

Indeed Plotinus in inspired moments can get still
further away from his system's exigencies, and can give
all but faultless expression to his religious experiences.
"We are not cut off from God or severed from Him, even
if our bodily nature interferes and drags us away to itself,
but we breathe and consist in Him, since God does not
N

give and then withdraw, but He ever lifts and carries us, so long as He is what He is. There too," in union with Him, "the soul rests, after she has fled away from Evil to the place which is pure from evils. And the true Life is there; for the life here and without God is but a trace of life in imitation of that Life." I have left out a bit of systematising, nor will we press the passages in which Plotinus teaches the pre-existence of the soul. The following has never ceased in its appeal:

"The good of the soul is there—in that life with God, and a Longing Love (*Eros*) is innate in the soul. For, since the soul is indeed other than God and yet from God, she loves and longs for Him of necessity; and, when she tarries there, she possesses Heavenly Love, whereas (straying) here below, she becomes, as it were, a common courtesan."

The remaining passages that concern us are indeed very splendid, yet they are in part very excessive, where they press the Soul's union with the One to a sheer deification of the soul, which, according to the system, means a complete absence of all desire and all thought —and condition beyond all beauty and every virtue—an utter standing still. And, yet, the intense emotion of Plotinus shows unmistakably how little adequate, here especially, is his system to the facts experienced by himself, for he promptly calls this condition "a striving after contact, a seeking after union." And similarly he tells us, on the one hand, that "such a life of Gods and men is a liberation from all the fetters of this earthly life—a life without the pleasures which spring for the earthly soul from this earthly life, a flight of one to the One." Yes; but, on the other hand, that other life is a happy, a blessed, *the* blessed (*eudaimon*) life—the life of men who have become blessed in their likeness to God and their union with Him.

If we are wise, we will, then, not worry over-much about what is, or is not, according to the Plotinian system, but we will listen to the heart-beats, the sighs heavenwards, of the great spirit Plotinus, and these will then tell us unmistakably that Plotinus is drawn, is lifted, is penetrated and environed on all sides by the great experience, indeed the great fact, of the overflowing Pure Beatitude of God.

2. Our second, *the Israelitish-Jewish current*, contrasts strikingly with the strength and still more with the defects of the Hellenic-Hellenistic current. Indeed, especially in their beginnings, these two currents stand to each other, roughly, as complementary extremes. If we have found it difficult to discover any Personality behind the Ideas which seem of themselves to excite Plato's noble and beautiful emotions, so we will find it often far from easy to discover nobility and beauty in the intensely Personal God as apprehended or conceived by the Israelites—the Jews before the preaching of the Prophets. And if, for our purpose, we have had to use a large and generous imagination and sympathy to reach, across the intense abstractions and intellectualism of the Greeks, the Reality, the Personalist God who was at bottom affecting them, and who alone sufficiently accounts for their rapturous joy as it culminates in Plotinus: so also will we have to reach, with a similar large and generous sympathy, across the intense concretions—the vivid pictures of awful volitional power, fierce emotions and eruptive self-determinations—to an apprehension of God as, centrally, the vigilant protector of His people, the unescapable sanction of their rights and duties, and—this is, of course, our point—of a nature, passionate indeed, but not suffering. The entire Israelitish conception of God circles too exclusively around Jahveh's awful power and unapproachableness to admit of suffering within Him even by implication. True, Jahveh appears as *anthropopathic*—as possessed of thoroughly human psychic emotions; He is not only a spiritual personal being who thinks, feels, wills, loves; but He can be angry and fierce, He can act and

can change His mind concerning His action. And, though
He is holy, this holiness is not yet perceived to be necessarily and always ethical, but appears simply as a quality
of the divine nature above and beyond all explanation or
expectation. Thus He can smite some fifty thousand of
the men of Bethshemesh, because they had merely looked
into the Ark; so that the survivors said: "Who is able to
stand before the Lord, this Holy God? And to whom shall
he go up from us?" And they at once eagerly sought out
others who would receive the Ark into *their* midst (1 Sam.
vi. 19–21). God's providence is still so little discriminated
that He Himself is felt directly to send, not only physical
evils—famine, pestilence, plagues, but also such great
and public moral evils as the defeats in battle of King
Solomon and the division of the Kingdom (1 Kings
xi. 14, 23; xii. 15). Indeed, David can pray to God to
mislead Absalom through the foolish counsel of Ahithophel
(2 Sam. xv. 31); and, further back, David can suppose
that it is God who has stirred up Saul to drive him out
and kill him (1 Sam. xxvi. 19).

But, if all this be so, was not God deliberately conceived
as Himself partly evil; and, if as in part evil, was He not
also conceived as in part suffering? Moral Evil, emotional
Evil—Sin and Suffering, are they so far apart, especially
in so early and undiscriminating an age? I do not doubt
that the answer is No. We cannot press these, doubtless
quite logical, implications as perceived and accepted by
the Israelites, or even as what would have been endorsed
by them had it clearly been put before them. For God is
placed too high above every comparison with man, He
is too holy in the sense of unapproachable, for these
worshippers of His to feel that He is not sufficiently
conceived as holy in the sense of ethical. He is thus not
deliberately or intentionally conceived as anti-moral or
even simply as unmoral; the question of morality in God
does not, so far, arise clearly and systematically at all.
And though His unapproachable power is represented

as discharging itself in volitional outbursts accompanied
by intense passions, though He may be said to "suffer"
anger, indignation and the like, these emotions here as
little connote suffering in the ordinary sense in the one
thus moved, as the fierce flow of desolating lava from a
flaming volcano can be conceived as suffering within the
tumultuous mountain. Indeed, certain touches in this
early conception of Jahveh appear to be in fact derived
from such natural phenomena—they are *physicomorphic*
features. Thus, though evils, which later on are distinctly
perceived to be moral, are at this stage still held to be
sent by God, and though fierce passions accompany such
and other actions of God, God is too powerful, too
portentous, to be held, even by the most slightly willed or
accepted implication, to be, in Himself, either Evil or
Suffering.[1]

It is those spiritual giants, the Prophets, who introduce
the necessary distinctions, softenings, spiritualisations.
Thus the Census which, in 2 Samuel xxiv. 1, is suggested
to David by God, who punishes the execution of the
suggestion by a pestilence which causes seventy thousand
deaths, is, in 1 Chron. xxi. 1, written after the Prophets
had accomplished their discriminative work, suggested to
David by Satan. And indeed Amos and Hosea, Isaiah of
Jerusalem, Jeremiah and Ezekiel, unfold before us, step
by step, magnificent pictures of the ethical greatness, the
supreme moral holiness of God, Who is now seen more
and more to be the God of the whole world and to care
tenderly for all things that He has made. Isaiah's exquisite lyrics of the Lord's Vineyard and Ezekiel's great
description of God as the Good Shepherd, who risks so
much in the reclaiming of His straying sheep and lambs,
seem on the very point of moving on to suffering—to
Suffering in Sacrifice—within God. Yes, but they nowhere
really thus move on. And, again, there is the utterly glorious

---

[1] The above sketch is mostly based upon Bernhard Stade's cold but
competent *Biblische Theologie des Alten Testaments* (1905), pp. 84-91.

poem concerning the Servant of the Lord. Here, indeed, is Suffering most clear and certain. Yes: but this Sufferer is not the Lord, but the Lord's Servant—the Jewish people, the martyr nation. True, the Prophets have made our problem somewhat more difficult, if (as I believe to be the case) the conception of Elkana, the "Jealous God," springs from them; for we have seen how sensitively hostile are Plato and Plotinus to any such emotion as really in God—evidently because they felt it to be evil: and were they not right in so feeling? And, again, what thing external or internal produces greater suffering in its patient than does jealousy? Yet we must not forget that this conception arose unforcedly during the fierce (but, in substance, most just and salutary) polemic against the Canaanitish worships and their contagion amongst the Jews, and that, as we shall find, a deep and abiding truth is conveyed under this doubtless unattractive imagery. In any case, the Prophets are, in this as throughout, not nearer, in intention or even in actual fact, to attributing Sin or Suffering to God, but distinctly still further, than were the pre-prophetic Israelites. It is also true, no doubt, that, with the great deepening and widening of the apprehension of the outward-going activity and feeling in the life of God effected by the Prophets, we have an increase of difficulty in at all picturing such a life, if we are not to attribute genuine suffering to it. Nevertheless, even in the most tender of the prophetical pictures, God still stands too high above our human nature, if not in this human nature's highest aspirations, at least in their costingness, to be conceived as a Sufferer. Does not the pleading pathos of the picture of the Suffering Servant arise precisely from the contrast between the Sufferings of the Servant and the Joy of the Master, a Joy which indeed is full of sympathy, of prodigal conferments of peace and of fruitfulness, yet is free from suffering?

I believe the Prophets to have, in this, been the faithful and vigilant guardians of a great and most precious truth,

3. Our third, *the "Patripassian" current*, differs most strikingly from both the Hellenic - Hellenistic and the Israelitish-Jewish currents. For here we find God intensely Personal, as against the Greeks; and we find God a Sufferer, an intense Sufferer, as against these Jews. What historically went before the "Patripassianism," and what followed after it, shall, as regards our question, be taken in our third stage. Thus we take "Patripassianism" here without its occasion—the antecedent great fact of the life and sufferings of Jesus—and without its provocativeness—the subsequent great reaction and discrimination of the doctrine of the Two Natures. But this will in nowise hinder our sufficient understanding of the doctrine. St. Paul (1 Cor. ii. 8) tells us (in about A.D. 53) of "the rulers of this world" who, unwittingly, "crucified the Lord of glory": I believe this verse to stand alone in the New Testament as to its "Patripassian" sound. But, in about A.D. 110, St. Ignatius of Antioch writes far more clearly: "There is one Physician. . . . God become Flesh, true Life in Death, at first capable of Suffering (*pathētos*), and then incapable of suffering (*apathēs*), Jesus Christ our Lord" (*Ad Eph.* vii. 2). And, referring to God: "Him Who is invisible, but Who for us became visible, Him Who is impassible, but Who suffered for us" (*To Polycarp*, iii. 2). Noetus of Smyrna, in about A.D. 180, taught, as Hippolytus of Rome informs us, a quite explicit "Patripassianism." "He," Noetus, "declared that Christ was the Father Himself and that the Father was born and suffered and died." He, Noetus, argued: "If I confess that Christ is God, He is the Father, or He would not be God. Now Christ suffered, Christ Who is God Himself; hence the Father suffered, for He, Christ, was the Father." "Cleomenes and his followers," Hippolytus reports further, "declare that He Who was nailed to the wood of the Cross . . . He Who was pierced by the lance, that this was the God and the Father of the Universe." This is an exact anticipation of our recent "Patripassians." And,

finally, the Christian poet Commodian writes: "God, the Lord, hung upon the wood"; "God so suffered that the Creator of the world can be declared to have been crucified," and "Who is that God whom we have crucified?"[1]

Harnack's very interesting discussion of the rights and wrongs of "Patripassianism" (especially on pp. 657 and 661) curiously overlooks the point which this address especially attempts to establish; for he nowhere apprehends that, though this outlook was doubtless the expression of an intense, naïve, and massive faith in God, in Christ as God, and in the immense worth of sanctified suffering, it really omits, indeed traverses, a profoundly important *religious* element—the Joy, the Pure Joy, of God. Harnack writes as though the whole *religious* worth were on the side of "Patripassianism," and as though only philosophical and other, not directly religious, needs had decided its defeat. I am convinced, on the contrary, that only a non-"Patripassian" view could defend and transmit the very deepest note of the *religious* consciousness.

III

The above three currents, which we recognised as the all but most important for our inquiry, and which we have considered as generously as possible, leave us now with, and bring us to, the two deepest, most inclusive and most fruitful currents of all—the current between the Israelitish-Jewish and the "Patripassian" currents, which consists of the words, deeds, implications and temper of mind of Jesus, as these are portrayed by the Synoptic Gospels, and then the current which attains to its full strength after and partly in conflict with "Patripassianism," and of which St. Athanasius and, for our special purpose,

[1] Harnack's *Dogmengeschichte*, ed. 1888, vol. i. pp. 658, notes 3 and 4; 665; 660, note 3; 669, 670.

more concisely, the Council of Chalcedon are the chief
spokesmen. The short presentation and analysis of these
two currents will readily lead us to our final array of the
main reasons for and against Suffering in God, and then
to our last, general and discriminative statement concerning the whole matter—a statement lit up and humanised,
I hope, by a concluding personal anecdote.

1. It is now a view fairly widespread amongst serious
scholars that, almost entirely restricted, as we are, to
the older constituents of our first three Gospels, for literal
information as to Our Lord's very words and acts, we
really do and can know but very little as to what He
Himself actually taught, did, and was. But such a view
cannot be pressed with regard to the main features and
characteristic lines of that wondrous teaching, because
of the undeniable fact, and because of certain consequences
from the fact, that the ancient record in question contains
the vivid presentation of three large elements of that life
and teaching, which very soon became occasions of difficulty, repulsion, and of consequent omission or softening
on the part of the next two generations of Christian
chroniclers and theologians. The genuine experiences
and spiritual growth, the temptations, the suffering, the
humanities of Jesus generally; the diabolical possessions
and exorcisings found and performed around Him; and
belief in, and proclamation of, a Proximate Second
Coming of Jesus, now fully revealed as the Glorious
Christ: these three things permeate that ancient record,
and these same things are, the first and third, entirely
absent from the Fourth Gospel, and the second is there
omitted as far as ever possible without a sheer breach of
identity with the early documents. And, again, of these
three things, only one—the Diabolism—is (late) Jewish;
the Suffering Messiah and the Proximate Second Coming
are new and special to Christianity and, in the intensity
of their presentation by that earliest record, largely special
to the very earliest Christian teaching and belief. Those

earliest witnesses and chroniclers did not evade, did not
soften down, what was new to them and what could not
but startle and scandalise the Jewish consciousness within
themselves and in their auditors. But if this be so and
who can deny it?—then it becomes a piece of gratuitous
scepticism to throw doubts upon the historical accuracy of
such large features, either positive or negative, of Jesus'
life and teaching there portrayed as simply carry on, or
at most develop, elements, ancient or recent, of Jewish
belief, doctrine and practice. Hence we cannot reasonably
accept the Suffering Messiah and the Proximate Second
Coming as really primitively Christian, and reject the
casting out of devils as an unreliable tradition.

Now, if all this be sound, it follows straight away that,
if Jesus had taught or implied Suffering in God, those
same witnesses and chroniclers would not, for all the
strange, un-Jewish, anti-Jewish character of the doctrine,
have ignored or softened it. Indeed, the early appearance
of "Patripassianism" shows clearly how easy, for the
vehement reaction and simplicity of converts, was the
transition from a Suffering Messiah (the very doctrine
of which these earliest witnesses are full) to a Suffering
God, manifested in, or at least preached by, that Messiah
and His sufferings. We thus secure a second, a particular
reason, for holding the complete absence of all "Patripassianism" from the earliest record absolutely to correspond to the actual teaching, doings, temper of the
historical Jesus. But a third reason for the same conclusion remains. The omissions and softenings of St. John's
Gospel with regard to the actual sufferings of Jesus, and
indeed also with regard to His teaching concerning the
Suffering Messiah, are readily intelligible if Jesus did not
teach or imply "Patripassianism"; but they are the
strangest of puzzles, if He taught or implied any suffering
in God. For St. John's Gospel very clearly minimises all
suffering, either endured or taught by the historic Jesus,
because the writer feels such suffering to be difficult to

reconcile with the divinity of Christ—a fact now more
fully realised. But if Jesus really taught or implied "Patripassianism," *that* ought to have been, and, I doubt not,
would have been the direction in which the Fourth Gospel
would have differed from the other three—it would have
emphasised the Suffering of God, not minimised the
Suffering of Jesus. Nor can we urge the fact of the "Patripassians," as though they should count as much in this
matter as the Fourth Gospel; for, subtle as is the Fourth
Gospel in its softenings or omissions, it still stands considerably more in the line of historical dependence and
in the sense as to what really happened, than do the
"Patripassians" in spite of all their popular short cuts and
emotional simplifications.

If we go through that glorious earliest record carefully,
we find it separately, and still more conjointly, presents an
outlook irreducible to a "Patripassian" view. And how
immensely richer and more satisfying in all its touching
simplicity of form is this outlook! There is in Jesus'
outlook a complete absence of the sorry rationalist alter-
native: "Either God sympathises, and then He suffers,"
or, "God does not suffer, and then He does not sympathise
or care." Here, on the contrary, God clothes the lilies
of the field, cares for the very sparrows, numbers every
hair on our head; yet all this, not with defect or suffering for Himself, but from the superabundance of His
peaceful power, His serene sympathy. From this, His
immensely generous providence, we are to learn to be
merciful, that is, to be *perfect*, as our heavenly Father
(Luke vi. 36; Matt. v. 48). Again, there is in Jesus' outlook a view of suffering contrary to that which sooner or
later, more or less, possesses our modern "Patripassians."
We have seen how hard Hinton labours to find all suffering either only an imaginary evil or, indeed, so essential to
all goodness on earth or in heaven, in man or in God, as
to become practically indistinguishable from good. Yet
that earliest record is full of the physical cures effected

by Jesus—many of which are neither preceded nor followed by a spiritual renovation. Indeed, on this point, it is Wellhausen, not Hinton, who penetrates into the real spirit, the noble sanity, of the place occupied by sacrifice and suffering in the teaching and mind of Jesus. "Jesus is far removed from the opinion that he who loves God, does not desire that God should return his love. Jesus teaches us to bear the cross, but He does not teach that it is sweet or that disease is health. The eventual reconciliation between faith and sight, between morality and nature, forms everywhere the background of His outlook; even if He could have dispensed with such a reconciliation for His own person, it is for Him a self-evident necessity, as the objective requirement of justice itself." [1]

And, finally, there is in Jesus a note of joy which accompanies, indeed informs, the whole temper, the speaking, doing and being—a joy from and about God. That earliest record is steeped in the vivid impression of this joy in Jesus; it appears to be closely connected with the impression of sinlessness which He made upon His contemporaries. In God there is no Suffering and no Sin; and in Jesus Christ, Who was and is in a unique closeness, in a unique kind of union, with God, Joy and Sanctity shine out in unique fashion and degree. "Which of you convinceth me of sin?" says Jesus in St. John's Gospel (viii. 46). Nor can we reasonably take this belief in His sinlessness to have been a consequence drawn later on, by the time of that late Gospel, from that no more primitive articulation of the belief in His Divinity. For if the Fourth Gospel links up His Sinlessness with a full articulation of His Divinity and an elimination, as far as possible, of all Suffering in the Christ: the Epistle to the Hebrews combines the Sinlessness with great Sufferings, and betrays an obscure and inadequate manner of conceiving His Divinity. "We have a high priest that hath been

[1] *Abriss der Geschichte Israels und Judas* (1884), p. 100.

in all points tempted like as we are, yet without sin."
And "Christ in the days of His flesh, having offered up
prayers and supplications with strong crying and tears
unto Him that was able to save Him from death, and having
been heard for His godly fear, though He was a Son, yet
learnt obedience by the things which He suffered; and
having been made perfect, He became the author of eternal
salvation" (iv. 15; v. 7–9). Even if this Epistle was,
perhaps, not written before A.D. 90, these passages very
certainly convey very early, I take it strictly primitive,
impressions and convictions. It was, then, the twin profound impression of His Sinlessness and of His Joy—it
was these forces so abundantly attested in His transformation of the psychic and spiritual life and health of
countless men and women: it was this, more than any or
all more minutely measurable miracles, which conveyed
to His contemporaries the fact of, and became the occasion
of their faith in, His more than human character.

But if this be the historical situation, then Jesus Himself
cannot have known, or believed, God to be even potentially a Suffering God. Indeed, there is the account of
His great rejoicing, which, though unusually rich in echoes
of the preceding sapiential literature, and though in both
its parallels differently and unsatisfactorily connected with
the antecedent passages, only expresses vividly what the
whole bearing of Jesus, conveyed by the many other quite
unchallenged texts, has fully prepared us for. "In that
hour Jesus rejoiced in the spirit and said: I thank Thee,
Father, Lord of heaven and earth, because Thou hast
hidden these things from the wise and understanding,
and didst reveal them unto babes: yea, Father, for so
it was well-pleasing in Thy sight." Surely, if Jesus rejoices
at this revelation of the Father, He rejoices still more
in the thus revealing Father; and, if Jesus rejoices in the
Father, it is because that Father, because God, is Joy
perfect and unutterable. Thus the God seen and rejoiced
in by Jesus is the same as the God, in the abyss of Whose

light and in the ocean of Whose eternal felicity St. Bernard, some eleven centuries later, rejoiced to believe that his lately-deceased, dearly-loved brother Gerard now subsisted, since God is Joy and Love, and "though God is incapable of suffering, He is not incapable of compassion, He Whose especial prerogative it is ever to have mercy and to spare." Thus also now, in that blessed life, brother Gerard does not suffer, but he does sympathise. For "thy affections have not been diminished, but only changed; nor because thou, Gerard, hast put on God, hast thou left off caring for us: since God Himself cares for us." [1]

Indeed, we have also a most impressive passage both in Mark (xv. 34) and in Matthew (xxvii. 46), in which the last utterance of the earthly Jesus appears as the utterance of the Psalmist's words, now repeated by Jesus, as a piercing death cry, upon His Cross: "My God, my God, why hast Thou forsaken me?" Professor Loisy has written much to show that none of the words of Jesus on the Cross are historical—that His followers, all kept back by the Roman soldiery at a considerable distance, could not have heard anything except the loud, inarticulate cry at the last. Yet I do not see why one or other of His disciples should not, later on, have been able to gather information of this kind from one or other of the soldiers. And certainly, if there is a strictly historical utterance amongst the seven "words" reported, it is this cry of desolation which very soon became a difficulty to all but the "Patripassians." Yet note how utterly superficial is any "Patripassian" satisfaction found in this passage; for, press the situation and take it according to their doctrine, and you get Jesus, Himself, and especially in His Sufferings, the full manifestation of the Father, quite ignorant that the said Father is Suffering—that His deepest nature is at that moment Suffering, Sacrifice, Forsakenness of the acutest and most massive kind. Jesus' cry which, at the least, is in utter accord with His entire outlook and temper, is dismayed

[1] Sermon xxvi. 5, on the Canticle of Canticles.

precisely because God Who for Him always means Joy,
Strength, Support, appears now to be absent—to have
allowed His place to be taken by utter Sadness and
Desolation. Thus both the great Rejoicing and the great
Desolation point equally to God experienced and conceived
as Joy full and overflowing.

2. Yet it is true that man thirsts, not only for sympa-
thising Joy, for a Divine Sympathiser, but also for a
direct Fellow-Sufferer, for one who suffers as you and I.
This thirst finds full satisfaction in the life, especially
in the Sufferings of Jesus. It was doubtless at least as
much in order to possess such a direct downright Sufferer
in God Himself, Who would thus be our immediate
model and fellow-martyr for and at our best, as because
thus the Divinity of Christ was most simply apprehensible
and preachable, that "Patripassianism" arose. Yet somewhat as the love of earthly lovers impels them at times to
desire the abolition of all distinction even of the bare
consciousness between each other, and yet such abolition
would abolish, at the same time, the joy of the mutual
self-surrender and, indeed, everything wherewith to love
and which to love: so, in other ways and degrees, the
vehement believer may long to abolish all difference in
the two natures of Christ, to have Him all and sheer
God, and especially to find His Sufferings to be direct
Sufferings of God Himself. Yet here also such violent
simplification would, in the long run, spell grave damage
to the very emotions which so largely helped to produce the movement concerned. The solemn definition of
the Two distinct and differing Natures of Christ, of
22 October, A.D. 451, by the Council of Chalcedon, is certainly full of difficulties, if we attempt to apply it in exhaustive detail to the life and work of the historic Jesus. Yet
not all the able and suggestive arguments of Professor
Harnack succeed, I am convinced, in establishing a better
general scheme—a more adequate apprehension and distinction as to the root of the matter before us. And, indeed,

it is plain that not a few of Harnack's most baffling difficulties occur also in any attempt to analyse the ordinary
indwelling of God in the average human soul, where and
when such soul is supernaturally awake—an indwelling
which St. Teresa came to hold, with the full encouragement of her Dominican adviser, to mean not the presence
of Grace, i.e. of certain effects and gifts of God, but the
presence of God Himself. For, here also, what precisely
is God's operation, what precisely is man's? Or rather,
what precisely, in each supernatural act and state of this
soul, is furnished by God and is furnished by this soul
itself? No mortal mind can achieve this; indeed no mortal
mind can furnish us with even a general, but vivid and
satisfying picture of such a co-operation. And yet, for these
our ordinary human cases, certain great, immensely
important facts and laws can truly be apprehended and
discriminated: we stammer out a real knowledge of
realities, although we do not succeed in fixing a clear and
complete scientific analysis of these same realities or even
of our "confused," dim, but real knowledge of them.
In a similar way the Two Natures doctrine can and does,
I believe, stammer out and protect a nucleus of truth
which we still, in this our study, discover to be of priceless practical worth.

The Chalcedonian formula has, upon the whole, been
more satisfactorily attended to as regards the Divine
Nature than as regards the Human Nature; and limitations, obscurities, weaknesses, growths, temptations, which
are interwoven with human nature as such, have been,
for the most part, too much ignored or explained away,
even though they still stand on clear record in the Synoptic
Gospels. Yet the predominant motive of this trend was,
I believe, far less a fear of forgetting the Divinity over
the Humanity than anxiety lest men should, little by little,
come to deny, or at least to ignore, the Sinlessness of
Jesus, even as man. And this motive was indeed an ex-
cellent one and should, surely, operate within us still.

For that Sinlessness is a most precious fact and most valuable conviction. True, it is not easy to maintain the Sinlessness of Jesus, whilst admitting those other conditions and happenings; but, then, neither is it easy to maintain the deep Sympathy of God without Suffering in God. Both combinations are difficult, yes; but both combinations are supremely important and astonishingly enriching; indeed the two, taken widely and wisely and vividly together, enable us, I am convinced after a half-century of experience, to produce a wealth and elasticity, a resourcefulness and power of outlook and motive with which no other conviction can seriously compare. And these two combinations, taken together, of course concern, quite centrally, the entire question of Suffering in God —they answer the question as no other position does or can. I trust that the following array and examination of the main reasons on the two opposite sides will make the pre-eminent inclusiveness of the view here adopted clear.

3. The chief objections against the exclusion of Suffering from God appear to be three.

(i.) Real Sympathy means Real Suffering.

Here we first require a careful distinction between suffering precedent to the sympathy, suffering of our own as necessary to make us sufficiently understand the suffering of the other man, and suffering subsequent to the sympathy—the pain, even physical but chiefly psychical, which such sympathy produces and involves. Now this latter, the subsequent Suffering, cannot be pressed with regard to the Sympathy in God, unless we are prepared to hold that what is equivalent to our emotions in God works the effects, in Him the Bodiless Spirit of Spirits, which follow for us mortals, possessed of bodies, in and through our nervous and other physical systems and influences. And, as to the preceding Suffering, it is only partially true, even of us little men, that we can possess true sympathy only in the proportion that we have actually

o

suffered sufferings identical or similar to those which now solicit our sympathy. Father Damian sympathised, he who had never suffered leprosy, with the sufferings of the lepers more, doubtless, than the average sufferer from leprosy sympathised; and this because his imaginative faculty, his altruistic emotions and the like were so much in excess of what that average leper possessed as to counterbalance, very largely, his, Father Damian's, lack of direct experience of leprosy. How much more must this be true of God, of Him Who is omniscient; of Him Who, according to most sound theology, alone can and does directly reach the human heart and will.

(ii.) Real Personality ultimately involves systems of Emotions which organise Feelings. We claim that God is Personalistic—consists of Persons. But where is such a system in God, if God is Joy alone? But there *are* other Emotions in God, besides Joy: there is also Love, this the primary Emotion, and Delectation; and these three Emotions are evoked in Him, and are applied by Him in countless degrees, ways and combinations—from the mutual love of the Three Persons in the Godhead for each other, then through a rich hierarchy of intelligent creatures, doubtless many realms of whom are more intelligent than man, on through mankind, the animal and the plant world, indeed to all extant things whatsoever. Also there are secondary, consequential attitudes of feeling and of will which we can, which indeed we apparently must, attribute to God, and these add to the articulation of the whole emotional life of God. Unless there exists a system only where its constituents are of the same number as are the constituents of our own system, there *is* a system, and a far nobler system, in God. Aquinas was already busy with these questions in his Theological *Summa,* and most of his allocations remain sound and instructive, even in view of so recent and probing a work as Shand's *Foundations of Character* (2nd Edition, 1920).

(iii.) "Real Personality is an achievement, through Suffer-

ing at least as much as through Joy." Yes, certainly in
man, and presumably so in every finite intelligent being.
But it does not at all follow that Perfect Personality is
thus intrinsically successive and discursive. Indeed, the
deepest aspirations and implications, the most comprehensive and permanently fruitful experiences of religious
souls all, in the last instance, require or indicate not
Comingness but Givenness—the Realised Ideal.

4. The objections to the presence of Suffering in God
appear, indeed, to be far more fundamental and far more
widely and variously operative—the acceptance of Suffering in God leads to far more doubtful or definitely dele-
terious results or concomitances than can, I believe, be
justly urged against the denial of such Suffering.

(i.) Suffering is intrinsically an Evil. It is impossible
to read much of the literature which insists upon the
presence of Suffering in God, without being struck with
the trend—I believe the inevitable trend, once Suffering
has been admitted into God—to treat that Suffering as
but a seeming Evil. The reason of this transmutation of
value is plain enough, viz. that no ingenuity can long
reconcile the healthy religious instinct of an ethically
developed soul to the conception of a God evil be it only
in part. True, even Hinton, perhaps the most relentlessly
consequential, certainly the boldest of these thinkers, does
not make the Unincarnate God actually a sufferer; God
Unincarnate—God Who, in both His conditions, is the
supreme hero, the perfect Utiliser and Transfigurer of
Suffering—is able, in the Unincarnate condition, to transform, without leaving a tell-tale fragment of suffering
untransfigured, to turn all what, if left alone, would make
Him suffer, would show Him to suffer, into utter Joy.
Indeed, Joy everywhere and of necessity—by its very
nature—is, according to Hinton, *overcome* Suffering—is
Pain rightly met and transfigured; hence, since he admits
that God Unincarnate is actually Consummate Joy, God
must have worked up the utmost material of Suffering by

the utmost heroism. Yet the overpowering trend towards the negation of all intrinsic reality in Suffering is shown by numerous utterances, especially in his, Hinton's, four volumes of *Manuscripts*, which declare outright that all Pain and Suffering are sheer misunderstandings on the part of the sufferer, are wrong volitional attitudes, etc.; as also in the complete exclusion, when he is in full swing, of any complementary movement, of any motives, towards the diminution of Pain and Suffering other than through this right conception of its nature. Nothing could be more marked than the contrast between this one movement of Hinton and the two movements of Jesus. Jesus cures pain and disease as though they could not be utilised, whilst Jesus also trains and empowers souls to utilise their sufferings, as though they were incurable; Hinton, on the contrary, when at the height of his peculiar enthusiasm, appears acutely alarmed lest you should, by any curative movement, diminish the material for the utilising movement—that is to say, lest you should reduce the conditions absolutely essential to heroism, which is the only true Joy, whether in heaven or on earth, in God or in man. There is thus in this outlook, in spite of its very large element of truth and of beauty, something strained and hectic, something that Matthew Arnold, at his fine best, would readily have scented out as wanting in *centrality*.

(ii.) Suffering and Sin are, indeed, not identical, yet they are sufficiently like to make the permanent treatment of Sin as intrinsically evil exceedingly difficult where Suffering is treated as not really evil at all. Here Hinton is again most tragically instructive. In his *The Coming of the Law* (in *The Lawbreaker and the Coming of the Law*, 1884, pp. 209–325) we get the impassioned pleadings of a fine mind and an ardent altruist—a mind carried away by very plain, very plausible, very false and pernicious principles—false and pernicious because taken out of their congenital contexts, and pressed ruthlessly to their now quite unchecked, uncorrected conclusion—to Free

Love between the sexes. Three principles—all three very
true principles, so long as they remain part and parcel
of a much larger whole—here work the ruin, without
any misgiving (except as to what the public may think),
indeed with enthusiastic certainty on the part of their
enunciator. "There is no such thing as simply external,
simply bodily chastity"; "the service of others is the one,
sole test and measure of ethics and of religion"; and "to
do what is wanted," *that* is the one thing to do. Thus
all professional bad women would be abolished, since the
most innocent girl would remain innocent, would indeed
attain to her true spiritual stature, by service, which alone
constitutes the value of acts—by supplying the wants now
catered for by those branded as fallen. Thus the new
world would be established in which "the bodily relation
between man and woman would be no more 'sensual';
so that there would be no ground for its avoidance," on
the part of anyone, "any more than for avoiding fresh
air or flowers" (p. 231). It is surely ghastly to note how
principles, thoroughly, even nobly, true within the limits
imposed upon them by the systems to which they intrinsically belong, can, and here do, work such appalling
havoc. It is clear, I think, that the most operative in the
mischief here, amongst Hinton's three principles, is the
quite unqualified principle of service. Hinton's early,
indeed congenital, horror of all self-regard anywhere,
in any sense, to any extent, for any purpose, here finds
at last its full assuagement. It lights up with warning
beacon-lights the danger of all Hegel-like extensions of
Our Lord's great teaching (as to losing our soul and so
finding it) into a cosmic principle, a principle taken as
true apart altogether from *what* we sacrifice and *to what*
and *for what*. The truth of the matter is assuredly far
more complex, and a certain kind and degree of self-
regard is as essential to all sane morality and all full
religion, as is a certain kind and degree of self-sacrifice.
The Good and the Right cannot possibly consist primarily,

still less completely, in their being done for others. To circulate counterfeit coin does not make it genuine.

No; we imperatively need deeper, more numerous, more central tests. Suffering and Sin must, neither of them, be sublimated into mere subjective false notions of our own. Love, even our love for God, must remain, and we must continue to desire it to remain, a *mutual* give and take. And Self-Love, Self-Regard, must be estimated an evil, not directly according as it is, or is not, a love of any Being for himself, but according as the self of such a Being deserves, or does not deserve, such love. Hence, however little we may be able to picture God's love for Himself, in a humanly attractive way, we will not and cannot cease to hold that these our human words involve a profound, all-decisive truth. We will, thus at the very source, escape the feverish movement so all-pervasive of Hinton, and will not turn all Being into Becoming, nor measure all things by Process never by Product. Indeed, God will be apprehended, loved and served by us neither as Process nor as Product, but as overflowing Being, as Perfect Reality, as the Real Ideal. "In His Will"—in His Nature and Being as they already are, as they ever have been, not in any Becoming of Him, but in the Being of Him—"in His Will is our peace."

(iii.) Liberty exists in various kinds, and the Perfect kind—Perfect Liberty—excludes Choice. This is a position which practically all the most recent Broad High Church literature has, alongside of many a wise insight, most unhappily denied. William Temple (now Bishop of Manchester), Walter H. Moberley, and with these fine minds scores of lesser lights, have insisted that the possibility of Evil is involved in the very nature of all Freedom; and hence that our very nobility, as free willing beings, involves our possible baseness. The reasons for the prevalence of this view are, doubtless, apologetic; for, given this doctrine to be true, the problem of Evil is

greatly simplified: Evil then becomes the reverse of the
shield of Good according to the very nature of things—
a nature which, Aquinas has already clearly taught us,
cannot be contradicted even by God Himself. We can
thus have Good and Evil (at least potential Evil), or we
can have neither; but we cannot have one without the
other. And, indeed, there certainly exist some clerics—
not any that I have named—who do not shrink in conversation from finding, not only Suffering, but also Sin
potentially in God, precisely because He is the Supreme
Liberty and Supreme Goodness.

Yet we have here a very certainly erroneous doctrine.
St. Augustine already finely formulates the real truth in
this matter: "It is indeed a great liberty to be able not to
s n; but the greatest liberty is to be unable to sin." If
we watch ourselves and others, we shall find that, as we
grow better, we become less liable to commit, we are less
inclined to commit, we get further away from the ability
to commit, evil: do we therefore grow less free? At all
times, since the fuller awakening of the moral sense, men
have taken offence, and this in proportion to their religiousness, at the notion that God indeed persistently
chooses the Good, yet cannot escape the need of thus
choosing for Himself between Good and Evil. Was this
refusal of Choice to God an age-long, universal, though
quite unconscious denial of His Freedom? Surely, no.
Perfect Liberty goes with Perfect Nature; an act of
Perfect Freedom is an act which spontaneously, joyously,
completely, expresses such a Perfect Nature. The more
the act is thus, the less it even could be otherwise, the
more free is the act, and the nature which this act expresses.
We men are, indeed, able to sin and we actually sin, and
yet we are free. Yes: but we are free not because of, but
in spite of, such ability and such acts: we are truly free
only in proportion to our not committing, not willing, not
wishing, Sin—Sin which is a negation of our true nature.

Again, our actual human virtue and human pathos is,

indeed, penetrated through and through by our peculiar degree and kind of liberty: not only our freedom but its imperfection—the often tragic cost and the never quite complete triumph of the Good—gives us our specifically human shape and size. We do right when we give a great place to this in our religious teaching, not only as to men in general, but, as regards the cost, even to the Human Nature of Christ. Yet we are wrong indeed when we do not give first place, determining position and influence, to the insight and conviction that there exists another Nature possessed of Perfect Freedom—the Nature of God, and that in Him, there exists neither Sin nor Sadness, nor even the possibility of any such thing.

(iv.) The conviction of the Otherness of God is, in the long run, as essential to full, powerful religion as any and all conviction of the Likeness of God. Belief in Suffering in God is generally commended to us as necessary if we are really to feel God like unto us, if for our feeling He is truly to be our Father, indeed more or less our elder Brother. For not only our average toil and doing, but especially our highest ethical and spiritual achievements, appear to be essentially bound up with Suffering —Suffering heroically borne or heroically overcome, yet still Suffering. Is God, then, to be so different from man as to be less than man? God is Love, is He not? Is His Love, then, to be but nominal? At least, to be less costly, hence less heroic, hence again less sublimely good, than is our own? "He who did most, shall bear most": would not God thus alone be a worthy leader? Heroism would thus be overflowingly in God and be but poorly imitated by us mortals even at our best. Browning has, of course, magnificently presented the case for this view. And, indeed, this view cannot be all false if the Christian doctrine of the Incarnation be true, which insists upon genuine, indeed immense, Suffering within one of the two natures of the one Person, Christ, Himself the fullest revelation of God vouchsafed to man.

Nevertheless I find it impossible to believe, I will not say in the falsehood, but even in any permanent unattractiveness, of the doctrine that there is no Suffering in God, as such. Sympathy, yes, indeed, overflowing Sympathy— a Sympathy which we cannot succeed in picturing vividly without drawing upon our own experiences of ourselves, where sympathy and suffering are so closely intertwined; but no Suffering in God; and Suffering, indeed overflowing suffering in Christ, but as Man, not as God. Surely, poets, even the deepest poets, require not seldom some discounting of their more enthusiastic views, by philosophers and theologians; the correction of Browning here suggested would be a relatively small one.

With the two admissions—proclamations—of Sympathy in God and Suffering in Christ, we can, and I suggest we should, retain ample food for the other, I submit still more fundamental need and implication of the deepest religious thought and religious emotion, of Pure Joy, which would continue to attach to God as such.

(v.) And, finally, Religion itself requires the Transcendence of God in a form and a degree which exclude Suffering in Him. I have purposely in this paper concentrated upon Suffering and Sympathy, and Suffering and Sin —upon the intimations of the religious sense that God is Joy, and upon the needs of this same sense that God be Joy. But I believe that, if fully pressed, this outlook involves, philosophically speaking, the following conception of the Absolute and of the relation between the Absolute and God, Metaphysics and Religion. I believe, then, that religion, at its deepest and in the long run, is not and never will be satisfied short of pressing on to, short of intimations from, the really Ultimate. It will persist as a conviction in the real, present existence of the Absolute, intimating this Its existence in the necessary implications of our thought, emotions and action, and in our most incurable dissatisfactions in Æsthetics, Ethics, Metaphysics. This Absolute is felt, is indirectly experienced, as still the centre, so to speak the core, of God. But there are two conditions attaching to this Absolute as soon as ever It acts outwards, so to speak. It cannot violate either Its own Nature within Itself, or the traces of this Its Nature within anything It creates or initiates. Such incapacities are not Imperfect Liberty, no limitation, in the true sense of the term, at all. Aquinas, who teaches this point with emphasis, declares that it is more proper to speak of things that cannot be done, than of God as incapable of doing certain things. And, then, there *is* a limitation, which, in its degree, is a genuine limitation— a limitation which inevitably accompanies God's creative activity, and which, as such, is willed by Himself in His creative volitions. He has directly willed Creation, and has deliberately accepted such degree and kind of Self-limitation as this Creation involves.

But—and here is the special implication of the outlook commended—the religious sense, at its deepest and in the long run, will not, must not, be restricted to the Self-limited Creative God, or (worse still) to the persuasion that the whole of the Absolute—that God in and for Himself—has been and is absorbed in God as Creator. The religious sense, on the contrary, must be allowed to press on to, to be moved and fully satisfied only by the Ultimate, the Absolute. This Absolute, however, is not conceived, or indirectly experienced by, such Religion, Plotinus-like, as without interiority—without richness or articulation, as above all Beauty, Truth and Goodness; but as overflowing with a life articulated within Itself— a life which, indeed, freely willed Creation, a Creation whose joy indeed adds to Its Joy, yet which in Itself, apart from such Creation, is full of Joy. Thus Religion would neither be a translation, by the religious sense, of the Ultimate facts of reality, these being furnished by Monistic Metaphysics—a sentimental Father-God taking the place of the real, utterly impersonal, so to say, also inwardly Absolute; nor even would Religion, though objectively true within its proper range—the Creative God—persistently ignore the Absolute. But Religion would essentially be busy with both—it would press on, through the Creative God, to the Absolute—to God within Himself, and would, within both ranges, bring real facts to our knowledge, facts none the less real and knowledge none the less certain because neither religion itself, nor, indeed, philosophy working upon these intimations, succeeds in bringing them to scientific clearness and complete interconnection.

The thirst of religion is, at bottom, a metaphysical thirst, and the intimations of religion are, ultimately, metaphysical intimations. Here it is where such minds as that of the Dean of Carlisle are so disappointing, when they attempt to describe and to analyse religion: the pressure, the passion of the religious sense in its metaphysical quality, is to such minds a sheer puzzle and acute annoyance.

Let me then conclude with a statement, as inclusive, precise and yet short as I can make it, with regard to the problem of Suffering and God; I will, however, now include certain preliminary points and certain applications which have not been discussed, but which, I trust, will approve themselves through their close appropriateness to the entire outlook.

A man never knows, or is even dimly aware of, himself alone; his consciousness of self is always with, and on occasion of, the consciousness of something other than himself. But any and all knowledge, or any rational awareness possessed by man, not only involves certain direct experiences, but also certain "ideas" as Kant calls them—certain convictions which are not directly experienced, yet which are rendered actual by the experience, and are absolutely necessary to the experience as a rational and informative event. We experience things as contingent, as partial, as successive, as causes, as effects —especially as contingent. Yes: but we do so experience them, because the things directly experienced wake up in us the "ideas" of the Absolute, the Whole, the Simultaneous, the Uncaused, the Uneffected. Now Kant, in his richest and most constructive vein, teaches that not only what we directly experience corresponds to extant realities, but that also such "ideas" as are simply necessary to render possible such experience correspond to extant realities; that we can and should be certain also, and especially, of the latter kind of reality. Now the ethically and religiously awake and observant spirit is full, not only of direct moral and religious experiences, but also of "ideas" or convictions which awake on occasion of these experiences, and which alone make them possible in the form in which we experience them. Here also, and here especially, what is directly experienced as contingent, partial, successive, as caused or effected, and further as imperfect, as unsatisfying, is so experienced because of the "ideas" or apprehensions which awake simultaneously of the Absolute, the All-Inclusive, the Simultaneous, the Perfect, the Utterly Satisfying. And it is thus that, as against the foreground of our little frail and mixed love and joy and delectation, our small beginnings towards the fullness of spiritual being, there contrast, and by their contrast light up and give their poignant meaning to, this littleness, frailty and mixedness of our love, joy and delectation, Perfect Love, Unmixed Joy, Entire Delectation. It is quite plain and entirely certain that were man a purely changeful, transitory, contingent, rootless and accidental being, he could never know he was such, still less could he suffer, as he most certainly does suffer, from the very thought that he possibly may be only such. The Contrasting Other is real and certain—more real, richer far in reality, and quite as certain as the contingents felt to be such, since it is that Contrasting Other which gives them, for our mind and feeling, that pathetic and utterly unsatisfying character of contingency.

Now God is that Perfect Love, Unmixed Joy, Entire Delectation. He is all this, not as a bundle of separate qualities, however consummate each quality may be, but as a living, spiritual, Personalist Reality, Who Himself is all this overflowingly. I believe this to be a true account of the fundamental religious experience and apprehension. But if so, we will not admit the presence of any Evil, be it Sin or even only Sorrow, be they actual or even only potential, in Him Who thus dwarfs for us all our little human goodness and earthly joy by His utter Sanctity and sheer Beatitude. And all this Goodness and Joy God does not become, does not acquire: He simply *is* it. We will be watchful against the blurring over of the contrast between our self, as experienced by us, and other, contingent things, always experienced by us at the time: those things and we are not identical, never were and never will be. How much more, then, will we be on our guard against any real blurring of the contrast between God and ourselves. His Otherness is as essential a part of the facts and of the power of religion as His Likeness can ever be. True, God is full of loving care for us, His creatures; He knows us each and singly in all our particularity, and can and does help us to become more like unto Himself. But this Sympathy is not Suffering; and, again, we never will, indeed never can, become really identical with Him. He has allowed real, direct Suffering to come as close to Him, in the humanity of Christ, as, in the nature of things, Suffering could come. Let us be wise and sober, and rest satisfied with that deep Sympathy in God and this deep Suffering in Christ. Let us be satisfied, not only because this, and not more than this, appears indeed to be the truth, but because we thus keep secure the only quite wholesome, the only sufficiently deep, outlook for our own utilisation—the outlook for which the Ultimate Intention, as indeed already the First Cause of all things, is not Sin or Suffering or Want, but Delectation, Joy and Holiness. We will admit indeed great tracts of dreariness, suffering, sin, in our human lives, possibly also more or less amongst other intelligent creatures of God; but all the more will we treasure the pure and distinct, the personalist and abounding Holiness, Joy and Delectation of God. Even if we could find no explanation whatsoever for the existence of Evil in all its degrees and kinds, this would not abolish the reality of the evidences for, our deep need of, that Absolute Goodness, Joy and Delectation which, in our experiences, reveals to us our mixed, and largely evil, and pathetically unsatisfying, existences. We will, indeed, utilise all the suffering which may come to us in atonement for Sin and for the attainment of Joy; but we will not strain the facts of life into revealing, as the cause of all suffering, the provision of occasions for heroism and heroic joy. Still less will we find the possibility of Evil to spring directly from Liberty as such. On the contrary, we will adore in God the Perfect Liberty which spontaneously and joyously always wills alone its own Perfect Nature. We will thus rest content with an outlook, obscure and fragmentary in parts, but with tracts of glorious richness, variety, drama and tension, the whole lit up, sustained and vitalised by a continuously renewed conviction of the Perfect Goodness, the Pure Joy of God.

I began with a short anecdote from the life of the bee; let me end with a longer anecdote from my own personal experience. I give it, not as something which others may not have experienced more or less similarly themselves; indeed I would beg my hearers to substitute their own similar experience for my own. Neither do I give this experience as a direct proof of the truth even of its central point. Such experiences, even when most genuine, are assuredly not infallible, are indeed rarely of equal soundness in all their information. I give this experience because it may help to light up the general position of this address with a homely, human radiance, and because it proves at least this much—that the vivid conviction of the Pure Joy of God is as capable now as in the days of Dante, of St. Francis, of St. Bernard, of St. Augustine, of St. Paul, and of Jesus Himself, to steady and subdue, to saturate and to satisfy our restless hearts and utterly exacting spirits.

It was on a Good Friday forenoon in Rome, I think in 1899, that I woke up with the sunshine streaming into my bedroom—I had somehow not been called by any of my people or of the domestics. Although I hurried through my toilet and through my breakfast, it was turned eleven o'clock when I reached the nearest church—all the service already over and the doors locked. I tried two other churches—the same result. Sad and lonely, empty-headed and dreary-hearted, I turned into the Villa Borghese, and there, in an ugly, newly-planted, still very shadeless tryst, with much sand about and an already baking sun, I sat down on the ground and relieved my aching back by leaning against one of the young trees. Many green lizards were soon frisking close around me—otherwise nothing living was to be seen or heard. I sat there thus —I suppose for half an hour or more—dull and dead, conscious of nothing but myself, so I felt; of that mass of failures, disappointments, pettinesses, with a dim background, though, of men at large hardly more inviting or inspiring than myself. And all this then articulated itself into special grievances and antipathies: Churchmen and Agnostics, Jews and Protestants, also such souls amongst them all as were dear to me at other times—all seemed empty, irritating, oppressive. And then—I know of no transition or connection — then — well, suddenly, ah, another, in very truth another outlook, an utterly other state wrapped me round. I felt—I seemed to see—now without any straining, without apparently any action of my own—one great, tender goodness and heroism pass before me after the other—the souls which, in this "eternal" Rome, had meekly suffered and had manfully agonised for God; also thinkers, and men of action, seekers after God. There were Peter and Paul, Caecilia and Agnes of the Catacombs, Rabbi Akiba dying a witness to God in the great Circus, Marcus Aurelius lonely on his throne,

Plotinus uttering winged words to his students, Augustine
now growing utterly weary and restless under his sins, so
near to his utter renunciation of them, and so on and on,
with many another figure long dear to me. And all of them
were marked by Suffering—and more or less marred by
Sin. But then, behind and above all these, appeared the
Master of Masters, Suffering Love gently, pathetically
triumphant—Jesus Christ, Our Lord, on this the day of
His utter Passion. And yet, somehow, even this, especially
this utter woe, this day of that woe, they seem best expressed just simply as Good—as "Good" Friday, better
than in the Italian or French or German "Holy" and
the like. For was it not *good*, supremely *good* for us?
Wholesome, fruitful, renovating, all-transfiguring? The
Suffering, even here, was certainly an evil, but then its
utilisation, how good that was! And besides, here, no
Sin! Somehow here the intense Suffering led on to Joy
—to the infinite Good that had sprung from this infinite
Sorrow. And, then, came the final state of soul and outlook:
God, God in Himself. And here, in contrast with the first
outlook, where fellow-creatures had appeared so largely
suffering and so truly sinful, and even in contrast with
the second outlook, where Jesus Christ had appeared, sinless indeed and Joy-bringing, yet also bowed down with
suffering, appeared Joy, pure Joy, an Ocean of it, un-
plumbed, unplumbable, with not one drop of Evil within
it—not one drop of Sin or Suffering or of the possibility
of either. And I did not want it otherwise—far, far from
it! God was too much our Friend, for us not to rejoice
that He does not suffer; and this Joy of God is too much
our sustenance, it too much shows us, contrastingly, our
indigence, a sight of ourselves which constitutes our
specific dignity, for me, for any of those great lovers of
His, to wish His Joy mixed or limited or conditional.
And yet this Pure Joy was utterly compassionate, utterly
sympathetic; It bent down to, It entered into, the hearts
of those great little ones; It was, indeed, at work all around

me at that moment. What else, in the last resort, made those dear little emerald lizards so happy there, close to my feet? And then all ended with my receiving a happy impression that all the dreariness, which had preceded all this happiness, that that too, that it, especially for me just then, had already been an effect of that contrasting Joy of God, or rather of my very dim but real apprehension of that Joy.

For indeed dreary and petty, oppressive and imprisoning, is our poor little life, on its surface and apart from God and from His merciful condescensions towards us. But we would not know our misery, we would not feel it as such, were there not Saints and Heroes around us, and Christ our Lord above us, and, encompassing all and penetrating all, God—not a Sufferer, but indeed the Sympathiser, God Joy, the Ocean of Joy, our Home.

P

VIII

THE FACTS AND TRUTHS CONCERNING GOD AND THE SOUL WHICH ARE OF MOST IMPORTANCE IN THE LIFE OF PRAYER

VIII

THE FACTS AND TRUTHS CONCERN-ING GOD AND THE SOUL WHICH ARE OF MOST IMPORTANCE IN THE LIFE OF PRAYER

I

THE FACTS AND DOCTRINES CONCERNING GOD WHICH ARE OF ESPECIAL IMPORTANCE IN THE LIFE OF PRAYER [1]

I FIND it impossible to restrict myself here to explicit tests of Scripture or to the Dogmatic Definitions of the Christian Faith. On the other hand, I will only put forward certain positions which have behind them large affirmations or assured implications of Scripture and great Fathers and theologians of the Church—positions which, if, in recent centuries or in our own times, largely ignored or explained away, nevertheless express the never extinct Christian and Catholic experience. Working within these lines and drawing also upon my own fifty years of endeavour in these matters, I find the positions concerning God, which require full and intelligent adoption in our life of Prayer, to be seven.

I

God is a stupendously rich Reality—the alone boundlessly rich Reality. His outward action throughout the Universe —His creation, sustentation and direction of the world at large—is immensely rich. Still deeper and more delicate is this richness and reality in God's Incarnation and

---

[1] An Address delivered at Beaconsfield, 26 October, 1921.

Redemptive Action. Yet His Being, His Interior Life, are in no wise exhausted by all this outward Action, nor does this action occasion or articulate His character. We indeed, we little mortals—they too, the greatest of angels —we become our true selves, we articulate our spiritual characters, by apprehending, willing and serving God. But God is God, already apart from His occupation with us. These are the great facts which I believe to be specially revealed to us in the dogma of the Holy Trinity—facts of which we have an especial need in these our times. The whole of the Negative Theology, where it is sound and not really agnostic or pantheistic, is but an attempt to utter vividly this stupendous richness of God.

Our prayer will lack the deepest awe and widest expansion, if we do not find room within it for this fact concerning God. We will thus retain a strong sense that not even Jesus Christ and His Redemption exhaust God. Christian prayer, indeed Christian theology, are thus not Soteriology, practical or theoretical. Here Fénelon's great letters to the Carmelite nun, Sœur Charlotte de S. Cyprien, are admirable in their tender devotion to Christ free from all excessive Christocentrism.

2

God is the author of, and God is variously reflected in, all (innocent) Nature as well as in all Supernature. Here is the doctrine which was central in the outlook of Aquinas and Dante, of St. Francis and of Giotto. It was very largely forgotten or denied afterwards, during the later Middle Ages. And, although the Renaissance and then the Protestant Reformation were (variously wise and wild) protests against the abuses of the later Middle Ages, these movements were themselves largely infected by the impoverished philosophy and the thin theology of these same later Middle Ages. The signs are multiplying that man will return, with such improvements as may be wisely desirable, to that wonderfully rich outlook of the Golden Middle Age, where God's outward action moves on two levels—the natural level and the supernatural level—a Good and a Better or Best—two *kinds,* and not merely two degrees, of Goodness. *We thus recognise in man's actual life a polarity, a tension, a friction, a one thing at work in distinctly another thing*—like yeast in meal, like salt in meat, like coral insects and whole coral reefs in the huge ocean—an ocean so different from themselves. We thus also acquire an explanation, and one which is not discouraging, of the fact that it is a difficult art to prevent religion from overstraining us and from thus leading to a very dangerous reaction against itself. For thus we see that the Beatitude of Heaven—the Direct Vision of God, that the sincere forgiveness of our enemies, the love of them, and that the eager acceptance of suffering, are graces and dispositions beyond, and different from, God apprehended as the dim background or groundwork of our lives, and from the honesties and decencies of average domestic and political life. Such honesties and decencies are also good, and they are necessary for us all, in various degrees and forms; and this, also, as the occasions and material for the supernatural to utilise and transform—the Mountain and the Plain, the Edelweiss, and Alpenrose, and the cornfields and potatoes; here all appear, and this in fruitful contrast and congenital inter-aid.

Such an inclusive and yet discriminating position brings also much help to our prayer. For in prayer, also, it brings a tension, to the verge of strain; and a *détente,* to the verge of relaxation. In both these movements of the soul God can, and God should, be envisaged—in the *détente,* the God of nature, the source of all that is wholesome and homely; and in the tension, the God of supernature, the source of all that is ardent and heroic. We thus escape dullness, monotony and the like—these subtle dangers of the spiritual life.

3

God alone is fully free. Here is another ancient doctrine which calls aloud for resuscitation. It is already clearly formulated by St. Augustine, and Aquinas elaborates it in its fullness. But the later Middle Ages largely lost it, and Protestants to this hour have, in this point, merely extended and hardened the later Mediæval obtuseness. Indeed, even the present Broad High Churchmen of the type of *Foundations* have, for the most part, elaborated an apologetic with regard to the dread fact of Evil which deliberately eliminates the great doctrine here envisaged. St. Augustine tells us: *"It is already a great freedom to be able not to sin. But the greatest freedom consists in the inability to sin."* And Aquinas elaborates how Perfect Freedom consists in the spontaneous and joyous self-expression of a perfect nature. Thus God cannot will, God possesses no inclination to, Evil; and this absence of choice springs from precisely the perfection of His Freedom.

The persistent and vivid apprehension of this fact will greatly help our prayer. For thus only are we adequately humbled before God, since the difference between God and man is thus, essentially, not a difference, however great, in performance but in *nature.* Far beyond the range of our actual sinfulness extends the range of our potential sinfulness—of the imperfection inherent in our human degree and kind of Freedom. Whereas God is not only not actually sinful at all—He is incapable of sin, incapable of temptation to sin.

But there exists, not only God Pure, but also God Incarnate, Jesus Christ. Here, again, there is no actual sinfulness, and here also the sinlessness is a most wholesome occasion of humility to ourselves, the manifoldly sinful. In Jesus Christ the closeness of the union of His human nature with the Divine nature—with a Divine Person—renders actual sin impossible even in that Human nature.

Nevertheless this human nature in itself is, even here, not above real temptation. "He was in all points tempted as we are, yet without sin," says the Epistle to the Hebrews (iv. 15). Here, again, it is important for us to understand that even such temptation—temptation without sin—is an imperfection pertaining to a certain kind of freedom—to the human kind of freedom—and not a necessary condition of all freedom, of freedom as such. For thus in Prayer we can, we will, look up to, adore God, the Perfect Freedom, which contrasts so grandly with our own poor little freedom—even with our freedom where this exists in us, and is used by us, at its very best.

4

God is the Supreme Good—of the stone and of the plant, of the animal, of man, of the angel, but in what wondrously various degrees both of self-communication on the part of God, and of consciousness on the part of the creature, as to this gift from God, and still more as to the Giver, God Himself! In proportion to the depth and the breadth of any and every creature's nature, the creature possesses, or can attain to, the consciousness that God is its sole ultimate rest, sole pure delight. Religion, as distinct from ethics, flies straight at once to this great ultimate fact, to this unique personalist reality, to God as Beatitude and Beatifier. Thus the religious soul, in proportion to the strength of its religion, always reaches beyond all abstract law, all mere sense of duty and of obligation. St. Augustine is the great doctor of this our divine rest and our divine delight.

Our prayer will be immensely enriched and expanded by a persistent cultivation of this sense of God as our true home. For thus the rivalry between God and creatures for the possession of our hearts will become less and less a struggle between a mysterious obligation and a clear fascination, and more and more a competition between an ocean-wide, all-penetrating joy, when our souls come to their true, deep selves, and pleasures feverish, fleeting and shallow, when we allow ourselves heedlessly to be carried along by our superficial selves.

5

God, we have thus already found, is, indeed, not all unlike man. For how, if God were all unlike him, could man apprehend God, and love God, and try "to be perfect even as our heavenly Father is perfect"? Yet God is also *other than man*. Other, because He, God, is a Reality, an Identity, a Consciousness, distinct from the reality, identity, consciousness of any of His creatures or of the sum-total of them. And God is other, because this His distinct Reality is, by its nature, so much higher and richer, not only in degree but in kind, than is the nature of man or of any other creature. "Man is made in the image and likeness of God." Yes, but we must not press this as an exhaustive norm, as though God were simply man writ large—man's better and best instincts and conditions on an immense scale. We shall doubtless be much nearer the facts if we think of God as the living Source and the always previous, always prevenient Realisation, in degrees and ways for us ineffable, of our ideals and ever imperfect achievements— a Realisation which must not be taken directly to contain concretely what our conditions and strivings contain ideally. I am deeply convinced that the truth, and hence the fascination of Religion, as really requires some such emphasis on the *unlikeness* of God as it requires emphasis upon the likeness. So, for instance, "God is Love" is a central truth proclaimed by the New Testament and by all the saints of God. And so again, "God careth for us"—that God is full of sympathy for all His creatures, and for man especially, Jesus Himself never ceases to proclaim and to illustrate. Yet we must beware not to press this further, so as to mean suffering in God. For suffering is an evil, and there exists no evil in God: the religious instinct spontaneously and unchangeably hungers after God as Pure Joy. With St. Bernard, in his classic lament on the death of his darling twin-brother Gerard, we will hold that there exists the deepest *compassio*, but no *passio* in God.

Yet our hearts long also (though less strongly, I believe) for downright fellow-suffering, when they suffer and when they are exhorted to suffer well. Such fellow-suffering (deeper than ever we ourselves could suffer, and in One Who shares with us the evil of suffering, but without any admixture of the far greater evil of sin) is supplied by the Humanity of Our Lord. The Humanity of Jesus Christ, we have already found, brings temptation as near to God as is compatible with Godhead. And now we find this same Humanity of Jesus brings suffering as near to God as is compatible with the same Godhead. Indeed, the sufferings are so great as to require, for their sustainment by His human nature, the presence and action of the Divine nature, of the Divine Person which has conjoined itself to, and which informs, this human nature.

Our prayer will profit greatly if we thus hold firmly and fervently this double truth: of the *Pure Joy of God* and of the *Deep Suffering of Jesus*. For we will thus neither diminish God to a man of but larger size than we little men are, nor will we dehumanise Jesus by ignoring the immense sufferings, as well as the storm and stress—the temptations—of His earthly life. The definition of the Council of Chalcedon, difficult as it may be to apply it in any great detail, will thus continue to enshrine for us, also as praying souls, an imperishable truth: Jesus Christ is both truly God and truly Man.

6

All we have so far said implies or leads up to the great fact and truth: that *we men need God much more than, and*

*very differently from, the way and degree in which God needs
us men.* God is the Absolute Cause, the Ultimate Reason,
the Sole True End and Determiner of our existence, of
our persistence, of our nature, of our essential calls and
requirements. God is all these things for man. Man is
not one of these things for God. Man comes to his true
self by loving God. God is the very ocean of Himself—
of Love—apart from all creation. Thus the positions
between God and Man, and between Man and God, are
entirely uninterchangeable. Hence the most fundamental
need, duty, honour and happiness of man, is not petition,
nor even contrition, nor again even thanksgiving; these
three kinds of prayer which, indeed, must never disappear out of our spiritual lives; but *adoration.* Probably
the greatest doctor and the greatest practiser among
souls well known to us in these respects, of such over-
whelmingly adoring prayer, is St. Augustine. Never, in
spite of his tenderly anthropomorphic devotion, does the
great African forget this profound non-equality, this
non-interchangeable relation between God and man. Our
prayer will greatly deepen and widen out, if we also
develop such a sense—a sense which is now continually
exposed to the subtle testing and sapping of the pure
immanentisms and the sentimental anthropocentrisms
which fill the air.

7

The Prevenience of God thus appears as the root-fact
and the root-truth of all our previous positions. God not
only loves us more and better than we can ever love
ourselves, *"carior est illis"*—to the Gods—*"homo quam
sibi,"* already Juvenal told us; but God loved us before
we loved, or could love, Him. God's love of us rendered
possible and actual our love of God. This is emphatically
proclaimed by the First Epistle of St. John, and is a
favourite doctrine of St. Bernard. Thus the great Cister-

cian Abbot bids his monks rise never so early for their
night choir prayer in coldest mid-winter; they will find
God awake, Him the awakener; they will find Him
waiting for them, always anticipating even their earliest
watches. How scandalously much is this great fact forgotten in our days, even by otherwise alert preachers to
educated congregations! I had much talk with an Austra-
lian nonconformist minister upon this point, some ten
years ago; and he determined to preach it before such
a congregation—a large one in London. He afterwards
reported to me that his discourse had made a great stir,
crowds of his hearers flocking into the vestry to declare to
him that they never in their lives had heard such doctrine,
and how wonderful and awakening it was!

Our prayer will certainly gain in depth and aliveness,
if we thus continually think of God as the true inspirer
of our most original-seeming thoughts and wishes, when-
soever these are good and fruitful—as Him Who secretly
initiates what He openly crowns.

I take these to be the seven great facts and doctrines
concerning God — His richness, His double action,
natural and supernatural, His perfect Freedom, His
delightfulness, His otherness, His adorableness and His
prevenience. These seven facts, vividly apprehended, will,
even singly and how much more if seen conjointly, each
penetrating and calling forth the others, bring much depth
and breadth, much variety and elasticity into our prayer.
This, however, only if we understand plainly that there
is no occasion whatsoever for us to constrain ourselves
positively on these points. I mean that, though a Christian's
prayer will suffer in its Christianity, if it consciously and
systematically excludes, still more if it denies, any of these
facts, yet no one soul, at any one period of its spiritual life,
will feel equally attracted to them all. It will be quite
enough—indeed it will be the only wise course—if each
particular soul, at any one period of its growth, attends

positively, affirmatively, and lovingly to two or three, or even to but one of these facts. Thus not any one soul, but the society of souls, the Church of Christ, will simultaneously apprehend and apply all these facts and truths. The Church's several constituents and organs will supplement each other, and will, collectively, furnish a full perception and a full practice of these great facts of God.

II

THE FACTS AND TRUTHS CONCERNING THE SOUL WHICH ARE OF MOST IMPORTANCE IN THE LIFE OF PRAYER [1]

MUCH in human psychology and epistemology has been rendered more clear during the last thirty years or so, and some very ancient misconceptions have now been finally cleared up. Yet the presentation and the penetration of the processes operative in the life of prayer, which we owe to a St. Augustine, a St. Bernard, a St. Teresa, remain unsurpassed, indeed, on the central points, unapproached to this very hour. I take the points which concern the human mind and spirit, indeed man's complex organism generally, in so far as they come largely into play in the life of prayer, to be again seven. The due allocation and utilisation of the seven psychological facts and laws will, very largely, depend upon the degree to which we have adequately and vividly apprehended the seven great facts and truths concerning God. Indeed, a certain amount of overlapping and repetition is unavoidable as between the two series of facts, where each set of facts is, doubtless, in itself, very distinct from the other set, yet where the one set has to be apprehended by, and has to be put into close relation with, the other set.

[1] An Address delivered at Beaconsfield, 27 October, 1921.

I

The decisive preparation for prayer lies not in the prayer itself, but in the life prior to the prayer. That is, distractions and dryness, indeed even the real fruitlessness in and of our prayer, spring largely from our faulty dispositions, doings and driftings when out of prayer. The effects of such faultinesses pursue us when we come to pray. The cure for such faults committed out of prayer, and for their effects upon and within prayer, lies in the very wise ordering, and in the very faithful execution of such ordering, of our active life.

Fénelon pointed out to the Duc de Chevreuse how overburdened, and how racketed and distracted was the Duke's life, outside of his direct and deliberate praying; and how greatly that over-burdenedness, when out of prayer, damaged his recollection when in prayer. Fénelon advised the Duke to begin his day with quietly running through in his mind the chief things he would probably have to do, or would probably be solicited to do, during that coming day. That he should then and there reduce the number of such things as much as was wisely possible. And that, when he came to the actual doing of these things, he should clip his action of all unnecessary detail and development. *In this way he would succeed in placing each action within a circumambient air of leisure—of leisure for the spirit of prayer and peace.* This would be like the ordering of a wise gardener, who carefully sees to it that the young trees he plants have sufficient spaces each from the other—have sufficient air in which to grow and expand. I have myself greatly profited by striving to practise this advice.

St. Catherine of Genoa's method of life has also helped me much. She would quietly concentrate, each moment, upon that moment's special content—upon God's gift and will of special suffering or joy, of determination, effort, decision and the like, conveyed within that moment.

Such a scheme follows out something similar, within the spiritual life, to the action of the sun upon the sun-dial in physical life. The sun successively touches and illumines this, and then that, and then the next radius of the dial. Or, again, the scheme reminds one of Goethe's old mother, Frau Rath, who, when one day an acquaintance, ignorant of Frau Rath's condition, called at her door and asked to see her, sent down a message to the visitor that "Frau Rath was busy dying." Indeed, a genial, quiet death to self lies in every minute, when the minute is thus taken separately as the dear will and the direct vehicle of God.

2

The ceaseless interdependence of Soul and Body. The more any state of soul—any *psychosis*—is mental, still more is spiritual, or at least the more the agent or patient feels the *psychosis* to be thus mental or spiritual, the less, as a rule, is the neural accompaniment, the neural limitation, and the neural cost of this state perceived at the time by the experiencing soul. Yet such accompaniment, limitation and cost are certainly present, even in the most genuine and highest of man's spiritual actions or states; indeed, the neural cost appears, roughly, to rise in proportion as the action, at the time, fails to bring with it any sense of cost at all.

Fénelon is admirably awake to this important fact, when he warns Madame de Montberon not to indulge, beyond a certain limited time, in the prayer of quiet—a prayer which greatly helped and refreshed her; and this because of the neural cost of such effortless-seeming prayer.

One quite general, yet very helpful preparation towards the practice of sobriety in prayer, and hence towards escaping, as far as possible, the acute reactions liable to follow upon such very delightful prayer, is admirably preached and practised by Jean Nicholas Grou. This fine classical scholar, and deeply spiritual writer and leader of souls, urges *the importance of the soul's possession and cultivation of two levels and kinds of action and interest*—a wholesome natural interest and action, and a deep supernatural interest and action. The soul will then possess and will cultivate a genuine interest in politics or economics, in language or history, in natural science or philosophy— in these, as part of its bread-winning or as quite freely chosen studies. And we will thus, when in dryness and even in anticipation of it, possess a most useful range of interest to which to turn, as our disporting ground, in relief of the dreariness or the strain of our directly religious life. I believe Grou's spiritual writings remain so fresh, because (given his spiritual experience) he never, as he tells us himself, wrote on religious subjects except when the spiritual light and fervour were within him; whilst at other—the far more frequent—times he translated Plato or emended the texts of Livy and Horace.

Some further hints towards the bearing and the utilisation of desolation, as part and parcel of every at all religious life, and of every at all complete self-knowledge possessed by the liver of such a life. Thus St. Teresa, especially in her Autobiography, gives us admirably vivid descriptions of her times of dryness. On the other hand, I was surprised and disappointed when, some fifteen months ago, that deeply sincere Indian convert, the Sadhu Sundar Singh, told me that, never since his conversion thirteen years before, had he ever suffered one moment of spiritual dryness. I believe, with a very experienced psychologist and philosopher friend of mine, that this opinion indicates a strange lack of self-knowledge, perhaps also of what is precisely meant by such dryness, on the part of this devoted Christian. If, then, spiritual dryness is indeed inevitable in the life of prayer, we will be much helped to bear these desert stretches, by persistent recognition—hence also, indeed especially, in our times of fervour—of the normality and the necessity of such

Q

desolation. We will thus come to treat desolation in religion as we treat the recurrence of the night within every twenty-four hours of our physical existence; or as bodily weariness at the end of any protracted exertion in our psychic life. When desolation is actually upon us, we will quietly modify, as far as need be, the kind and the amount of our prayer—back, say, from prayer of quiet to ordinary meditation, or to vocal prayer—even to but a few uttered aspirations. And, if the desolation is more acute, we will act somewhat like the Arab caravans behave in the face of a blinding sandstorm in the desert. The men dismount, throw themselves upon their faces in the sand; and there they remain, patient and uncomplaining, till the storm passes, and until, with their wonted patient endurance, they can and do continue on their way.

There are generally a weakness and an error at work within us, at such times, which considerably prolong the trouble, and largely neutralise the growth this very trouble would otherwise bring to our souls. The weakness lies in that we let our imagination and sensitiveness be directly absorbed in our trouble. We contemplate, and further enlarge, the trouble present in ourselves, instead of firmly and faithfully looking away, either at the great abiding realities of the spiritual world, or, if this is momentarily impossible for us, at some other, natural or human, wholesome fact or law. And the error lies in our lurking suspicions that, for such trials to purify us, we must feel them fully in their tryingness—that is, we must face and fathom them directly and completely. Such a view completely overlooks the fact that such trials are sent us for the purpose of deoccupying us with our smaller selves; and, again, it ignores the experience of God's saints across the ages, that, precisely in proportion as we can get away from direct occupation with our troubles to the thought and love of God, to the presence of Him Who permits all this, in the same proportion do and will these trials purify our souls.

3

The great difference, in spiritual range and depth, in special *attrait* and peculiar calls and gifts, *unchangeably inherent in each soul's vocation to what it is, and still more to what God would have it become.* True, certain differences, perceptible on the surface, between soul and soul, largely spring from some changeable causes or defects. And, again, at the opposite end, the ultimate limitations as well as the possible final calls of individual souls are completely known to God alone, and to the soul itself, with some real knowledge, only and when it has advanced considerably on the spiritual way. Still, even the soul which is but a beginner can, with a little reflection and some good advice, save itself either much unnecessary failure, or, again, much vagueness and superficiality of endeavour, if it sorts out, roughly and for practical purposes, those acts, habits, intentions, self-conquests, etc., which specially appeal to it in its deepest, most peaceful moments, or which are specially called for by its particular character in the peculiar circumstances of its life and call: if it fixes upon *these* dispositions and virtues, and makes *these* things the central objects of its prayers and endeavours. It will work at these things—at least for a while—on a relatively wide and deep scale, and, as to the other virtues and dispositions, it will be content with not completely neglecting them. If we are faithful and humble in this concentration and cultivation, we shall come to discover any serious mistakes we may have made in our original choice, and we can then correspondingly widen, or narrow, or shift, the field, or alter the methods of our operations.

All this directly concerns our prayer also. For all such choosing of the field of our spiritual self-cultivation, all our labours in this field, all our little successes, many failures, and long awaitings of *some* fruit: all this should be *saturated with prayer*—by the spirit of prayer and by definite prayer, vocal, mental or of quiet. And, again, these several kinds of prayer, or combinations of kinds: these too, of course, should be chosen with due care and circumspection, according, again, to the *attrait*, the need, and the experience of the particular soul, which, however, must never be allowed to eliminate all vocal prayer.

Bishop Creighton wrote a fine letter, given in his *Life*, on the wonderfully rich variety which characterised the spiritual life of the Mediæval Church at its best; and, indeed, such varieties continue to flourish in the Roman Catholic Church. When Frederick William Faber preached the panegyric of St. Ignatius Loyola, on the occasion of the Feast of the Founder of the Jesuits, in the Jesuit church at Farm Street, he spent an hour in unbroken, sympathetic, indeed fervent, exposition of this saint's spirituality, and only in his last sentence did he introduce the necessary limitation and expansion: " This, then, my dear brethren, is St. Ignatius's way to heaven; and, thank God, it is not the only way!"

A friend of mine, who loved her garden, told me how only one of the many gardeners employed by her had succeeded with every one of her roses. She asked him what was the secret of his success. He told her that the other gardeners treated all her roses, not unwisely, but too generally—they treated them all in precisely the same way; whereas he himself watched across the months each rose-bush separately, and followed out, for each plant, that plant's special *attrait* as to soil, manure, sun, air, water, support, shelter and the like. So with souls: let us, without undue self-occupation, learn to discriminate between them and, again, between them all and ourselves, so as both to respect and encourage *their* ways, however different from our own, and to persevere and improve in *our* ways, however lonely these ways may be.

4

The Incarnational side of religion may never be despised nor forgotten, but must always be assigned *some* definite place and power within our spiritual lives. The approach to God and the condescension of God, the Invisible, Pure Spirit, on occasion of, in, and with the Sensible and Visible—the Historical, Traditional, Social, Sacramental—must remain and be cultivated within our souls.

The fact is that Pure Mysticism is but Pantheism; and that Pantheism is, on principle and incurably, a non-moral, a supra-moral and a non-personalist position, within which there is really no place for a distinct and definite God, for Sin, for Contrition, for the sense of our being creatures, and for Adoration. All attempts to interpret the whole life and teaching of Jesus, as simply the supreme unfolding of Pure Mysticism, suffer shipwreck against the great convictions which colour all the words and deeds of Jesus, that the consummation is indeed proximate, but not present; that its beginnings can indeed already be seen, but not its fulfilment; and that even these beginnings, and still more the fulfilment, are the deed of God, the immensely Personalist Power, and not the work of mankind, still less just the operation of the world-whole. The supreme revelation of the omnipresent, non-successive God, took place, in unique fashion and degree, in such and such years, and months and days and hours, and in such and such places, of human history. And so, similarly, with His lesser, yet still real, self-communications.

Now there is no doubt that *the prayer of quiet*—that *a certain formless recollection and loving feeding upon the sense and presence of God*—of God, as here and now—is a most legitimate prayer. Indeed, for the souls which possess the call to, and capacity for, such prayer (and their number is, I believe, not so very small), this form of prayer will feed and fortify their spirit more than would, *at the times when such prayer can healthily operate,* any number of vocal prayers, formal meditations, or Church services. Nevertheless—and this is our present special point—such prayer of quiet will remain safe and

wholesome only if *some* daily vocal prayers, and *some* more
or less frequent Church attendances and sacramental acts
and receptions, continue active within this same soul's
life. I know well that such sensible and spiritual practices
will, to such a soul, bring with them, at least at their
beginnings, a feeling of incongruity, of oppression, of
contraction, sometimes only dull, but at other times very
acute. Yet every such initial discomfort, if only the
sensible-spiritual acts be chosen with reasonable reference to this soul's special call, and if these acts be bravely
faced and persevered in, will (if not promptly, at least
in the long run) be followed by an increase, very real, and
mostly also clearly perceived, of the substantiality, and of
humble, childlike quality in the prayer of quiet, and in
the entire character of this same soul.

Let me illustrate what I mean from my own direct
experience. After practising a daily three-point meditation for some twenty-five years, the new Helper sent me
by God advised me that my prayer should now be mainly
informal—more of the prayer of quiet type; but that
there should always remain short vocal prayers morning
and night, Mass and Holy Communion twice a week,
with Confession once a week or once a fortnight; and
(perhaps most characteristic point of all) one decade of
the rosary every day—this especially to help prevent my
interior life from losing touch with the devotion of the
people. After over thirty years of this mixed *régime*, I
am profoundly convinced of the penetrating sagacity of
this advice.

Let me, then, suggest that we should each of us discover, with sufficient detail, what is the form of prayer
to which God appears to call us; let us give ample room
and opportunity to this particular form; but let us also
organise, most carefully, a certain regular amount of the
other kinds of prayer and worship.

5

The right attitude towards the Sex-instinct, and as to what is, for the Christian, the sin of sins.

Original Sin was generally considered by Catholic Christians, up to the advent of the great Jesuit theologians, as a *stain*, a vicious habit present within human souls from the moment of their conception and birth into this earthly life. And especially St. Augustine, following and still further accentuating the attitude of St. Paul, found this vicious habit to lie centrally in the vehemence of the sex-instinct. Not even St. Augustine dared censure the sex-instinct as such; as a Catholic Christian, he could not cast a slur upon marriage in its essentials. He declared a moderate, readily controllable sex-instinct to be right; only the vehemence, such as now characterises this instinct, was evil and part of original sin.

But the great Jesuit theologians found even this much to be untenable: how could an instinct, without which men would certainly not face the grave burdens of bringing dependent families into the world, be too strong, if we grant that the perpetuation of the human race really matters? So these Jesuit theologians placed the evil, not in the instinct, nor even in the vehemence of the instinct, but simply in the weakness of the reason and of the will called upon to control and moderate that vehemence.

Certain difficulties attach also to this view. Yet this view is satisfactory in that it removes all grounds for pains of conscience as to the presence of the sex-instinct, however strong this sex-instinct may be (apart, of course, from such strength as it may possess owing to the bad or slack life led by the soul which thus experiences the instinct).

Now I believe it to be of great importance that we should realise, vividly and persistently, that human purity is not only consistent with the presence of this instinct, but, at bottom, requires it. There doubtless can exist creatures of God without such an instinct. But man ceases to be human, unpossessed of such an instinct. Human purity is thus essentially a virtue operating within the body— a fleshly virtue.

Yet Mr. F. R. Tennant's books, so wholesomely suggestive on this point, should suffice to warn us how easily we can be led on to think of the body as ultimately the occasion of *all* our sins, as well as of our virtues; or, at least, to make impurity be, in our minds, *the* sin, the type and measure of all sin. For, with Tennant, *all* sin is but an *atavism*, a lapse back into the animalism from out of which mankind has raised itself. Impurity is a direct atavism— a gross, simple atavism, whilst *pride* is an indirect atavism —a subtilised, compound animalism. But this, I do not doubt, is a strangely inadequate view, both as to the sheer facts and as to the specifically Christian position. For the facts readily show that the occasions, the effects and the reactions of our consciousness with regard to Impurity, are all different from the occasions, the effects and the reactions of Pride. It is very distinctly *not* the animal within us which leads us to pride and self-sufficiency, whereas it is, quite as distinctly, the animal within us which does lead us to sloth, gluttony and impurity.

And as to the Christian outlook, its genius is sensitively keen and final concerning which is the central, the most heinous sin. *The central sin, for the Christian, is Pride and Self-sufficiency*, distinctly more so than Impurity and Sloth.

I take the occasion, the very possibility of such pride and self-sufficiency, to spring, not from the body at all, but from the delicate poise of our imperfect freedom. We possess a real, but only partial independence; we own a limited power and a limited self-determinative freedom, and even these our fundamental qualities we owe, not to our own making or finding, but we hold them as gifts, as creations of God. The very deep doctrine of the Fall of the Angels grandly illustrates this

position. The Angels are without bodies; yet this does
not lift them above probation, but merely makes their
testing a testing in Humility instead of Purity. And, again,
this absence of bodies does not make the alternatives
or the Fall of these Angels to be less. On the contrary,
it makes them greater.

I can only say that these two convictions, as to the
nature of human Purity, and as to the rank of Humility
amongst the virtues of all the creatures of God, have
greatly helped my prayer. For the conviction as to Purity
has freed me from much previous scruple and depression;
and the conviction as to Humility has, I feel, anchored
me more deeply and more securely in the Christian
Ideal, in the Christian life, and in the rich Christian fact
—the life and spirit of Jesus Christ, Our Lord.

6

A right attitude towards Temptation and towards Sin.
Such an attitude springs from two vivid perceptions: a
keen sense of the difference between Perfect Liberty, as
we found it to characterise God, and Imperfect Liberty,
as it exists in man and, indeed, doubtless in all the higher
and highest creatures of God; and an equally keen sense
of how all-penetrating and all-characterising is, for man,
the effect of this his Imperfect Liberty. The first sense,
as to the Imperfection of our Liberty, will save us, as we
have seen, from all pride, not only in our perhaps actually
being some kind of Byron or Don Juan, but even in our
ability thus to fall away from what we should be. And the
second sense, as to the special character conferred upon
all our moral and spiritual life by this our betwixt and
between position of Imperfect Freedom, will keep us
awake to the fact that, for our special human kind and
degree of virtue, Temptation is indeed necessary, in the
long run and upon the whole, for the perfecting and
testing of our moral and spiritual life. Temptation—

Temptation to sin—is necessary; but not the Commission of sin, not sin itself. Both these facts find their supreme illustration in the earthly life of Jesus. His Sinlessness —the unquestioning conviction of His sinlessness—appears in the oldest documents, but also His Temptedness. This temptedness disappears already in the Fourth Gospel. Yet the Synoptic Gospels (especially St. Luke), and the Epistle to the Hebrews, give varied and quite unforced expression to the reality of these temptations and to the primitiveness of the belief in their reality. We thus secure the text: "He was tempted like unto ourselves in all points, yet without sin." This, for the Humanity even of Jesus Christ. And we affirm the doctrine "without Sin, without Temptation, without Suffering"—this, for God—indeed even for the Divinity of Jesus Christ. "Credo in Deum Impassibilem," declared the Council of Aquileia.

I wish we could all vividly realise how all grave sin, actually committed by us, leaves—at least for and during this our earthly life—scars and limitations upon our souls, even after our most generous penitence. Thus St. Augustine did not simply profit by his sins. They became, indeed, the occasions for a grand humility and for the keenest sense of the mercy of God. He became, in spite of his past sins, a greater Saint than is many another saint whose sins were far fewer or far smaller. But Augustine the Sinner, even when he had become Augustine the Penitent, did not surpass, not even equal what—everything else being equal—would have been Augustine the Innocent. He would then, for instance, not have so closely grazed Gnosticism in his treatment of marriage. So, too, the noble founder of La Trappe, the vehement de Rancé, did not simply profit all round by his former sins, heroically repented of though they were. His aversion to all critical historical work, as part of the lives of monks, is doubtless an excess, and an excess which forms part of the reaction from his former worldly life. Here, too, the

model of all models is Jesus Christ Our Lord—Jesus, and
not even St. Paul. Our Lord's Humanity really grows and
grows "in favour with God and man" amidst real temptation. But Jesus commits no sin; nor is there any trace of
a reaction, still less of any excessive reaction, from a sinful
life, or, indeed, from any single sin. And this Sinlessness
does not spell weakness, but the fullest power.

Let us penetrate our prayer with these discriminations,
and let us beware of loose thinking about the profitable-
ness of sin, which, alas, even great poets such as Robert
Browning have, at times, encouraged. I am very sure
that, if we keep persistently awake to the contrast between
ourselves, the tempted and sinning, and Jesus, the sinless
but tempted, and again God, the living Reality beyond
all sin and temptation, we shall greatly strengthen and
fruitfully articulate our prayer.

7

*The Divinely intended End of our Life is Joy overflowing
and infinite, a Joy closely connected with a noble asceticism.*
There is a wholesome, a strengthening *zest* attached
to all action which is right and appropriate for the agent;
and there is an unhealthily weakening *excitement*, which
accompanies or follows all activity that is wrong or in-
appropriate. Hence one great end, and one sure test of
right living and right dispositions, is the degree to which
such living and dispositions make zest to prevail in our
lives and make excitement to disappear from them. Now
there is no zest comparable to the zest, the expansion,
the joy brought to the soul by God and the soul's close
union with Him. True, here below, we require to the
end a filial reverence, fear, restraint; virtues which, in
the beyond, will continue deepened, in the life of Adoration. True, again, we must never cease to fight Self, to
flee from Self. "The love of God, even to the contempt
of self," must more and more supplant the "love of

self, even to the contempt of God." We never may directly seek mere pleasure. Yet it is also true that we possess, deep within us, a spontaneous affinity for God. Nature draws us to God, as the dim, though most real background and groundwork of our existence; and Supernature raises this semi-conscious affinity to an active hunger for direct and clear vision, for a true participation in the Supernatural Life of God. Hence we must, in our practice, beware of deciding, as to what precisely to think, to do, to be, in execution of God's will for us, directly and simply in favour of what we do not like, or what we like least. We ought, instead, quietly to concentrate our thoughts upon God—upon His will and His various calls, and upon discovering which of such forms and degrees of moral and spiritual life most draws the soul in the moments of its greatest clearness and peacefulness, as to what is somehow meant for it. There will be plenty of opportunities for a large and deep asceticism within the life thus chosen, when we come, as assuredly we will, to have patiently to hold out, and laboriously to advance along the road— a road which, nevertheless, will be *the* road to Peace and to Power for the chooser.

We will not, of course, rule out, for ourselves or for others, the practice, or at least the spirit, also of bodily austerities. The spirit, and even some mild amount of the actual practice, of such austerities is, indeed, an integral constituent of all virile religion: the man who laughs at the plank bed and the discipline is a shallow fool. Indeed, some souls are, undoubtedly, called to more than the minimum indicated, and only find their full peace and persuasiveness in some such bodily asceticism. Thus there was a Sacred Heart nun, of whom I heard some time ago, who dearly loved, and anxiously watched over one of the pupils of the convent school, a beautiful young woman. This young woman, soon after leaving the school, took to an evil life and became a wealthy man's mistress. The nun knew well how unavailing would be, in this case, any direct appeal to the girl's religion or conscience. So she wrote to the girl that she was sure the girl loved her and wished her to live for many a year. Well, she merely wanted the girl to know that, on every day during which this her immoral life should last, she, the nun, would scourge herself till her feet stood in a pool of her own blood. That she had already carried out this plan daily since she knew of the girl's condition; and that nothing could or would stop her but the girl's own written announcement that she had left the man. The days went by. At last the girl wrote. The nun had gained her point. Is not that grand?

Yet it is Love, God, that first should be in our hearts; and if that Love then impels us to such deeds, we will attempt to do them, to feed and to express our love of that Love, and not otherwise. There is an admirable letter on asceticism generally from Fénelon to Madame de Maintenon. My own daughter, a Carmelite nun, spoke simply the spirit of her great Order, when, some little time ago, she answered an Anglican married lady, who declared herself repelled by all such mortifications—how could they ever form a part of the Christian life? Did not God Himself send us crosses, sufficient for all purposes, through and within our duties? Why arbitrarily add to these? The nun answered that she did not, indeed, find any trace of an *attrait* to such mortifications in her questioner—let her cheerfully leave such things alone and serve God joyfully along her way. That these things are never more than instruments or applications of the one spirit and way of love and of service. But that the lady would be unwise did she go further—if she condemned all such things for everyone. God's calls, within our one great common vocation, are many and various. Souls exist which are as truly called to such mortifications, as her soul was *not* called to them. Who are we, to lay down the law and the limit to God?

In either of these two paths, as Denifle draws out

finely in his great Luther book, the general direction, the End and the Measure are the same—the love of God above all things and the love of our neighbour as ourselves. And this love of God, where uninhibited and full, brings Joy—it seeks God, Joy; and it finds Joy, God. I used to wonder, in my intercourse with John Henry Newman, how one so good, and who had made so many sacrifices to God, could be so depressing. And again, twenty years later, I used to marvel contrariwise, in my intercourse with the Abbé Huvelin, how one more melancholy in natural temperament than even Newman himself, and one physically ill in ways and degrees in which Newman never was, could so radiate spiritual joy and expansion as, in very truth, the Abbé did. I came to feel that Newman had never succeeded in surmounting his deeply predestinarian, Puritan, training; whilst Huvelin had nourished his soul, from boyhood upwards, on the Catholic spirituality as it flowered in St. Francis. Under the fine rule by which the Roman Church tribunals require, for Canonisation as distinct from Beatification, that the Servant of God concerned should be proved to have possessed and to have transmitted a deep spiritual joy, Newman, I felt and feel, could indeed be beatified, but only Huvelin could be canonised.

Our prayer will greatly benefit by the great facts and discriminations we have been considering. Without in any way forcing, or escaping from, our real *attrait*, our prayer will thus possess a double virile asceticism. We shall feel ourselves, even if personally not called to very definite or to large bodily mortifications, in spiritual touch with, and supplemented by, those who are; and, again, we will deliberately hold ourselves as pledged to much renunciation of facile pleasures, as the condition and cost of our own abiding Joy.

IX

THE CATHOLIC CONTRIBUTION
TO RELIGION

IX

THE CATHOLIC CONTRIBUTION TO RELIGION [1]

I HAVE been asked, as a Catholic, shortly and plainly to unfold a topic which, as a Catholic, I feel to be like snakes in Ireland. Neither do snakes exist in Ireland, nor, in strictness, do Catholic contributions to Religion exist. Catholicism, as such, always aims at, and always more or less achieves, a recognition, utilisation and harmony of *all* the great insights and forces of Religion. In hardly a case is even the aim, let alone the achievement, as completely inclusive and integrative within the large whole of Catholicism, as is ideally possible. We shall indeed also find certain inveterate, widely prevalent habits of mind and of procedure, now largely peculiar to Catholicism, which somewhat limit and much obscure the inclusiveness here insisted on. Yet, in all such failures, the fault lies, not in the Catholicism, but in the limitations, faults and sins of its human teachers or learners or critics—usually of all three. I will, then, at first, write somewhat aside of my title, in attempting to draw out the fundamental implications, needs and demands of the human spirit, when touched by Religion, and to show how these conditions are met more and otherwise by Catholicism at its best than they are met elsewhere. But I will bring a certain justification to my title when I finish, by indicating the chief obscurations specially suffered by Catholicism in its average representation.

[1] Published in *The Student Movement*, December 1921.

I

I take the chief requirements of the religious instinct amongst mankind at large, and their full awakening and assuagement by Catholicism, to be as follows.

First, Spirit is awakened on occasion of Sense—when Sense responds to stimulations from Realities other than itself. George Fox, or all Quakers, or Mystics generally, may ignore or deny this great fact, or it may be difficult to trace in such cases. Yet the fact is general and *in possession*; no competent psychology will henceforth deny it. Catholicism alone, in its deliberately Sacramental outlook, stands, fully consistent and persistent, for this great fact of Spirit *and* Sense, Spirit *in* Sense, Spirit *through* Sense.

Next, Spirit is awakened by Spirit—one human spirit by other human spirits. The great religious spirits, whom we really know, all largely presuppose predecessors— their very ascent and advance implies such a ladder, such a springboard. Catholicism, in its traditional system, alone remains ceaselessly aware of this sacred torch-race across the ages.

Thirdly, all this occurs not in mere parallels of vertical action. But all this awakening, nurture and direction of spirits takes place within a great social and spiritual Organism, which itself possesses a certain mysterious yet very real person-like identity and influence—a whole extant from the first in those subjects and their activities, as the several parts of this whole. Catholicism, in its Institutional outlook, stands uniquely firm for this deep fact of the Personalist Organism. All the deeper Psychology, Theory of Knowledge and Sociology are now full of such a sense of parts constituted by their special wholes —wholes which are by no means the mere sum-totals of so many self-contained individuals.

Fourthly, Man is incurably *amphibious*; he belongs to Two Worlds—to two sets of duties, needs and satisfac-

tions—to the Visible or This World, and to the Invisible
or the Other World. This duality precedes and reaches
further than even the duality of Good and Evil. Both
these worlds spring from but One God, and are intended
to be brought to an eventual harmony. Yet this harmony
is the soul's ideal end rather than, as a rule, the soul's real
beginning. This harmony will never become an identity
of its several constituents; in heaven itself there will be,
not only Grace, but also Nature, good of its kind—transfigured, supernaturalised Nature, yet Nature still. And
on earth the soul will ever experience, indeed require,
friction, tension, alternation, a mutual supply of materials
and stimulations between the Seen and the Unseen, the
Good and the Better or Best—Nature and Supernature.
Catholicism vigilantly requires such an interrelation of
two worlds and of their several tasks.

Fifthly, there is the duality of Suffering and Renunciation and of Possession and Joy, and the fruitful integration of both within a larger whole. No conception
of Religion as, at bottom, an Abstract Law or a Joyless
Duty can abidingly prevail. Man is made for overflowing
Joy, though not for shallow Pleasure; and man's thirst
for God, as man's sole full Delight, must somehow be
combined with a deep Detachment and Purity of Love.
Christian Asceticism, its grand range from virile tone
and tension to delicate tenderness and expansive happiness, is being re-discovered by psychologists of the first
rank. Catholicism insists upon such comprehension with
a special breadth of range and a special elasticity of
adaptation; for it persistently includes the body, and dis-
criminates the one call of all men to holiness into various
forms of married or celibate devotedness. And the Asceticism here mediates a supreme Acquisition: the Roman
Church tribunals require the presence of Spiritual Joy
for the formal Canonisation of any of God's servants.

We thus find a close interpenetration, in the fullest
Religion, between numerous and varied levels and ranges

of human apprehension, assimilation and application of God's several gifts and calls. But, as a sixth characteristic (which, at bottom, is but a wider application of the third), this Unity is not merely a resultant or a superadded quality, however necessary for the fruitful action of those several ranges and levels. But this Unity, from the first, penetrates and gives a special character to all these, as its parts and differentiations. Now the first and widest of such integrations is that of Sense, the Visible, within Spirit, the Invisible. The entire Unity, at its various levels and even in its crown, will thus possess a visible Incorporation and Instrument, as well as an invisible Force and End. Catholicising Protestantism recognises the Priest and the Bishop as such incorporations and instruments of the unity of the Parish and of the Diocese. Yet the logic of such positions presses on to the recognition also of a similar incorporation and instrument of the Church as a whole—i.e. the Pope. For either the Unity of the Church is constituted by the Spirit only, and then also Priest and Bishop are not essential; or the unity of the Church is constituted by Spirit *and* by Sense, and then the Pope is as essential as are Priest and Bishop. The various other Personalist Organisms— the Family, the Guild, the State—all possess Visibility with Visible Heads: the Father, the President, the Sovereign. Why not also the Church?

And, finally, Religion, in proportion to its religiousness, is everywhere profoundly evidential; it affirms real contacts with a Reality which both occasions and transcends— which exists independently of—all these contacts. Presence, *Isness*, as distinct from the *Oughtness* of Morals: this is the deepest characteristic of all truly religious outlooks. Catholicism is specially concentrated upon this profound Otherness, this Over - against - ness, this *Contrada*, this *Country*, of the Soul. Not the recognition of all the previous requirements of Religion constitutes Catholicism, if the recognition of this final characteristic be lacking. For Catholicism recognises those requirements as primarily responses to, as effects of, previously extant Realities, which thus awaken man's spirit to their existence and to his need of them as extant. The doctrine of, and the devotion to, Jesus Christ, truly present, God and Man, Body and Soul, in the Holy Eucharist, thus forms, most characteristically, the very heart of the Catholic worship.

II

The seven characteristics just considered appear essential to Religion, as it is everywhere more or less groped after; and they appear to be really present within Catholicism, in a unique manner and degree. Why, then, do so many men of good faith keep outside, and indeed bitterly hostile to, the Catholic Church? And why are not a few within it more or less sullen, nominal adherents? Does not the reason lie perhaps, after all, in the very Catholicism of the Catholic Church?

The answer is doubtless, for the greater part, that most men not actually within the Roman Catholic Church are markedly ignorant or misinformed, both as to Religion at large and as to the Church's faith in particular; and that the men we have in view within the Church have not sufficiently woken up to the uniqueness of its powers and peace. Yet there are also three widespread and ancient facts which largely obscure the evidences and the attractions of the Church. I take Dante, and the persistent immense general influence of this profoundly Catholic seer, for the purpose of locating these three obscurations.

No man ever loved the Church, or served the Church, better than Dante. But Dante's enthusiastic loyalty goes to the Church's rights as co-extensive with her services; these rights extend no further than love, service and influence on the Church's part, and a corresponding docility and obedience on our own. Temporal power, political domination, earthly riches—such things belong to the State, not to the Church. Here Dante is supported by a very galaxy of Catholic Saints and Seers, from Christ Our Lord downwards unto now. Yet the, more or less direct, seeking after these earthly things persistently infects not a few Churchmen; and the consciousness, amongst men at large, that this is so, gravely limits the Church's influence—an influence which ought to be so great precisely also within the higher politics.

Dante again, as part of his Catholicism, not only declares, in a general way, the several rights and duties, and the harmony, present or eventual, of Faith and Reason, and of Theology and the other Sciences; but the Reason and the Sciences which he thus joyously upholds are actually the richest Reason, and the furthest advances of the Sciences of his day. Entire Sciences have arisen since Dante, especially has the Historical Sense and Method grown strong, largely through the work of Roman Catholic pioneers; yet the average official theology lags, angry or suspicious, behind these rich increases or renewals of human knowledge which men at large cannot forgo.

Yet even Dante is not free from the third obscuration. Hobbes pictures the Papacy as "no other than the Ghost of the deceased Roman Empire, sitting crowned upon the grave thereof." Assuredly, the substance of the Papacy is no such thing. But a certain survival of that Pagan Empire cannot seriously be denied in the temper even of Dante and of the average Church official. This regimen aims, above all, at prompt, visible conformity in the masses of the Church's actual adherents, and this with the least immediate difficulty. And thus insufficient room is left for the ample patience and the delicate discriminations so necessary for all fruitful Scholarship and Science. In directly practical acts, this temper appears in the form for reconciling a Jew, where he is made to forswear idolatry, an error from which the Jew is, in a sense, even too much removed. Yet official representatives of the delicately

discriminative spirit are never entirely lacking in the
Church. So with Pope Innocent XII., the Pope of
Browning's *Ring and the Book,* who authorised Bossuet
to declare the Church ready to receive back the Protestants with only positive declarations on their part—
i.e. without any direct repudiation of their previous
claims, teachings or experiences.

None of these obscurations, then, reveal themselves,
when pressed, as necessary parts of Catholicism, although
the wielders of the great powers recognised as legitimate
by the same Catholicism will, as but human beings, ever
be tempted to such excesses or deviations. Protestantism
as such has, upon the whole, been less tempted and less
entangled in these respects. This, I doubt not, because
Protestants, revolution-wise, so largely cut the knots of
problems, and did not untie them; and, more fundamentally, because they indeed attempted many criticisms and
contributions, and even achieved some abidingly valuable
ones, but, less even than the average Roman Catholic
officials, attained to the rich inclusiveness and the patient
tension of all complete and classical Catholicism.

X

THE DIFFICULTIES AND DANGERS
OF NATIONALITY

X

THE DIFFICULTIES AND DANGERS OF NATIONALITY [1]

I PROPOSE, first, to take the instincts of Nationality, as far as possible, separately—that is, roughly, as they function, or seem to function, without the religious checks and sublimations, and to consider *four great causes of defect or excess or abnormality* at work in these instincts. I will then attempt to draw out the *four special perceptions and powers in Christianity* which are the born correctors and completers, the four natural supernatural antidotes, to those subtle poisons.

But, before beginning our detailed study, let me put to you, as a vivid instance of the strange blindness which, in this matter of Nationality, can hold captive even cultivated and otherwise alert intelligences, what befell myself some twenty-five years or more ago.

The publishing house of Macmillan had kindly presented me with a two-volume work on *The King's English*, then just published by them, from the pen of an Oxford scholar of unmistakable competence. I could and did learn many a most accurate detail from him. Yet the fundamental position and express object of the work turned out to be an aberration so strange as to constitute by far the most instructive, the warningly instructive, part of the whole undertaking. The author wanted to prove, and evidently thought that he did prove, that the English language had always suffered—had always lost without any compensating gain—whenever it had admitted

[1] Published in the *Challenge*, 4 and 11 August, 1922.

255

any foreign elements or foreign influences into or upon itself. Danish and Norwegian, Norman-French, Renaissance Latin and Greek—before and alongside of these, Popery, especially Popery, in all its degrees and forms; all this and the like had always damaged, and had done nothing but damage, the English tongue. The English tongue could and can subsist of itself without a touch of foreign aid; indeed, only thus does and can it retain and develop its unique power and beauties.

What astonishing obtuseness! As if the English language were not (in its grammar and fundamental vocabulary) the language of the Angles and Saxons—those Teutonic races which came and brought this language with them from the Continent, from those dreadful foreign parts. This language, in the mouths of these, its early speakers, was in no sense or degree a native product of Britain; it was as "foreign" as were, later on, the Norman-French language and the Norman-French people, when these, in their turn, invaded England. And as to "Popery," this was not more "foreign"; it was considerably less "foreign" in and for Britain—once we allow some kind and degree of Christianity—than, say, this author's Protestant or Unitarian conception or reduction of it, which came to England so much later and so very largely from abroad. The book thus ended by unconsciously suggesting the parallel of an account of the Egyptians, or of the Aryan Hindus, coloured peoples one and all, which would undertake to show how, always and everywhere, the marriage of these peoples with any coloured races had gravely deteriorated them. Let us, then, wake up, and keep awake—first of all, indeed, against the constant danger of our falling thus fast asleep over this question, a sleep in which we would not judge of influences according as they may be good or bad, and as they may be truly and profitably assimilable by ourselves, but simply according as we may class them—often with grotesque inaccuracy—as sheer native-grown or as more "foreign" than the highly "foreign" elements of ourselves which thus reject these latest claimants.

I

It is especially from Walter Bagehot that I have learnt how useful, indeed, how necessary, a stage in man's development has been, not only a measured, wise, and noble sense of Nationality, but, indeed, also its naked, direct, unabashed form, where the martial virtues predominate with not a little of fighting and of killing. It is the same Bagehot again who, with his wondrously vivid thinking and writing—especially in his valuable *Physics and Politics*—has taught me how very large has been the share of man's innate imitativeness in producing, certainly not the great races, with their deep physical differences each from the others, but those less differentiated smaller groups which we call nations; that is, not the Indo-Germanic, the Semitic, the Negro, the Mongol and Redskin races, but the ancient Greek, the ancient Roman proper, the Frenchman, the German, the Englishman. That imitativeness has, very certainly, contributed more largely to the formation of the national types indicated by the latter string of names than have external nature, geographical position, climate, or any other condition or constituent we can find, even though such conditions and constituents, doubtless, also played their part. And in *Physics and Politics*, and in the hardly less penetrating *Metaphysical Basis of Toleration*, Bagehot traces to this same imitative, gregarious instinct much the greater part of the average intolerance or persecution which so persistently besets the human groups—the human flocks of various ages, sizes and characters, which we call schools and nations. The same instinct which readily, though for the most part quite unconsciously, leads the majority of the boys in a school, or of the men in a nation, simultaneously to copy the boy or man amongst them who, through a certain real or accidental, deep or superficial, wise or foolish originality of his own, forcibly strikes their imaginations and tastes, flares up in hot resentment against any infraction of the fashion and standard of correctness thus introduced and now sacrosanct.

"My dear fellow, I simply cannot walk with you to the pier to-day—with you wearing that quite incorrect tie," said a fellow-youngster to me, over fifty years ago, in a South of England watering-place. It would, of course, be absurd to maintain that all the differences, or that the central differences between civilised nations at any one important moment, amounted only to the clash between such differing automatic imitations and their consequent instinctive persecutions. We shall find three further, ever deeper and tougher, roots of such differences. Yet these further three roots do not prove that the root of unchecked, thoughtless imitation is not also extant and operative. And given that this root would be a very commonplace agent, and seeing that we are all so very largely commonplace, it seems to follow of necessity that the operation of this root must be very extensive.

II

Now, if we penetrate further into the motives which lead the average member of any one group or nation to starve out or to persecute, according to his ability, the average member of another group or nation, we shall find, I think, two intrinsically different kinds of irritation. There is at work, at one moment, or to some degree, an irritation, not only against a type really contrary to, and incompatible with, the type which the irritated national has found to be true and fruitful for his own life—or, at least, against a type which he sincerely believes and strongly feels to be thus incompatible; and, at another moment, or to some other degree, there is at work an irritation against simply any other type which (though differing somewhat from the type nationally followed and endorsed) is, nevertheless, quite compatible with it. These two irritations are, at bottom and in their eventual articulations, very distinct the one from the other. For even after the supervening of circumspection, of comparison, and of selection, there can and should be, not, indeed, persecution, yet certainly not adoption—there should be starvation (in so far as any participation of our own is concerned) of any type seen by us to be essentially incompatible with what we have come fully and definitely to perceive as abidingly true and precious; whereas a type seen by us to be different from our own, yet which is not seen to be incompatible with our own type, should be left unmolested—indeed, should be met with as much sympathy and encouragement as may be possible to us here and now.

Here, again, it is impossible to trace all antagonisms, hatreds, wars between nation and nation, solely to the narrow and illegitimate kind of intolerance, or even to such intolerance combined with the first force at work within us—the power of thoughtless imitation. But that this, our second force, is a force indeed, it would surely be futile to deny. Thus, besides inevitable, objective, worthy antagonisms (all this, for any one point in, or any one side of, the controversy), there exist mixed, avoidable, subjective, petty antagonisms, or, again, differences which are not sheer incompatibles—which, indeed, constitute genuine supplements or wholesome correctives each to the other. How much, e.g., of the antagonism between Frenchman and German springs from the ready lucidity of form and comparative indifference to the solidity of the content in the Frenchman's thinking, and from the probing, if often stolid, solidity of mind and the absorption, away from questions of form, in the subject-matter, so common in the German's rumination! Yet these two things are neither of them evil; they are both good;

and the ideal human being would possess both these sets
of qualities, each set, and each quality in each set, in their
proper place, function and degree.

III

And then there appear, at the third depth, differences
which (early in the history of any two nations, or in the
history of the one group, already a nation long ere the
other group existed as a nation at all) were in themselves
largely differences—peculiarities—of the sort or sorts
hitherto studied by us, but which, through certain, mostly
long vicissitudes of history, have hardened into all but incurable antipathies, even though, here again, we have a cause
which never thus acts simply by itself. How largely, e.g.,
though doubtless not wholly, the Frenchman's state of soul,
deep down when not also on the surface, has, with respect
to the Englishman, been influenced and hardened by the
Hundred Years' War, that episode of three generations
and more, which looks so splendid in Shakespeare, yet
which no responsible historian has, now for many a day,
dreamt of holding to be justifiable! Englishmen have
learnt to admire the "witch," Joan of Arc, as warmly
as any Frenchman admires that touching saint. Nevertheless, the past rarely, perhaps never, ceases to obstruct,
where it was evil, any more than it ceases to aid where
it was good. So, again, the Irishman, with the unforgiving,
unforgetting temperament of the true Celt, has his natural
temperamental differences from the far less remembering
Anglo-Saxon, hardened into sullen, or fanned into fiery,
hostility by facts of long (even if of long ago) oppression
or neglect. And I note that the Frenchman's and the
Irishman's never more than slumbering suspicion and
hostility, however understandable, however apparently of
a character to provoke regret for the past in the Englishman, do not, indeed cannot (of themselves and as between

average men) make either Frenchman or Irishman more
attractive to the Englishman—indeed, they certainly
operate in the opposite direction. This, partly for the
quite general human reason that also the Englishman
readily likes those that like him, and is repelled by suspicion and hostility; partly for the reason more special to
himself, that he is too little prone himself to centuries-
long and irreconcilable resentment, not to be readily
bored with men who live with so sleepless an intensity.
"It is, ma'am, so very tactless of him to come amongst
us like this, so soon after the Massacres," said a Mac-
donald housemaid to her mistress, a friend of ours, who
lived at Glencoe, when the late Duke of Argyll, then
Lord Lorne, visited that part of Scotland, full seven
generations after that lamentable act of the Campbell clan!

Yet the most striking instance of a strong mutual antipathy caused, beyond all doubt, very largely by a special
history of well over 2000 years at least, are the Jews.
Here we have not, it is true, a nation in the strict sense
of the term, or rather in the ordinary conditions, since
for eighteen centuries and a half, indeed, largely since
before then, the Jews have been scattered over the face
of the earth. Yet we have in them a race, with laws, traditions, habits, ideals of its own, far more compact and
sui generis than any nation, properly so called, that has
ever existed upon earth. And, here again, it is easy to see
how little the peculiarities traceable to the tragic mal-
treatment of this wonderful people—how little its suspi-
ciousness and servility of demeanour, soften the Gentiles'
feelings towards the Jews.

IV

And then there is, finally, an influence at work, in all
our present-day Nationalisms, of an immensely penetrating as well as massive and most formidable kind.

s

Its danger lies, on the side of the motive of the individual man's adherence, in that men, even not ignoble men—indeed, precisely the nobler sort of men—will readily allow themselves to be carried away to ideals or proceedings of a stunting and sterilising kind, when they act not as individuals, but in crowds, and for the supposed good of the whole or of the many, which they would never entertain for their own strictly private ends. And the danger, on the side of the contents of the Nationalism which I have now in view, results from the history of some nineteen centuries, of which the following are the four main tributaries and stages. The first two stages either retarded the self-development of the several Nationalities, or (in part simultaneously) trained men and large groups of men in what will have again to form part of the deepest safeguards and transforming influences for the Nationalisms now so alarmingly awake. There was, first, the great training furnished by the Roman Empire for some three and a half centuries beyond the end of Our Lord's earthly life. And there was, next, the Christendom which, roughly from the Coronation of Charlemagne in A.D. 800 up to, say, A.D. 1300, worked with a power and fruitfulness less equable, but deeper and richer, than did ancient Rome. In both these conditions, of some four hundred and five hundred years respectively, the interdependent, social, co-operative instincts (or, at least, ideals) were, upon the whole, in the ascendant. By social I mean here social as between large groups of men as groups. Then there came the Renaissance and the birth of the strictly modern Nations, with their supposed utter mutual independence of each other, and their supposed omnipotent Governments—two wild and poisonous suppositions. Here the entire self-sufficingness, pure selfishness, and boundless competitiveness of the several Nations and States becomes the fashionable doctrine. With Hobbes, we find a conception of the State in full parallel with that of the individual man, and of both as purely pre-

datory. The single man is a wolf to his fellow-individuals
—a single wolf amongst and against the other single
wolves, until the omnipotent State undertakes to do, for
these single wolves, the prowling and preying upon the
other packs of wolves with a perfection of force and of
cunning utterly beyond all private competition. And then,
finally, but, perhaps, most forcibly of all so far, comes the
Industrial Movement from, say, A.D. 1780 to this moment
—a movement which, for five generations, has always
increasingly withdrawn men from healthy and truly
human, because moderate, open-air and intrinsically
interesting work, and has crowded them, away from the
lovely country, into huge factories and hideous cities, for
labour of the most mechanical and soul-destroying kind.

Now the Nationalism of our day readily takes over
and fills itself with this Industrialism. And thus we get
the omnipotent State of the Renaissance (all the more
omnipotent now, under the rule of bare majorities in
place of the individual despotic kings), filled and inflamed
with the cupidities of boundless money-getting and of
immense material prosperity. Nor would it be true to
insist that such absorption in money-getting is special
to but a small band of profiteers. After reading specially
hot and specially windy demagogic utterances some months
back, I passed through a London slum, which in one of
its shop windows advertised a shilling booklet, *How to
Become a Capitalist.*

Very certainly the instinct of Nationality pure and
simple will not save men from such debasing fevers;
it will, on the contrary, if left alone, but drive such fevers
still further into the very blood of men.

V

Let us now turn to Religion—to Christianity in especial—
and seek to discover what it can, what (when most sensitively loved and lived) it *does* do towards checking, trans-

forming, transcending the four main weaknesses of the National Instincts. We thus ask: "What does and can Christianity effect here against the predominant gregarious imitation and thoughtlessness? Against the narrowness and intolerance of types, merely because they are not the Nation's own? Against the impotence to amend, indeed, the proneness to increase still further, the antipathies chiefly caused by long injustices in the far-back past? And, finally, against the keeping of even noble characters at the level of a predominantly materialistic patriotism?" We shall find, I think, the following four strengths and cures in Christianity for those four weaknesses and diseases of Nationalism.

I

Christianity, as every religion in proportion to such religion's religiousness—Christianity, with a depth and delicacy, tenacity and tension surpassing those supplied by any of the other religions, is primarily busy with Ultimates, with Ends. Christianity has itself been by far the greatest awakener and articulator of the thirst for such Ultimates, and the only full assuager of this same thirst. It is, indeed, entrancing, for such spiritual sense as there may be within us, to note how, without a break anywhere, Our Lord lives and moves and has His Being in those Ultimates; how He is Himself the full revelation, the grand yet utterly touching incorporation of those Ultimates, as they bend down to enter into, and elevate—if we but allow them—our poor little mediacies. Humanitarianism, when quite genuine and truly operative, is doubtless both a wider and a deeper principle than is Nationality; and Humanitarianism, precisely of this genuine, operative kind, has received no stimulation or awakening even approaching in fullness to that effected by Jesus Christ. And yet, in all Our Lord's utterances and actions, even the love of *man*, however sincere, however pure, stands always in subordination to, is the effect and test of, the love and the service of *God*. The movement is here, not from man, or even from all mankind, as the final and adequate end of man's service, to a more or less hypothetical, or at least to a background God; but from God, as Himself the final and adequate end, to God's will and creation, God's love and care— to men, myself and others. Thus God, Himself man's final and adequate end, appears here, not as the philosophical Absolute, nor as a popular term for the totality of things, nor as some dry principle requiring a learned training to seize at all; but as a Personalist Mind and Love and Power, Who cares for the very birds of the air and the lilies of the field—indeed, Who knows the number of the hairs upon our heads.

Now, if there is one thing such a faith should be able to effect, it is a certain fundamental thoughtfulness, a certain emancipation from the childish tyranny of thoughtless imitation. It was assuredly amongst the marks of the deep spiritual *flaire* possessed by Cardinal Newman, that, in his Oratory Church at Edgbaston, he used to preach so fiercely to his young men against their "second-rate imitations of polished ungodliness." It might easily seem a venial fault to ape, however vulgarly, such worldliness in matters of no great import. But Newman saw, even in such imitation, the mark of a soul spiritually asleep. And, very certainly, the Cardinal did not mean to require any abstract thinking from these young men. He but wanted them to awake to another, to quite another, set of living models—to make them deeply aware of certain great living and breathing types—above all to the immense force and figure of the Overlord and Master, Jesus Christ. There is a wonderful passage in Matthew Arnold's *Culture and Anarchy*, where, after we have been long immersed in the crowd of men who "do what they like"—whose ideal is so to do, and who are driven hither and thither by their restless and yet monotonous prejudices and passions, without any deeper reflection, without unity, without growth in their inner lives—there rises, there appears behind them, in touching contrast, in lovely splendour, the great figure of Christ, of Him Who never did His own will. Countless souls, thank God, even amongst the least orthodox, the least complete or exact in their articulated belief, have been awed and softened and sobered, have had some unity and meaning and growth brought to them by this greatest of figures and forces, the ever-living Christ. Thus we know that John Stuart Mill is right, when he tells us that we cannot reach a loftier or more exacting standard than "so to live that Christ would approve our life." To live thus, and in so far as we live thus, is to break through the obsession of sheer imitation. For now we are absorbed away from mimicry of shoddy mediocrity into loving and living the Best as far as ever we can.

2

Against intolerance of national types Christianity brings us, with unique power and penetration, the insight into, the further and deeper formation of, the Organism. In the teaching of Jesus, as continuously as God comes first and man comes second, man appears, not as a simple individual who derives his light and life directly from God alone, alongside of other single individuals who similarly derive *their* light thus directly. Man here is never just a single man—a single grain of sand amongst other grains of sand upon the seashore. But man here is always the father or brother or son of a family; the servant of a master, or the master of servants; a sower, a vintner, a fisherman—connected with his field, his vineyard, his nets and boats, the lake or the sea. How deep, how very deep, all this is! Why, even the last thirty years have added much to our insight into this great mysterious fact, that the fundamental social groups—the Family, the Guild, the State—possess a *personalist* character and influence of their own—that they are not simply the sum-total of the individual units which compose them and seem to exhaust their significance. We can, and we do, blame families and states. And now the law, in our own and in other countries, is coming to acquit and to condemn, not merely this or that trade unionist, but this or that trade union. It is especially those two great geniuses, the German von Gierke and the Englishman, the late Frederick William Maitland, who have drawn this out with unforgettably luminous erudition.

Now to such Organisms belong also the Nation and the Church. True, the Nation hardly appears in the direct teachings of Jesus Himself, and the Church figures there less in the lessons as to the Kingdom of Heaven than in the organisation of, and the commission to, the little preaching band—the Twelve Apostles, with Simon Peter at their head. Yet what I am now seeking is, nevertheless, abundantly present in principle throughout all Our Lord's sayings and doings, for, though He does not explicitly draw out a full list of the essential groups, He everywhere teaches and illustrates the great *organic* fact and conception of them all—that man stands within these great groups, getting far more than giving; that he is very largely constituted by the very groups to which, at his best, he brings irreplaceable further riches.

And this great *organic* fact and conception we soon find systematically articulated by St. Paul, who appropriates and applies to the Church the great Stoic conception of individual men as severally so many variously necessary members of the One Universal City of Humanity. It is here, in St. Paul, that we get the unsurpassed insight into the Church as a living Body, in which the individual believers contribute each his own much or little, his nobler or less noble seeming share towards the life and prosperity of the whole; and where each member participates in, and is particularised for service towards, the honour and deep significance of the whole. And this great scheme involves all sorts of co-ordination, super-ordination, subordination, and every kind of reciprocal check, supplementation, stimulation, service and support. True, even St. Paul does not articulate a similar organic view of the State nor even of the Family; and the feeling for Nationality is as little clear and strong in St. Paul as it is in Jesus Himself. Yet his references to, and his utilisation of, images derived from the Family and the State all involve a similar organic conception of these groups. And, as to the feeling for Nationality, for Nationality as distinct from the State, it appears plain that, given the then extant incorporation of Palestine, and, indeed, of all the other West Asiatic, the North African, and the South and West European countries in the all-powerful Roman Empire, geniuses of religion would, indeed, do all towards the salvation of souls within those political conditions, but would leave the attempts at nationalist revolts to the zealots. Indeed, the quite fruitful conception of Nationality (which always involves also Internationality) lay, as to the very beginnings of this most slow and costly question, still some fourteen centuries ahead. For it was necessary (if this question was to be formulated with sufficient vigour) that, first of all, definitely, indeed dangerously, independent Nationalities, that powerful, immensely *competitive* units should confront each other; only then would men be driven to seek for some *co-operative* system of which these units might be found, or made to be, the mutually supplementary members. Before the Renaissance, England and France, pretty well alone, furnished such clear units and such a pressing problem. But the late Great War has even recklessly spread and pushed this problem over the entire globe.

Mrs. Sophie Bryant has well described, in her fine article, "Nationality," in the *Encyclopædia of Religion and Ethics*, how every Nation known to history has demonstrably acquired its special character and value, never alone, but always through intercourse, friendly and hostile, competitive and co-operative, taking and giving, between itself and other nations near and far both in space and in time. Shut yourself off, if unhappily you can, from all other nations, and you become a Lama State, as in Tibet; harden yourself deliberately and finally against all and every influence from any one Nation sufficiently great to persist for some generations as such a costly entity at all, and you have atrophied or inflated your own Nationality, and, together with it, your personal nature, and this the more gravely, the more rhetoric you may pour over this breach and wound.

When John Henry Newman, as a child, watched the French prisoners from the Napoleonic Wars as they were marched through the streets of the City of London —he tells us this himself—he noticed how men amongst the dense onlooking English crowds would, quite seriously, lift up the French soldiers' greatcoats from behind—to discover their tails, so simply did these Englishmen believe Frenchmen to be apes. The national antipathy has, for the time, shifted away to against the Germans. We shall do well, there also, to watch against seeking in our antagonists, whatever may be their real special racial faults and sins, for the equivalents of monkeys' tails. For such frames of mind are of tragic damage for all concerned.

3

We have thus come close to the third defect and danger of Nationalism, or rather to the special power of Christianity in face of this third defect. What can Christianity show and effect against the wholesale taking over of racial and national animosities of appalling antiquity, a taking over at which even the youngest nationalities are astonishingly apt and able? Here, especially, Christianity is so plain and so direct with its quite unescapable facts, that the sole difficulty consists in getting men squarely to front these facts and not steadily to look the other way. The most fundamental of the doctrines specific to Christianity is, doubtless, the doctrine that Jesus Christ is truly God and truly Man. Yet, to become truly man, God had to become Incarnate in a particular human race, short of whatsoever might be sinful in this race. And we know, beyond the possibility of all reasonable challenge, that the race, thus chosen by God for His central condescension, was the Jewish race; Jesus, as man, is a Jew—a pure Jew. So was His great Precursor, so is His Blessed Mother, so are His Twelve Apostles, with Simon Peter, their Head, and so is the last, yet assuredly not the least, of the Apostles, St. Paul. Soon, it is true, the Greek and the Greek-speaking races, and almost as soon the Italic, the strictly Roman race, come to Christianity, and get from it and give to it infinitely much. Only much later—at earliest with the Goths, some three centuries after the Jews—do the Teutonic races come to Christianity. I do not doubt at all that we are right in believing that very valuable new materials and applications, for and of the Christian spirit and life, were brought also by these races. They had, and they have, the right and the duty of a large place and influence within the religion to which they owe so unspeakable a debt. Yet the greatness, the full adequacy of Christianity to the needs also of our own race, consists precisely in that the various great races—so also the Celtic and the Slavonic —have had their share in the articulation and application of its spirit, and that such great races as the Hindu, the Chinese, and the Japanese will, please God, still come, and, whilst gaining so much themselves, may also give of their specific best.

The greatness of Christianity consists in this its inter-nationality, yet still more in its supernationality. It never can, it never ought to, satisfy just simply what men of this or that particular race and time desire—*that* and nothing else. It must bring, it ought to bring with it, always a surplusage which any one race will not be able, here and now, to work up in any detail. Christianity is extant chiefly to make us grow, and not simply to suit us with clothes fitting exactly to the growth already attained by us.

Aquinas teaches that God, in His creative activity, aims at producing, as nearly as is possible by the sum-total of so many finites, an image of His own infinite richness, and hence that He creates no two leaves, no two insects quite alike—and that, the higher a creature stands in the scale of creation, the more nearly each individual is a species in itself. So, too, so especially in national types, can we believe in, and pray and work for, realities precious enough in their particularity to demand our endless care and cultivation. For myself, I am deeply grateful to God that I most truly owe, and that I am keenly aware that I owe, to all the great typical races and nations far too much ever to condemn any one of them root and branch. What, above all, would my Religion be without its Jewish figure? What would my Theology be without the Greeks? What would my Church Order be without the Italians? How much poorer would be my devotional life without the German *Imitation!* without the French Fénelon! without the Spanish St. Teresa! without the English Mother Julian! I want them all, and I rejoice in them all.

4

And yet it is only the fourth and last strength of Christianity, as it is drawn out in correction and completion of the fourth and last weakness of Nationality, which brings us to the deepest depth of the Christian help. We found that Nationality—a keen sense of Nationality, as Nationality has been developed and has been fitted with content across the centuries—tends to limit even noble men's outlook to the things and standards of this life; tends to fill them primarily with the endless competitions for unbounded temporal wealth and physical power, for the forcible predominance of *our* industries, *our* commerce. Well, as against this, Christianity can and does develop in man a temper, a state of soul, which so deeply and delicately, so sharply and steadily perceives and feels the difference between Time and Eternity, the Fleeting and the Abiding, Pleasure and Beatitude, the Contingent and the Final, the Creature and God, as to make such souls incapable of being paid off, in these deepest matters, with anything but the genuine coin. No doubt this world-fleeing movement will have to be alternated with, will have to find its stimulus and material, in a world-seeking movement; and only the two together, in their proper proportions and interpenetrations, will furnish the complete service of God by complete mankind. Yet we will have to be on our guard lest, beginning the social betterment of others, as the means to help these others to find time and inclination for God and for prayer, and as a means towards our own closer access to Him, we defer the setting aside of our time and thought for the other-world movement to the Greek calends. How much decency, leisure, and pay is the miner to have, till he is to be helped to love prayer and the thought of God? Ought not any and every man's mind and conscience to be developed simultaneously with his merely wage-earning activities? Does not that noble, large interest in the things that matter in themselves do more to moderate a man's desires for the visible good things of this life than all the Acts of Parliament that ever were or will be? How noble, to be deliberately content with little of such visible good things, so as, more or less from the first, to secure some leisure of soul for those very different good things— the things of the mind, of the conscience, of the spirit! I know of no other force which can bring such moderation to men except Religion; and the prosperity of the nations, even measured by at all wholesome this-world standards, so profoundly requires such moderate desires!

I will only now, as to this fourth and last help, insist

upon two special points which will, I hope, still more clearly bring out the ultimate facts, and the ultimate right positions to these facts, as I believe the facts are and the positions ought to be. The first point concerns the Millenarianisms which, in their irreligious form, are again so rampant. This point demands careful retrospection. And the second point concerns the central characteristic of any and every sensitively religious conception of the other life. This point requires a careful forecast.

It is at first sight strange, yet on consideration very natural, that the apocalyptic, prompt, and final change of the world—that the millenarian outlooks which (in the original sources whence believer and infidel get them, in the Old and in the New Testaments) are full of God; which there stand, not for man's work, but for God's gift; which indeed, in precisely this their proximity, suddenness and completeness of transforming power, express this lightning illapse from without and from above into human life and human nature, and not a slow, gradual growth upwards and from within of this same human life and human nature: that these outlooks so readily seem to dominate such anti-religious fanatics as Lenin and Trotsky. Nevertheless, this is not really strange, since the fanatic, and especially the anti-religious fanatic, is nothing if not intensely impatient and absolute. Such an one, then, finds in those apocalyptic and millenarian outlooks exactly what he wants—on one condition: that he empties them precisely of what gave them all their genuine spiritual worth—their perception that all that is best in our human lives, private or public, that especially what is necessary to preserve them and to crown them, is the pure gift of God; and, again, that God's gifts, as such, are, like His own inner life generally, outside of time and of succession. Now the warning which I think we believers here require is, not to attempt the revival of religious millenarianism as an escape from and a cure for secularist millenarianism, but to meet the secularist insistence upon the *periphery* of those apocalyptic outlooks by a renewed perception and acceptance of their deep, *central* truth. The Christian Church has had to soften the abruptness and proximity of those apocalyptic outlooks; but it has done so without damage to the depth of religion only where, as in its saints, it retains a profound, penetrating sense of the Givenness of all the best we ever have or ever gain—of that supernatural grace and joy which we can taste already here below a little, and which, if we are faithful, will uphold and penetrate us unfailingly in the beyond. By so doing, the Church retained and retains the central truth of those apocalyptic outlooks, whereas the irreligious millenarianists seize upon the form whilst carefully rejecting the content. Indeed, they place man and his natural powers in the stead of God and of His supernatural grace, and thus feed the human soul with windy, readily inflating, intoxicating error. The National and Nationalist movements continue to show a marked inclination for such dangerous Utopias; hence the need of a countervailing deep sobriety in the outlook of religious men.

And, then, as to the second point—the centre and the fundamental root of the Beatitude in the Beyond. We can, and we should indeed, persist in our forecast as to this point, in the Incarnational trend of Christianity, so that the Beatitude in the Beyond will be held to include the deepest human social happinesses, in so far as they deserve, or are capable of, transfiguration beyond all simple naturalism, by God's supernatural grace. The relations of parents and children, of brothers and sisters, of man and wife: they doubtless will not abide just simply as they stood on earth; yet not one of them but can, but will survive, in what it may have developed of spiritual, perennial worth too closely connected with these special, sweet relationships of earth not permanently to bear touching traces of where and how these heroic nobilities grew towards heaven. But if this be sound, then one does

not see why Nationality of the noblest sort should not
also exist, supernaturally transfigured, in heaven itself.
Thus that moving vision in the Revelation of St. John,
of men of every tribe and tongue and nation who stand
before the Lamb, would not mean—how can it mean?—
merely that these men *were* thus distinct, but have now
been redeemed from out of all those variations into an
utter sameness, an interchangeableness of robes: no, these
men will, for all eternity, retain, transfigured, what they
have on earth achieved, of a supernaturally valuable
kind, also as Jews, Greeks, and Romans, Englishmen and
Frenchmen, Germans and Italians, and the rest.

Yet the other element of the Life of the Beyond is,
more or less ever since the Renaissance, in far greater
danger of being overlooked or explained away: the centrality of God and of our satisfaction—our fullest satisfaction—there in and through the direct vision of God
and our assured close union with Him. That disappointed,
often reckless and excessive spirit, the German with the
French name, Paul de Lagarde, who insists that men even
in heaven will be there as Frenchmen and as Germans
(a position I have just conceded), has a wonderfully
probing poem, *After Death*, upon the point I here am
after. De Lagarde there pictures the soul as, at first,
dazed by the new conditions of its existence, but as soon
conscious as of a kind of motion—it is moving on to new
worlds, new scenes. And after a while it hears an angel
voice, which announces to it that henceforth its social
service shall function with practically no limits, no defects,
no failures; throughout eternity it shall serve its fellow-
souls, those down there still on earth, as well as these
here in heaven. *That* shall be its joy. But when the soul
hears this, a great pang of disappointment shoots through
it. It turns vehemently to God and, whilst protesting
that it will submit to whatever may be His holy will,
it implores Him to grant to it the assuagement of the
thirst which, at its deepest moments, moved and drew it,

down there in the previous life. Let it, oh let it see—not
souls, not its fellows primarily, but Him; let it lose itself
in Him, become as nearly one with Him as may be possible
for it, the little creature absorbed in the Creator, its true
life, its transfiguring love.

Pleasant Sunday Afternoons amongst our Nonconformist
fellow-Christians; even appurtenance to the Labour Party
of some of our Anglican Bishop friends; indeed, even the
Catholic Social Guild, as it functions amongst us grateful
subjects of the Catholic and Roman Church: how good and
how useful can be such things, as parts and parcels of that
man-seeking, world-seeking movement so necessary to the
religion of the Incarnation. Yet this movement will have
always to constitute only the second table of our Law of
Life. It will all turn to sheer fatuity and vulgarity unless
the Supernatural Life, unless God and our Life in and
for Him, forms indeed the very centre, the final home,
and the constant refuge of our deepest being. Here again,
here especially, Nationality clamours aloud for incorporation within, and transfiguration by, the wider, the deeper,
the ultimate outlook, Life and Reality as brought to
us by Christianity.

INDEX

T

INDEX

I.—OF PERSONS, PLACES AND DOCUMENTS

II.—ON SUBJECT MATTERS

and as science, 30–4; the mind's movement in relation to, 35–42; its phenomenal surface and religious interpretation, 43–8; its relations to Time, Duration, and Simultaneity, 49–55; Past and Present in, 64–5; its supreme importance in Religion, 66; its need ignored by Fox, 76–7, 82; attitude of men towards, especially in Roman Catholic Church, 103–11; influence upon Nationality, 260–3
Humanitarianism, 264
Humility, 159, 237

"Ideas," of Kant, 163; of Plato, 176; of Plotinus, 180
Immanence, contrasted with Abidingness, 144
Industrialism, 263
Infallibility, 20–2
Infinite, the minds sense of and search after, 63
Interdependence, of man and man, 159; of Soul and Body, 47–8, 228–30
Isness, of Religion, 164, 248

Joy: God as, 170; in and as God, 181, 186, 188, 192–5, 198–200, 205, 206, 208–13, 223; the Divinely intended End of our life, 239–42, 247

Kinesis, Aristotelian doctrine of, 50, 51, 179

Liberty (Freedom): conceptions of, 112, 113–15, 118; Perfect and Imperfect, 202–04; Perfect Freedom of God, 210, 220, 221; Man's Imperfect, 237
Love, of God and in God, 153–4, 160, 198, 204, 208, 212, 222, 224, 230, 240–2, 247, 265

Materialism, 136, 137, 142
Messiah, the Suffering, 190
Metaphysics, relation with Religion, 205–7
Morals, relations with Religion, 157–64; oughtness of, 164, 248
Millenarianisms, 273, 274
Middle Ages, 218, 219, 220, 262

Mysticism: Christian, 28; denies succession in the spirit's deepest experience, 49; its conception of "Action," 51; false, 53; German mediæval, 60; Pure, virtually Pantheism, 233

Nationalism and Nationality, defects and excesses of, 255–63; counteracted by Religion, 264–74; supernaturally transfigured in Heaven, 275–6
Natural Sciences, contrasted with Historical, 31–4
Nature, distinct from God, 120, 121; Nature and Supernature, 122, 130, 218–19, 247

Officiality (see Authority)
Optimism and Pessimism, the soul's experience of, 10

Panentheism, 39
Pantheism, 39, 119–21, 136, 137, 139, 143, 151, 158, 233
Pain, 168–9; see Suffering
Papacy, the, 71–3, 104, 125, 129, 248, 250, 251
Past and Present, 6, 12, 27, 64–6, 140
Patripassianism, 187, 188, 190, 191, 194, 195
Perfection, the soul's search of the Complete, 63; Fox's insistence on, 73, 74
Personality, full functioning of, 51; development of individual, 113, 114; of the Family, Guild, Commune, Church, State, 118, 246, 248; in God, 152, 163–4, 183, 187, 198, 199, 204, 220, 221, 233
Pluralism, 136, 137, 143
Prayer: seven positions concerning God to be adopted in, 217–26; the life of, 226; preparation for, 227–8; neural cost of, 228–30; attrait to different kinds, 231–2; prayer of quiet and Incarnational side of religion, 232–4; treatment of sex-instinct and temptation in, 235–9; adoration and asceticism in life of, 239–42
Prevenience, the Divine, 114, 116, 224–5

INDEX
287

and Hellenistic current concerning, 175–83; Israelitish-Jewish current, 183–6; Patripassian current, 187–8; teaching of the New Testament concerning, 188–95; examination of reasons for and against, 197–207; rejection of belief in Suffering in God, 207–13, 222–3

Suffering Servant, the, 186

Sympathy, in God, 191, 195, 197, 198, 205, 209, 213, 222, 223

Temptation, right attitude towards, 237–9

Temptedness of Jesus, 192–3, 221, 238, 239

Teleological conceptions, needed by History, 33

Time: definition of, 6; relation with Reality, 50; with History, 52, 53; Time and Eternity, 139–41

Tradition, in relation with Inspiration, 66–7

Theism: religious controversy no longer concentrated upon, 3; demanded by Religion, 121; obstructions or obscurations of, 136; intimations of, 138–154; virtues involved by, 159–164

Trinitarian Doctrine, 151, 152, 153, 198

Truth, differing attitudes of the soul and official Authority towards, 9; differing depths and levels of, 38–9; of the Creed, 110

Truthfulness, interior, 8–9; need and difficulty of, 160

Ultimates, Christianity busy with, 264

Unconditioned, the "Idea" of, 163

Uniqueness, 31, 39

Unitarian Body, the, 84–5

Unpretentiousness, virtue of, 159

Zest, contrasted with excitement, 239